SAS Trooper

Charlie's Dedication

To men without dogs, and dogs without men ...

The Royalties from sales of this book will go to the SAS Association and to the Cyprus Association for the Protection and Care of Animals (CAPCA) to support its 'Paws' Dog Shelter outside Paphos, something close to Charlie's heart.

SAS Trooper

Charlie Radford's Operations in Enemy Occupied France and Italy

CHARLIE RADFORD

and

FRANCIS MACKAY

Pen & Sword
MILITARY

First published in Great Britain in 2011 by
PEN & SWORD MILITARY
An imprint of
Pen & Sword Books Ltd
47 Church Street
Barnsley
South Yorkshire
S70 2AS

ISBN 978-1-84884-399-8

A CIP catalogue record for this book is
available from the British Library

Typeset by Concept, Huddersfield, West Yorkshire
Printed and bound in England by CPI, UK.

Pen & Sword Books Ltd incorporates the Imprints of Pen & Sword Aviation, Pen & Sword Family History, Pen & Sword Maritime, Pen & Sword Military, Pen & Sword Discovery, Wharncliffe Local History, Wharncliffe True Crime, Wharncliffe Transport, Pen & Sword Select, Pen & Sword Military Classics, Leo Cooper, The Praetorian Press, Remember When, Seaforth Publishing and Frontline Publishing.

For a complete list of Pen & Sword titles please contact
PEN & SWORD BOOKS LIMITED
47 Church Street, Barnsley, South Yorkshire, S70 2AS, England
E-mail: enquiries@pen-and-sword.co.uk
Website: www.pen-and-sword.co.uk

Contents

List of Plates

Charlie, Cecina, January 1945, before Operation COLD COMFORT, wearing Africa Star ribbon.

Scottish Women's Timber Corps uniform, 1944.

Memorials to Operation LOYTON personnel executed near La Grande-Fosse, Vosges, 15 October 1944.

Partisan hut used by 7 Stick showing 'polenta' pot and spoon, late winter 1945.

Operation ZOMBIE: 7 Stick, Asiago, spring 1945.

Charlie with Shannon c.1978.

Custodian 'Roberto', CWGC Padua War Cemetery, October 1995.

Grave of Major Ross Robertson Littlejohn MC, October 1995.

Grave of Corporal Joseph Patrick Crowley, October 1995.

Charlie with Rejane, June 2003.

Charlie about to lay the wreath at the execution site. SAS Pilgrimage, September 2004.

Moussey ceremony.

Moussey: SAS Graves and plaque.

Moussey: close-up of plaque.

Asiago Plateau: Val d'Assa, Val Portule, Partisan camp area, Camporovere.

Charlie outside the former German HQ, Asiago.

List of Maps

Preface

This is the story of one man's early life before, during and after the Second World War. It is unusual in that it describes the life and times of a Regular Army Other Rank, from Apprentice Sapper to Senior NCO, and his missions, not all successful, with the SAS behind enemy lines. This is not the full story of Charlie's life. His original manuscript ran to over 135,000 words, and even then only covered the first twenty-six years of a long and varied existence. The economics of modern-day publishing required a shorter account, so much of his early life in Devon and as an apprentice tradesman had to been omitted.

Charlie died before this book could be published and before I could get to Cyprus to meet him. And, sadly, after he first contacted me, it transpired that in 1995 and 2002 we were within a few miles, and hours, of each other in northern Italy. In 1995 Charlie and Jack Paley, veterans of 2SAS's Italian Detachment, were visiting the graves of dead comrades in Milan and Padua CWGC Cemeteries, and in 2002, with an old friend from Cyprus, Hugh Reid, Charlie was walking around his wartime stamping ground on the Asiago plateau, north of Venice. Charlie and Hugh used one of my Great War battlefield guides to explore the area and to visit the CWGC cemeteries on and near the plateau. On both occasions I was nearby, researching the role of British forces in that area during both world wars. In 1995 I went to Padua CWGC 1939–1945 War Cemetery to pay my respects to the graves of the two SAS men murdered by the Nazis in the aftermath of Operation COLD COMFORT/ZOMBIE and found someone had laid poppies ahead of me. The CWGC Custodian informed me that recently *'due vecchia soldati inglese, multo gentile'* had come to honour Major Ross Robertson Littlejohn MC and Corporal Joseph Patrick Crowley, 3 Squadron, 2SAS. Unfortunately, the cemetery visitor's book had just been replaced – they fill quickly in Italian CWGC cemeteries, mainly with Italian names, many with moving inscriptions. However, some months later Charlie contacted me via Pen & Sword asking if I knew anything about an SAS badge he had seen displayed in a small museum near Asiago.

We compared old diaries and, sure enough, had indeed been ships passing in the night. From then on we corresponded at length about the disastrous Operations COLD COMFORT and ZOMBIE. Eventually Charlie asked me to read the drafts of his autobiography, which so impressed me that I sent it to Pen & Sword, who thought it well worth publishing – and the rest you know. However, this book does not describe Operation COLD COMFORT in detail, but does cover most aspects of Operation ZOMBIE. Charlie knew little of the first and did not have access to the few official files held in London and elsewhere. We agreed to collaborate on a sequel to this book, covering both operations as fully as possible, and had, in fact, started work. Hopefully, the planned book will appear in due course.

As to the badge. It is, or was as of 2009, on show in the Museo Della Grande Guerra, Canove di Sopra, housed in a former station of the narrow-gauge railway mentioned later in this book. It is definitely not an early-war version, and appears to be a post-war bi-metal Service Dress cap badge. When last seen it was part of a group of British badges, including, for some reason, that of Kingston Grammar School CCF! None of the staff seemed sure how or when they arrived at the museum, as the organizer, Francesco Magnabosco, a former member of the Alpini, had died without leaving many notes.

Francis Mackay
Stirling, August 2010

Acknowledgements

Charlie wrote the words, Charles Hewitt and Henry Wilson at Pen & Sword liked them, their colleague Matt Jones edited my editing and Alex Swanston worked away at my maps. My thanks go to Margaret Burford, Ambleside, for clarification of wartime domestic life, and to Major Bob Bragg, Dronfield, a wartime contemporary of Charlie's at the Airborne Forces Depot at Hardwick Hall, for amplifying Charlie's descriptions of life there. Rosalind Elder, Vancouver, told me, politely but firmly, what Scottish Women's Timber Corps girls did, and did not, do in Highland forests during the war. Harry Doy, of Doune, identified sites where 2SAS trained in southern Perthshire. In Asiago, Vittorio Cora and Fausto Rebechin were as helpful as always about wartime life on their beautiful plateau, while in London, Jackie Smith, burrower of The National Archives, helped confirm details of Operations RUPERT, LOYTON, COLD COMFORT and ZOMBIE. Above all, we should all thank Chris Georgiou in Cyprus, who willingly agreed to the continuance of this project after Charlie's untimely death.

Glossary

AT – Apprentice Tradesman.

ATS – Auxiliary Transport Service: wartime predecessor of the Women's Royal Army Corps.

BD – battle dress: name given to the woollen serge blouses and trousers worn by British servicemen between 1937 and the late 1960s.

Bergans – durable rucksacks that became the trademark of the SAS. The original Norwegian manufacturer is still in business.

blanco – a coloured compound, powder or cake, used by British servicemen on webbing equipment during the Second World War, and made by the Mills Equipment Company Ltd, designers and primary manufacturers of 37 pattern Webbing, and sold in round cakes manufactured by Joseph Pickering and Sons Ltd, Sheffield. It was manufactured for eighty years and sold to over sixty nations for use by military and police services. Related verbs: blancoing, blancoed.

Cordtex – a type of detonation cord usually used in mining but which can be used in booby traps.

CQMS – Company Quartermaster Sergeant Major.

CSM – Company Sergeant Major.

CWGC – Commonwealth War Graves Commission.

DZ – Drop Zone.

ENSA – Entertainments National Service Association. Established 1939 to entertain British forces; part of NAAFI.

erk – wartime RAF slang name for its lowest rank, Aircraftman or AC, originally Air Mechanic. Probably a corruption of the Great War phonetic alphabet letters A, *ack* and M, *Emma*, with *ack* slurred into *erk*.

HMS – His/Her Majesty's Ship.

HMT – His Majesty's Transport: a merchant ship exclusively at the service of HM government on time charter.

Joe-hole – aircraft belly-hatch for dropping parachutists and supplies. 'Joes' were secret agents (possibly derived from 'Old Joe Soap', a British expression referring to anyone of unknown identity). At RAF stations handling Special Duties flights no one, not even the escorting officer, knew the name of the agent(s) to be dropped into enemy territory.

Kapok – a tropical tree, the fibre from which was used as a filling for life-jackets, flying suits and so on.

KIA – Killed in Action.

'Lili Marlene' – wartime German romantic ballad, dating from 1915, which caught the imagination of servicemen, and women, of all nations in a later war. 'Underneath the lantern / By the barrack gate / Darling I remember / The way you used to wait / T'was there that you whispered tenderly / That you loved me / You'd always be / My Lilli of the Lamplight / My own Lilli Marlene ... It is the Regimental Slow March of the British and Australian SAS Regiments and the Princess Patricia's Canadian Light Infantry. Heard at dusk, with or without 'drink taken', it can bring tears to old soldier's eyes.

LUP – lying-up position: rest areas during operations.

Maquis – Mainly rural guerilla bands of the French Resistance. A member was known as a Maquisard.

MO – Medical Officer.

MP – Military Police.

MT – Military Transport.

NAAFI – Naval, Army and Air Force Institutes: the official forces' trading organization.

NCO – Non-Commissioned Officer.

Organization Todt – Nazi civil and military engineering body named for its founder, Fritz Todt.

OSS – Office of Strategic Services: predecessor of the CIA.

PE – Plastic Explosive.

PFC – Private First Class.

RASC – Royal Army Service Corps.

RMP – Royal Military Police.

RQMS – Regimental Quartermaster Sergeant.

RSM – Regimental Sergeant Major.

RTU – Returned to Unit: dreaded punishment in SAS and other elite units.

RV – Rendezvous.

SBS – Special Boat Squadron.

SMG – Sub-machine-gun.

SOE – Special Operations Executive: British organization responsible for training and co-ordinating the operations of partisan groups in occupied countries.

S-phone – UHF secure radio-telephone system used between aircraft and ships and personnel on the ground. Mainly used to co-ordinate the final phase of parachute drops of agents and supplies.

Tilly – British service slang for Car, Light Utility 4 × 2.

WAAF – member of the Women's Auxiliary Air Force.

WO – Warrant Officer (WO2 – Second Class WO).

WRNS – Women's Royal Naval Service.

WVS – Women's Voluntary Service.

Chapter 1

Boyhood

I was born on 4 June 1923 in Bath, Somerset, shortly before my family moved to a small, dark, poorly furnished terraced house in Teignmouth, Devon. This was during the Depression, and we were quite poor. I remember going to a Teignmouth Council soup kitchen, where a ha'penny bought a bowl of pea soup and a thick slice of bread.

I idolized my father. He was short, and sometimes short-tempered, and had an interesting life. He joined the Somerset Yeomanry in 1911, married mother in 1912, made her pregnant before working his passage to Australia, worked throughout 1913 as a boundary rider on a remote New South Wales sheep station, and then in August 1914 joined the Australian Light Horse. He transferred to a 5th Division machine-gun company in 1915, and in 1916 saw action in Egypt against the Turks. He went to France in 1917, was gassed and wounded, then in 1918 was pensioned off in England as 'unfit'. Thereafter he rarely found work until 1929, when he became a Cunard steward – low pay but good tips. Before each voyage men lined up, hoping to catch the Chief Steward's eye, in return for a handsome tip when paid off. Father worked throughout the 1930s, so he must have tipped well!

In 1930 we moved into a new semi-detached council house in Mill Lane. It sat at ninety degrees to the road, giving splendid views over Teignmouth and the Teign Estuary. 'We' meant my maternal grandmother, bedridden after a stroke, Father, Mother, eldest brother Arthur, sister Kathleen, brother Roy, who had Down's Syndrome, and me. Mother had more than enough to do as all chores were done by hand. On washdays everything was boiled in a copper, laboriously mangled, hung out to dry, and then ironed with a heavy flat iron heated on the gas stove. She also had to do the laundry, shop, cook, serve meals then wash up, light fires, clean out the ashes, do housework, darn socks, feed the cat and dog, and care for an old lady who required everything: bed pans, turning to prevent bed sores, meals, bathing and hair washing.

Father spent his shore time growing potatoes, peas, beans, cabbages, gooseberries, loganberries and rhubarb in good red Devon soil,

1

enriched with horse manure. We had a healthy diet, albeit without much meat, apart from rabbit stew with dumplings, or sausages. Each October Mother would make half a dozen Christmas puddings in white bowls, with a white cloth tied tightly around the top, then boiled in the laundry copper for several hours and stored away until the festive season.

Arthur loved sport, and we often went by train to watch Exeter City play at home. In three years we never once saw drunkenness or violent behaviour, only good-humoured remarks like 'Where are you specs, ref?' From Exeter St Davids station we walked past Higher Barracks, the Devonshire Regiment's depot. I little thought that later I'd be inside, enlisting in the Army.

Because of Roy's condition I protected him, especially from teasing children. He had limited mental faculties. He could read, write and tell the time, but could not work out the correct change in a shop. Later, increasingly violent outbursts led to his admission to the Royal Western Counties Institution. It looked grand, with immaculate buildings and gardens, but Roy's group lived behind, in damp, gloomy, semi-derelict huts. Sadly, he died of TB there. I never felt so sorry for anyone in my life.

One summer, Sir Alan Cobham's Flying Circus came to town. There were mock air battles and bombings with bags of flour, but the big event was a parachute descent; hardly worth a second glance nowadays, but really dramatic then. We couldn't afford a five-shilling flight, but didn't worry: the thought of flying was beyond our wildest dreams.

Another summer event was community singing in the park. I have never heard of it happening anywhere else, but I may well be wrong. It always attracted a good crowd, although there were no chairs or benches, but on a warm summer evening it was pleasant to sit on well-mown grassy banks. We sang all sorts, accompanied by a piano: 'Danny Boy', 'The Rose of Tralee', 'Roses of Picardy', 'Long, Long, Trail A-winding' and 'Pack up Your Troubles in Your Old Kitbag'. All very nostalgic and heart-warming, especially for older people. I can remember, even after seventy years, the strong sense of community, probably only to be felt in small places. The evening ended with the National Anthem, with everyone standing up, showing proper respect. Respect for elders and those in authority seemed perfectly natural to us and was rarely questioned. In particular, our parents and school-teachers were shown this respect, also the local 'bobby', unlike today, where near anarchy seems to exist everywhere.

Another big event was Bonfire Night. For weeks any pennies earned or cadged went to the local shop's Guy Fawkes Club. Your fireworks were stored in a marked box until The Day. During the week beforehand we paraded the streets with a homemade Guy, a straw-stuffed sack wearing an old jacket with a carved turnip head and a hat gleaned from the rubbish dump. He sat in a soap box on wheels, while we begged passersby for a 'penny for the Guy'.

We mainly bought loud, cheap bangers: 'Little Demon', 'Thunderbolt', or 'Rip-Rap' jumping-jacks. In the days beforehand Teignmouth Council assembled a huge bonfire on waste ground. Once it was well ablaze, our Guys were tossed onto it, commemorating the attempt to blow up the Houses of Parliament. An interest in 'bangs' stayed with me throughout my Sapper career.

I remember clearly how simple life was in those days. No muggers, football hooligans, internet, e-mail, TV, mobile phones or hysterical tabloid newspapers. It wasn't Utopia, especially for the unemployed, but I am utterly convinced it was a better world.

I spent several happy years at West Lawn Boy's School, but failed narrowly to win a grammar school scholarship. A Mr Ballard generously funded a small group, thereafter referred to as 'Ballard's Boys'. However, our parents had to buy our uniform of grey flannel jacket and shorts, red- and black-striped tie, grey stockings, black shoes and red and black caps with the school badge bearing the motto 'Carpe diem'. I soon learned this was the first part of a phrase by the Roman poet Horace: *Carpe diem, quam minimum credula postero* ('Seize the day, trusting as little as possible in the future'), which I have always tried to follow! I liked French, taught by a tall, elegant Mademoiselle Bending, inevitably nicknamed 'Catcher', who always addressed us in French. She left after a year or so, and her replacement, Mr Thomas, a squat, nasal-voiced Welshman, looked like a frog, but nevertheless was very popular.

My grammar school days were really very happy, but unfortunately in 1938 Mr Ballard suddenly moved away, and as Father, like many other men, was unemployed, my schooling ended. Perhaps I was foolish, but I didn't mind, as all my Mill Lane friends were working. I had a sort of after-school job as a baker's delivery boy, reimbursed with cakes and being allowed to drive the van in back streets. As Arthur, a solicitor's clerk, and Kathleen, a hairdresser, contributed to the family budget, I felt I should do so too. I became a 'learner' at Lansdowne's Furniture Store, Station Road, for the princely wage of 5/- per week. Lansdowne's had large plate-glass windows displaying three-piece suites, beds and other furniture. Upstairs were carpets, linoleum, curtain materials and so on, and downstairs was a workshop for repairs and making coffins. Lansdowne's did a good line in undertaking.

After a while I was moved to collecting cash from customers who had bought furniture by hire purchase, or 'the never-never'. I soon found why it was so called. Armed with a receipt book, indelible pencil and a list of names and addresses, I set out one morning with a light heart, glad to escape the confines of the shop. Most of the addresses were in the poorer parts of Teignmouth, where people were most reluctant to part with money. The weekly installments were between 3/6d and 5/-, but wages were low. I was either fobbed off with promises to pay next week or my knocks were ignored. Perhaps one in four paid up without quibbling.

At this time I began going out with a very nice girl. We spent our evenings in one or other of the Victorian glass-panelled iron shelters on the esplanade, which are probably still there. We would find an empty one and nestle into a corner, kissing. This we would often keep up for a couple of hours. I went out with several girls in those days, but always came back to my seafront girl.

After some months I realized there was little future at Lansdowne's. After some years all I might become would be a salesman, which did not appeal at all. Then one day I responded to an Army advertisement for apprentice tradesmen. I always wanted to be a soldier, having read many books about the Great War, which should have put me off but didn't. It was obvious that another war was coming.

In due course I was summoned to Exeter for a medical and written examination. I passed both, with high marks in English, Mathematics and General Intelligence, and signed on for fourteen years: two in training, eight with the Colours, then four in the Reserve, starting as an AT (F) – Apprentice Tradesman (Fitter), Royal Engineers. Soon a letter arrived summoning me to the Army Technical School (Boys) at Fort Darland, Chatham. So ended my childhood.

Chapter 2

Army Apprentice

On 4 July 1938, American Independence Day, I lost my independence for ten years by joining the British Army. That morning, after a very good breakfast, I said goodbye to my family and walked to the station with mixed feelings of pride and apprehension, but determined to put up with whatever lay ahead.

On the train I met four other Devon lads bound for Darland. At Exeter, as I had passed Higher Barracks many times before, I guided them there. On arrival we filled in many bits of paper, then, after an officer read out the Oath of Allegiance, we each repeated it in turn. He then gave each of us a shilling coin, the 'King's Shilling', sealing our fate. We also received rail warrants for Chatham via London.

We arrived at Fort Darland late in the evening but we were immediately given bread, cheese and mugs of tea. We were then taken to a hut with iron beds and bedding, told to make up the beds and retire before 'Lights Out' was signaled by a bugle call at 2200 hrs. It was our first taste of army routine. More came next day.

At 0600 hrs we were woken by a bugle playing 'reveille'. After getting dressed we stood around wondering what to do next when in strode a broad-shouldered, clean-shaven man with a commanding manner and authoritarian voice. This was Sergeant Draper, our Wing NCO. He wore a well-fitting khaki Service Dress (SD) jacket with brass buttons shining like miniature suns and trouser creases so sharp they looked as if you could cut your fingers on them. He informed us we were in Three Wing, B Company, of the RE Apprentice School, and we would spend the day drawing kit and getting army-style haircuts. Afterwards we would get brown paper and string to parcel up our civilian clothes to be sent to our homes. But first, breakfast! It was excellent: eggs, bacon and sausages, with lots of tea, bread, butter and marmalade. Even after war broke out we were fed well, although margarine replaced butter.

Back at the hut we were shown how to make our beds. They were extendable, the bottom being pushed into the top half during the day to create more space. They had three small mattresses, or 'biscuits'. Two were placed upright against the bedhead with the other lying flat in front. Blankets were then wrapped neatly around the upright biscuits and the pillow and sheets concealed behind. The only other furniture was a wooden table and four hard chairs, all scrubbed white daily.

Once our beds were made to Sergeant Draper's satisfaction we marched to the QM Stores for kitting out. Every boy first drew a canvas kitbag, followed by two hairy serge SD uniforms with brass buttons, RE shoulder titles and 'flaming grenade' collar dogs. Next came a 'bus conductor'-style SD cap, with RE badge and leather chin strap; a khaki forage cap worn when working, a woollen scarf or 'cap comforter' and two sets of workshop overalls. We drew KFS (knife, fork, spoon), comb, brass button-stick, brushes for boots, clothes and shaving, a safety razor, a cloth 'hussif' ('housewife') containing thimble, needles, cotton and wool (for darning socks) and gym kit (cotton vest, thin blue shorts and canvas gym shoes). Then we got a white leather belt with brass buckle, greatcoat with brass buttons and shoulder titles, a rubber groundsheet-cum-waterproof cape, puttees, three pairs of grey woollen socks, two pairs of boots with laces, a large RE jack-knife with one single, very sharp blade, a marlin spike and a woven lanyard. Finally, we were given a 'walking-out' cane, topped by a silver sleeve and ball engraved with the RE badge. Everything was packed, carefully, into the kitbags onto which later we stenciled our name and number.

We then marched, or staggered, back to our hut to learn how to stow and look after our kit. As there were no electric irons for soldiers in those days we were initiated into the art of pressing uniforms between two sheets of stiff cardboard placed beneath our biscuits at night. Before that the insides of the creases were dampened with soapy water, and, initially, shaved with an old razor. When dried this produced a sharp and near-permanent crease. The cap badge was polished back and front, and a flat piece of metal, usually an old hacksaw blade, positioned behind the badge and inside the cap to raise the front of the crown. Then a clothes brush was dipped in soapy water and applied to the crown in a circular motion, causing the hairy surface to lie flat in a circular pattern. This all took time to learn, but the biggest challenge was creating a glass-like shine on our boots. This involved heating them with a candle, battering them with the handle of an old toothbrush, then applying spit and boot polish with a cloth, working in small circles over the toecap.

Fort Darland was built on, and named after, Darland Bank, a slope on the outskirts of Chatham. The camp was built in 1938 for the recently expanded Apprentice Tradesman Scheme, and opened for training in the spring of that year. It had a hospital, gymnasium, classrooms, kitchens, dining hall and workshops. The school's role was to train surveyors, electricians, fitters, carpenters, painters, blacksmiths, tin-smiths and metal turners and other RE trades. Boys also studied the Army First Class Certificate of Education. Our huts, each housing twenty boys, were in clusters of six built around the parade square. Each cluster had its own 'ablutions' – washrooms, baths, showers and toilets.

Many of the boys came from military schools, such as the Duke of York's at Dover, and Queen Victoria, outside Dunblane in Scotland, but they were called either 'Dukies' or 'Vickies'. They were either military orphans or sons of soldiers serving overseas, and entered the schools from age nine. There were also boys with families posted to overseas military stations, mostly India, but we had one from China, where his father was in the Shanghai garrison. The Indian pupils used many Hindustani and Urdu words, which soon became part of Fort Darland's *lingua franca*.

The school had two companies, A and B, each with three wings of 120 boys. A Company had been training for three months, and having finished their 'square bashing' was training in the workshops. Main-tenance of discipline was mainly left to boy NCOs, with ranks ranging from lance corporal to RSM. They did not get extra pay but had a private cubicle at the entrance to their hut.

In 1939 corporal punishment still existed for boy soldiers committing 'serious misdemeanours', such as smoking. They were first put on a charge by the NCO who caught them, then paraded before their com-pany commander. He awarded six strokes of the cane, subject to written approval from parents or guardians. To the best of my know-ledge this was never refused, as most parents supported the biblical adage 'spare the rod and spoil the child'. When approval was received the culprits were summoned to the Company Office and one by one had to lower their trousers and underpants then bend over the end of a table. Shirt-tails remained draped over buttocks to preserve some dignity. Then the Wing Sergeant applied the cane, sometimes forcefully – one of my friends still bore the marks a year later. Needless to say, this didn't deter anyone from smoking. It just made you more careful. In retrospect, I think that though the discipline was strict, it wasn't oppressive, and it stood us in good stead in service.

The day we were marched to the workshops none of us had any idea what was in store. We were shown into a huge corrugated iron-roofed shed. Down one side were two long lines of heavy wooden benches, each with a large metalworking vice, and a metal toolbox containing a ball-peen hammer, cold chisels and files. The rest of the shed was occupied by lathes, drills, milling machines and so on.

Each of us was assigned to a bench, given a steel slab measuring 9″ × 6″ × 1″ and told to reduce it to lesser dimensions by filing down two of the sides and chipping the other two with hammer and chisel. The noise made by some sixty trainee fitters hammering metal in a hangar-like shed had to be experienced to be believed. This cacophony went on for weeks, for when the steel had been battered into submission we were presented with a piece of cast iron and told to repeat the process.

Most of us managed to hit our thumbs in the chipping process, which didn't do anything to brighten our days. Our fingernails and overalls were soon blackened with the dust created by the iron filings, and outside the sun was shining while we were under artificial light. Soon we began to wish we were back on the square again.

Our metalworking instructor was a dour Scots warrant officer with a red face and a bulbous journeyman drinker's nose supporting 'granny' glasses. He seldom moved from his desk, but would summon a boy there and examine his work. He examined mine once, two pieces of angled flat metal, fitted together. He held it up to the light and said, 'I could crawl between them wi' ma bluidy overcoat on.' But eventually my work improved enough for me to be graded 'Fitter, Class Three' and moved on to using metalworking machines. We were also taught blacksmithing so that we could make our own chisels.

On Sunday 3 September 1939, while at compulsory church service, the air raid sirens started their unholy wailing. We had heard them before when sounded for practice, but now, on the day war was declared, we thought they must be for real. The padre stopped his sermon and we left the church hut quickly, but in good order, and entered the air raid shelters. The newspapers had predicted that German air raids would cause thousands of casualties, hence the frequent alarms in the weeks that followed, so we soon became blasé about them.

The war didn't impinge on our lives except for more frequent fire drills, and on the second day our bed sheets vanished forever. Maybe hospitals needed them for the thousands of casualties. For the next six years I only slept between sheets when home on leave.

The winter of 1939–1940 was one of the coldest for decades, with heavy snow lying until early March. One morning we paraded outside for morning PT but found the gym locked. Someone was sent for the key, but by the time he returned we were blue with cold, despite running on the spot as hard as possible. Next morning I had a sore throat and a high fever, so reported sick. The Army will provide a good funeral if you die, but regard anyone reporting sick with suspicion, and for ATs things were made as inconvenient as possible. Kit, plus bedding, had to be handed in to the QM stores: quite a chore for a sick person. Having done that, I plodded through the snow to the medical inspection room. Suddenly a Regimental Policeman bellowed '*You!* Put your bloody gas mask on!' I had forgotten that we had to wear our respirators for two hours that morning, for acclimatization in case of a gas attack. So on went the mask, but the heat of my fever made the eyepieces mist over, and I floundered into a snow-filled drainage ditch.

The MO seemed quite impressed with my temperature of 104 and I was soon in bed in the camp hospital. After two days my temperature was normal and I became an 'Up Patient', which meant helping out in the ward. It was pretty boring in the hospital. There were no pretty female nurses, only unsympathetic male orderlies, and there was neither radio nor reading material. I was more than pleased to get back to my chums in the barrack hut.

Gradually winter turned to spring and it was no longer necessary to put our greatcoats on our beds to keep warm at night. On the Western Front nothing had happened throughout the winter and many people hoped a political settlement could be reached. Then in April the Germans invaded Denmark, then Norway. British, French and Polish forces were sent to northern Norway but as the Germans had air supremacy the Allied forces had to withdraw. While that was going on the Germans attacked through Holland and Belgium and overran most of northern France. Then came Dunkirk, with 350,000 Allied servicemen and women miraculously brought to Britain. This had an important effect on our lives.

The evacuated troops needed accommodation, including Fort Darland, so we were sent on indefinite leave. I vividly remember the journey home as the train was jam-packed with soldiers and I stood in the corridor all the way from Chatham to London Bridge, then from Paddington to Teignmouth. As my train pulled slowly out of Paddington another was pulling in alongside, full of dirty, exhausted and very sad-looking French soldiers. Standing next to me was a full colonel, which illustrates how crowded the train was. I had a cold but no handkerchief, so kept sniffing. The Colonel suddenly said 'Here, my boy, take this,' and handed me his handkerchief, telling me to keep it.

At home, luxury liners had become troopships so didn't need stewards, and Father was now managing a NAAFI canteen somewhere on Salisbury Plain. Arthur was in the RASC and Kathleen the WRNS in Plymouth. But apart from there being soldiers everywhere, nothing much had changed. In fact, there were still quite a large number of holidaymakers from all over the country enjoying time by the sea, just as they had pre-war. But the war was making an impact, mainly through shortages caused by U-boats. Petrol was so severely rationed that many car owners put their cars on blocks for the duration of the war. Petrol was only allowed to doctors, farmers and other people with jobs requiring a car. A coloured dye was added to military petrol and the police would check cars to see if any unauthorized persons were using it.

Perhaps the hardest thing for civilians was food rationing. The food allowances changed from time to time but were never generous, such as the cheese ration, which was usually two ounces per person per week. Bread was never rationed but white bread was replaced with the dark and coarse National Loaf, much like today's wholemeal bread. Vegetables were generally widely available as thousands of people responded to the 'Dig for Victory' call. Many lawns were dug up and parks became new allotments for those willing to work them.

Meat was always in short supply and most people only had one meat meal in a week. Later on, this situation was alleviated by imports of American 'Spam', tinned luncheon meat. Inevitably, rationing soon produced a flourishing black market where anything was available – at a price. In city restaurants gourmet meals could still be had by those with the wherewithal to pay for them. The people who operated the black market, and sometimes made fortunes, were known as 'spivs'. There were strict laws and punishments for those who broke them, but they were seldom enforced. It has to be said that the spivs were frequently smarter than the police and in general carried out their activities with impunity.

One more burden the civilian population had to bear was the black-out. Every building had to be completely blacked out at night, street lights were out, and ARP wardens and police patrolled to ensure that not a chink of light was revealed. Vehicles travelling at night had metal hoods over their headlights with only a tiny slit, which provided a downward-shining glimmer. By 1942 it was claimed the blackout had caused more casualties than the Germans!

However, in late summer 1940, we stood alone against Germany and Italy. It was still the old Britain, conservative in its ways, including music. Popular songs had a patriotic flavor: 'There'll Always be an

England', 'White Cliffs of Dover', 'Wish me Luck as you Wave me Goodbye', and others in similar vein.

After six weeks at home I felt out of things, but eventually an official letter arrived ordering me to report at Beachley Camp, Chepstow, in Monmouthshire.

The camp, which was on the banks of the River Severn, had a more relaxed atmosphere than Darland. A blind eye was turned on boys who smoked, providing they weren't too blatant about it. At NAAFI breaks the majority of boys were outside the workshops smoking, irrespective of bad weather. By now cigarettes were hard to come by so one cigarette would be shared among four or five friends. Anyone taking too deep a drag was not popular!

One sunny Sunday morning we were loafing around outside our hut when a Heinkel 111, flying so low we could clearly see the aircrew, dropped a stick of bombs on the workshops. Then as it crossed over the camp the air gunner sprayed the huts with machine-gun fire, killing an AT lying on his bed. He was the only casualty, but there would have been many more if it had been a working day and the workshops had been full.

In general I had enjoyed my time at Beachley, but I was looking forward to getting into man's service when I turned eighteen.

Chapter 3

Trainee Sapper

In June 1941 I entered man's service and was posted to No. 55 War Party, No. 1 Training Battalion RE, in Clitheroe, Lancashire, but given seven days' leave before joining. I enjoyed good home cooking and going to the pub every evening with Father, who was running a canteen in a camp near Teignmouth.

On the third night I was woken by air raid sirens and looked out of the window. The moon was nearly full so the town was clearly visible. I could hear the uneven engine beat of a German bomber, then suddenly, very close, bombs exploded, followed by the crash of falling masonry. I dressed quickly and ran into the street. The bombs had hit the roadway, not, miraculously, the houses, and as far as I could ascertain no one had been killed or injured. Next morning I discovered that the front steps of the house opposite, where Arthur's fiancée lived, had been blown right through the roof of our house. Another bomb landed in the grounds of Teignmouth Hospital, just down the road, but fortunately only damaged the administration block, which was unoccupied at the time. Repairs by Teignmouth Council started almost at once. It was an eventful leave and time simply flew by, so all too soon I made the long, slow train journey to Lancashire.

The training battalion was housed in a disused cotton mill, with the spinning mules replaced by hundreds of two-tier beds. One floor housed No. 55 WP, raw recruits apart from some twenty ex-ATs. The first day was spent getting army haircuts and drawing clothing and equipment, including 1914-vintage SMLE (Short Magazine Lee Enfield), otherwise Rifle, Mark III, bayonet and scabbard. Next came webbing equipment: water bottle holder, waist belt, large pack, small pack, cross braces, ammunition pouches and bayonet frog. It had to be blancoed every night, a hated chore and one of the worst aspects of army bullshit. Every evening soldiers in barracks were in the ablutions blancoing their webbing, then desperately looking for a place to hang it up to dry.

Our mentors were one full and two lance corporals who insisted we address them as 'Corporal' while at 'Attention'. Some of the older recruits found this hard to take but probably later realized that it was necessary to instill discipline before moving on to other things. Next morning, at 0600 hrs, someone blew 'reveille', and seconds later the corporals were bouncing around, yelling 'Rise and shine, beds in line, piss pots out the window!', or 'Let go cocks, on with socks!' Part dressed, we raced to the ablutions, hoping for hot water and a free basin, washed and shaved, raced back upstairs, dressed properly, downstairs again, fallen-in to be marched to the dining hall for breakfast. Spam had replaced bacon and 'soya-links', skinless, meatless things made from soya beans took the place of sausages, accompanied by scrambled powdered egg, but we were ravenous and ate everything.

After breakfast it was back to the barrack room, then into the toilets for a quick smoke before clattering downstairs again for the first parade and much foot drill. This was old stuff to us ex-ATs, and we showed off not a little. A week of foot drill was followed by one of with arms, interspersed with what the Army persisted in calling 'musketry'. That meant learning to hold, aim and fire a rifle, albeit without live ammunition. We lay prone, taking aim at a small disc held by the instructor, also in the prone position, facing the trainee. There was a small hole in the disc through which he peered to see if the aim was correct. We had to repeat: 'Tip of the foresight in the centre of the V and in line with the shoulders of the back-sight. Take first pressure, and gently squeeze.'

We looked forward to the first day on the rifle range with keen anticipation, despite much speculation about bruised shoulders. That only happened if the rifle wasn't pulled tightly into the shoulder when firing. We fired from 200, 500, and 800 yards at paper 'bullseye' targets hoisted on iron frames from a deep trench in front of the 'butts', a high sand bank that stopped the bullets. After firing, the targets were lowered and examined for hits. Hits were classified as outer, inner, magpie and bullseye, and their position indicated to the shooter with a white wooden triangle on the end of a pole. A miss, or 'whitewash', was signalled by waving the triangle across the front of the target.

Afterwards, in the barracks, rifles were cleaned by 'boiling out'. This entailed pouring boiling water down the barrel, without benefit of a funnel, leading to not a few scalded fingers and much swearing! The barrel was then 'pulled through', using a cord with a brass weight at one end and a loop at the other, which held a piece of dry lint, known as 4 × 2 (its size in inches). The brass weight was dropped down the barrel, gripped and pulled until the 4 × 2 passed right through. The process was repeated with an oily piece of 4 × 2, the rest of the weapon meticulously cleaned, and it was ready for inspection. Inspections of rifles were frequent and taken seriously: a dirty or rusty rifle barrel was a serious crime.

Then we began the real sapper training – field engineering. It started with constructing shear-legs and tripods using stout poles and cordage. From these were hung pulley blocks, which when reeved (fitted with a rope) were used to lift heavy objects. Then came assembly of small and large box-girder bridges, all heavy and requiring manhandling into position over small gaps. Then on to the Bailey bridge, one of the great inventions of the war, and a British one at that. Basically it was constructed of three elements: cross-transoms, side panels and wooden decking. Baileys could be built with amazing speed, especially if there were already good bank seats in situ for the ends to rest on. The carrying capacity of a bridge could be increased by adding more side panels. Every man on a bridging site knew his job. For instance, he might be a member of a six-man panel party, or the 'hammer man' who fixed the heavy steel pins that held the panels together. We all got 'bridging fit' very quickly, if painfully, at that time. Building a Bailey bridge over a dry gap was a comparatively simple affair compared to building one across a river.

We also learned how to build pontoon, or floating, bridges, using metal box-like boats to support a flexible trackway. Our 'wet' bridging site was on the River Ribble, in Lancashire, and from constant use the banks were extremely muddy. To manhandle pontoons down to the river took a lot of sweat because they invariably sunk deep into the mud. More often that not, water leaked into them, making them even heavier. Once launched, the pontoons had to be manoeuvered into the bridge position, and if the launching site was not near the bridge we used oars, fitted into rowlocks on the pontoon sides, to get them into position.

We also learned 'boatmanship', handling assault boats, an essential and very important part of RE training. It included all kinds of knots and splices, and how to manoeuvre boats and pontoons on fast-flowing rivers. We would, in fact, have made quite good sailors in the Royal Navy. The odd chap fell in but since we wore lifejackets when wet bridging no harm was done.

The subject we probably enjoyed most was demolitions. Sappers not only learn how to build bridges but also how to destroy them. At that time the main British Army explosives were guncotton and Nobel 808 gelignite, nasty smelling stuff, which if handled too long induced severe headaches. We also learned how to use ammonal blasting

14

powder to blow craters. We became familiar with detonators, primers and fuses, but not over familiar – explosives and their appurtenances are dangerous if not handled carefully and expertly.

Another dangerous subject was mines – how to lay, and clear, mine-fields. All types of mines and their associated tripwires and igniters, British, German and Italian, were shown to us. The German equipment seemed to be better than our own.

There was one really strange episode at Clitheroe – the arrival of several hundred West Indian recruits. In peacetime they would have been segregated from white soldiers at meal times, but as space was short they used our dining hall, but were supposed sit in a separate area. They raised heated objections to this, and insisted on sharing our tables. Rather than have to put down a riot, they were allowed to have their way.

These volunteers were a pretty rowdy lot and mealtimes became noisy, to say the least. As the winter approached and the weather worsened they became very miserable, continually wearing their great-coats and balaclava helmets and refusing all orders to remove them. It was amusing to see them down at the river when ice formed on its edges, tapping it, saying 'Whassamatter wid dis water, man? He gone hard.' One day they all disappeared as suddenly as they had arrived, possibly transferred to the RAF.

Our training was now drawing to a close. In peacetime it would have lasted for eighteen months. We had done it in six, but we would obviously quickly gain more knowledge and experience on active service. We moved out of the mill into huts to make room for the next intake, but within a week we had all moved on, posted to various units. Two of us went to 109 (Army Troops) Company RE at Haworth, Yorkshire.

Postings broke up many friendships. I said goodbye to Roy Sheard from Rochdale: we had shared many a laugh in Chatham, Chepstow and Clitheroe. I never saw him again. He went to 276 Field Company RE in 51st (Highland) Division and served from Alamein to Berlin. After VE-Day, on 24 July 1945, near Hanover, he was shot dead by a trigger-happy Russian sentry and is buried in Celle CWGC.

Anyway, my colleague and I reported to 109 and were housed in Nissen huts, next to a farm outside Haworth. We were met by a corporal and immediately came to attention. He smiled, saying 'You can forget that nonsense here!' We happily followed him into a barrack hut where he allocated us beds, then showed us the dining hall, NAAFI and QM stores, where we drew palliasses then filled them with clean straw. There was a friendly atmosphere in 109, attributable to an easy-going OC. One bitterly cold night he returned late and was surprised to find no sentry manning the gate. Noticing smoke coming from the NAAFI chimney he found the sentry sound asleep in front of a nicely glowing stove! In most units the sentry would have received at least twenty-eight days in the 'glasshouse', but in 109 all he got was seven days' stoppage of pay and a severe reprimand.

I enjoyed a few weeks with 109, and would have happily stayed, but it was not to be. It was ordered overseas and as I was only eighteen I could not to go on active service. After a brief spell at an RAOC Depot I was posted to 102 (Army Troops) Company RE, a pre-war TA Glasgow unit temporarily based in Paisley, Scotland.

Chapter 4

Marching as to War

My new unit was billeted in Moor Park School, near Paisley town centre. The OC, Major Paul Postlethwaite, known as 'PP', was a Regular, not TA, officer, and worked hard to prepare us for war. He recognized that we needed toughening up so we slept on the school's wooden floors, resting on groundsheets, not even palliasses. As a Scots unit 'reveille' was played by a bagpiper who paraded the rooms blowing some God-awful dirge fit to wake the dead, never mind the living. Breakfast was 'burgoo', porridge without sugar. Enough said!

Another of PP's 'fit-for-war' ideas was unannounced route marches, in full battle order, webbing and weapons. One bright morning, instead of being dismissed to our duties after muster parade, we were marched out of the school playground, then turned east through the town. Unknown to us we were heading for Stirling, thirty long miles away. It was to be the first leg of what could be called my 'grand tour' of Scotland, some stages done on foot, a few in lorries. The British Army marches at 120 paces per minute (ppm), covering three miles in fifty minutes and then resting for ten. Light Infantry units march at 180 ppm, and Highland ones 112 ppm. To digress a little, the French Foreign Legion march at 90 ppm and can look quite menacing coming towards one. I imagine they march as fast as anyone else when needs must!

To return to our morning march. We didn't know it, but it was going to take about ten hours, not the usual three. The first two were quite pleasant, the weather was sunny but cool, and at the hourly halts housewives regaled us with jugs of tea and a chat-up. But suddenly the heavens released a downpour that continued all day. We donned our groundsheets, which doubled as waterproof capes. They were made of rubberized fabric and hung in uneven folds to knee length, which meant the rain saturated one's trouser legs.

In addition to a groundsheet every soldier had a long, voluminous waterproof anti-gas cape. They were carried, tightly rolled, on the top of the small pack, released by one tug on a tape. They made ideal

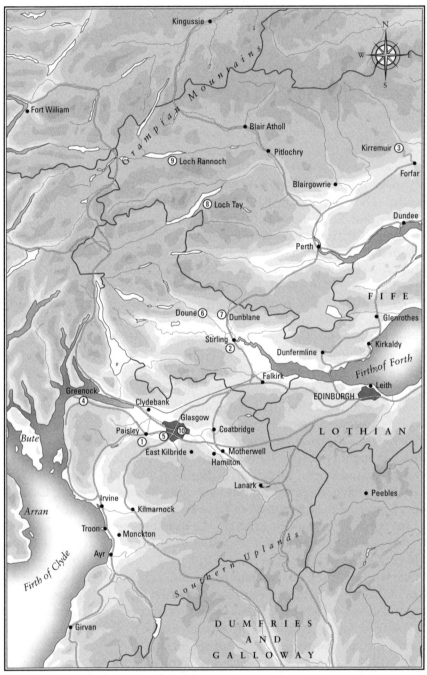

Map 1. Charlie's Scottish travels, in sequence … ① Paisley, ② Stirling, ③ Kirriemuir, ④ Greenock, ⑤ Monckton, ⑥ Doune, ⑦ Dunblane, ⑧ Loch Earn, ⑨ Loch Rannoch, ⑩ Glasgow.

raincoats but we were forbidden to use them as such until it became obvious gas would not be used.

So on we marched through the rain. The usual banter and singing dissolved into silence, broken only by the rhythmic crunch of hob-nailed boots on wet asphalt. Happily, at midday the cookhouse Tilly appeared with hot tea and two sandwiches per man, one cheese, the other jam. The normal lunchtime rest was forfeited by popular consent: no one wanted to hang about in the rain.

It was getting dark by the time we reached Stirling, and marched round it past the castle perched high above our road on its rock, before reaching the RE's Drip Road Bridging Camp on the banks of the River Forth. As we passed the below Stirling Castle we perked up, and there was much comforting speculation about warm, dry billets, but the reality was very different. We suddenly turned into a large muddy field with a heap of tentage and poles in one corner – so much for warm and dry! We quickly erected the tents before dark, gloomily wondering what the next surprise might be. Fortunately it was a nice one: the cookhouse Tilly again, with hot food and strong tea, which cheered everyone up. But we had an uncomfortable night, lying on damp ground without blankets. Next morning we returned to Paisley by 3-tonner.

Not long after there was a three-day 'divisional movement' exercise, not on foot but in lorries, with all our RE kit. After many hours our convoy halted for the night in the middle of a dripping-wet forest somewhere in the Scottish Highlands. We put up tents, and with our RE tools soon made wooden beds. Not very comfortable, but better than lying on wet ground. Next day we found ourselves driving through the small mill town of Kirriemuir. This was the only place on the trip I remember as we all knew the song, but didn't know the place really existed! It looked rather drab on a cold, wet Scottish Highlands' morning, and we were glad to return to our schoolrooms in Paisley, however hard the floors.

A few days later half a dozen of us were told to report to the QM Stores to exchange old BD for new. This didn't please us: the uniforms handed in were well pressed and carefully tailored whereas the new ones would be ill-fitting and impregnated with anti-gas chemicals, but orders is orders. Next morning we were minutely inspected, then driven, standing up to preserve our creases, to a huge empty bus park in Ayr. We joined detachments from every unit of the new First Army, formed for Operation TORCH, the North African landings. There were several hundred men on parade, in three long ranks. Eventually a large shiny Daimler glided onto the scene, we were called to attention, and out stepped King George VI. He was greeted by the Parade Commander and innumerable staff officers, then he and his entourage walked slowly along the ranks, occasionally stopping to speak to a soldier. We were wearing the First Army arm patch, a white shield bearing a sword superimposed on a red Crusader's cross. The king stopped and asked an NCO next to me if he knew what the patch represented. The NCO said he didn't, there was no reason why he should, they had only been issued the day before, but it was an embarrassing moment.

It was now obvious we would soon go overseas. This was confirmed when it was announced that everyone would be going on embarkation leave before 'going somewhere'. No other information was forthcoming. After a short but pleasant leave, I rejoined 102 and learned we were going on long sea voyage, destination unknown, leaving from Greenock, on the Firth of Clyde, a few miles west of Paisley.

At Greenock we boarded HMT *Strathmore*, a converted P&O liner. 'Conversion' meant that, apart from officer's areas, all cabins, restaurants and bars were removed. The resultant spaces became troop decks, with fixed mess tables and benches, washbasins and large wooden racks for daytime stowage of hammocks. At night the ends of hammocks were fastened to hooks welded to the deck head. As there were not enough hooks some unfortunates slept on, or under, mess tables. Troop deck portholes were welded shut to maintain blackout. This, combined with overcrowding, created a claustrophobic and fetid atmosphere, especially at night.

After inspecting, gloomily, our troop deck we traversed seemingly endless alleyways and companionways to reach our designated lifeboat station. We wondered if we should ever find our way back, but it soon became a familiar route. At the lifeboat station everyone received a Kapok life-jacket, to be carried at all times. We were happy to do this as they made comfortable pillows. We then heard about the 'do's and don'ts' of wartime troopship life. They included never showing light at night, and never throwing anything overboard. The first was commonsense, but the second wasn't until we learned that empty cigarette packets in the sea gave useful clues to U-boat lookouts. Full water bottles had to be carried at all times, and open decks were out of bounds at night. Finally, as we were to sail that night, we lined the ship's rails to have a last look at Britain. Sadly, for some that was true.

As dusk fell we went below for our first meal afloat. It was the usual tinned or dehydrated stuff, but we were used to such fare and ate heartily. Happily, *Strathmore* had a bakery, which produced superb bread, something we hadn't enjoyed for a long time. Then came a lecture on action if the ship was torpedoed – basically getting to your lifeboat station as quickly as possible, then awaiting orders. With these dire warnings giving us food for thought we gladly turned to the light relief of learning to sling our hammocks. There are knacks to that, and to getting in and out, and quite a few of us landlubbers came to grief until we learned them, but it provided much-needed laughs for all. Gradually the hubbub became subdued conversations, which died away to silence, broken only by the occasional snore. However, the lights stayed on, in case of torpedoing.

At some time during the night *Strathmore* trembled as her powerful engines started up and she glided out to take position in the convoy. At 0600 hrs the Deck Orderly Sergeant appeared, bawling 'Wakey, wakey, rise and shine!' and slapping the hammocks of the slow and lazy. We rolled and stowed our hammocks with the blankets inside, had a quick wash and shave before breakfast of tea, powdered egg and soya sausage, but with good fresh bread and *butter*! As the ship was still on an even keel, everyone ate heartily.

Fifteen minutes later we paraded at our boat station with life-jackets and full water bottles. Despite a sullen sky and slate-gray sea it was good to be out in the fresh salt-laden air, with plenty to see. We appeared to be in the middle of a large convoy, surrounded by troopships. Barely visible on the outer flanks were escorting corvettes and destroyers, which would suddenly increase speed and dart off in different directions.

On this first day at sea we stood at the lifeboat station for about three hours to allow the initial ship's inspection to be carried out by the Army OIC Troopship, accompanied by *Strathmore*'s First Officer, the Ship's RSM and a retinue of minions. As we entered the Irish Sea the wind increased, the waves started to build up and the ship started a gentle roll. Gradually the wind strengthened and the waves got so high that the nearest ships seemed to disappear into the troughs then slowly reappear on the crests of the following seas. As *Strathmore* followed suit many faces gradually turned pale, then green.

Once the inspection finished there was an immediate rush to the wet canteen, run in a lower deck cabin by a *Strathmore* crewman. He must have become very rich, selling thousands of sixpenny mugs of tea on each voyage. That was the only commodity sold, but soldiers can never have too much tea, and will brew up at any opportunity. The motto of one unit I served in was 'When in doubt, brew up.' In those days no British soldier in the field was separated from his enamel mug, usually carried on the waist-belt or a strap of the small pack, ready for immediate use. Strangely enough, I never saw US, French, Italian, German or Brazilian soldiers carrying mugs. Having drunk our first mug we went to the dry canteen, also run by a crewman in a small cabin. It only sold Canadian Sweet Caporal cigarettes and strong black plug tobacco, both in abundance.

We still had no idea of our destination but guessed it could be lively as we had on board most of 1st Parachute Brigade. Thick overcast made it impossible to work the ship's heading but a crewman said it was west. We maintained that course for three days before turning south. This was probably a ruse to fool U-boats, making them think we were bound for the USA or Canada. It also kept us away from the French coastal bases of German long-range Focke-Wulf 'Condor' recce aircraft. We were not really aware of any serious threat, but that month, October 1942, 808,000 tons of Allied shipping was sunk, mainly by U-boats. Unknown to us was the sacrifice of Convoy SL125, travelling from Sierra Leone to Liverpool. It was lightly escorted and lost twelve ships when attacked by a ten-strong U-boat wolfpack. A tragedy, but the price of our successful landings in French North Africa.

A 'ship's newspaper', a single typewritten sheet, was posted daily outside the former Purser's Office. It had the latest reports received by *Strathmore*'s Radio Officer, and the news was good. In a big battle at El Alamein, in Egypt, the Germans and Italians had been defeated and were in full retreat. This was a huge boost to our morale as up to then good news had been rather a rare commodity. As Churchill rightly said, Alamein was not the end, not even the beginning of the end, but it was, perhaps, the end of the beginning.

Apart from the ship's Army staff, *Strathmore* also carried Royal Artillery gunners as she was a Defensively Equipped Merchant Ship. She had several Oerlikon AA guns and a single stern-mounted 6-inch gun. In compliance with the Geneva Convention, DEMS could only carry a rear-firing gun, as if fitted with forward-firing ones they became Armed Merchant Cruisers, technically warships.

The bad weather may have been a blessing in disguise by restricting U-boat activity but it made troop deck conditions horrible. At one end there was a urinal, a long, deep trough, with a drain usually clogged with cigarette ends and vomit. Every time *Strathmore* rolled, gallons of stale urine and rubbish surged onto the mess deck. The effect of the sight and smell of this had disastrous results, especially at night when no one was allowed onto the open decks.

A further troop deck indignity was 'short-arm inspections', held at irregular intervals to ascertain that servicemen were 'FFI' (free from infection). The MO and his assistant sat behind a table with their victims in single file to one side. As each man arrived in front of the MO he would drop his trousers and underpants and his penis and pubic area were inspected, sometimes with the aid of a torch. He would then order the man turn around and bend over. The object, of course, was to look for signs of venereal disease or crab lice. If the MO was satisfied the man would then pull up his trousers and move on, making room for the next victim. We were accustomed to these lewd exhibitions but we were somewhat indignant when one occurred on our mess deck when we were having dinner. Perhaps it was in lieu of an ENSA show, but it didn't improve our appetite for soya links and dehydrated vegetables.

There wasn't space on board for foot drill but some mornings PT was done on the boat deck: running on the spot, stretching exercises and so on. However, the Paras, as is their wont, had to have boxing matches, using the forward cargo hatch as ring, albeit without ropes. Sadly, one Para was knocked down and was killed instantly when his head struck the metal hatch corner. At dusk his body, sewn into his hammock and covered with the Union Jack, was laid on a plank. *Strathmore*'s Tannoy sounded 'Still', and the 'Burial at Sea' service was read, beginning with the words 'We therefore commit the earthly remains of ... to the deep ...' Then the plank was tilted over the rail, the shrouded body slipped out from under the flag to splash into the cold grey sea, looking very lonely, while the ship ploughed remorselessly on. Traditionally it would heave-to, but not in a wartime convoy, with U-boats about.

Shortly after we learned our destination was Algiers, news that met with general approval. Our conversation centred on the imaginary delights of belly dancers. Some of the film buffs tried to imitate the French accent of Charles Boyer with the phrase 'Come wiz me to ze Casbah.' We were issued with paper BNAF (British North Africa Forces) franc notes, specially printed for the invasion forces.

That evening we sailed past the Rock of Gibraltar and into the Straits. We were allowed a few extra minutes on deck to see the twinkling lights of neutral Tangiers, an incredible sight after three years of blacked-out Britain.

The next two days had an almost holiday feeling as the sun was warm and the sparkling blue sea calm. Leaning on the ship's rail, we speculated whether or not the French troops in Algeria would come over to our side. Fortunately for our peace of mind we did not know that at that very moment German forces were being ferried into adjacent Tunisia by sea and air, nor that the build-up would continue for weeks and it would take six months of hard fighting before they were defeated.

Eventually, *Strathmore* approached Algiers and we saw a gleaming white city spreading from the sea up to the hills above. As we got

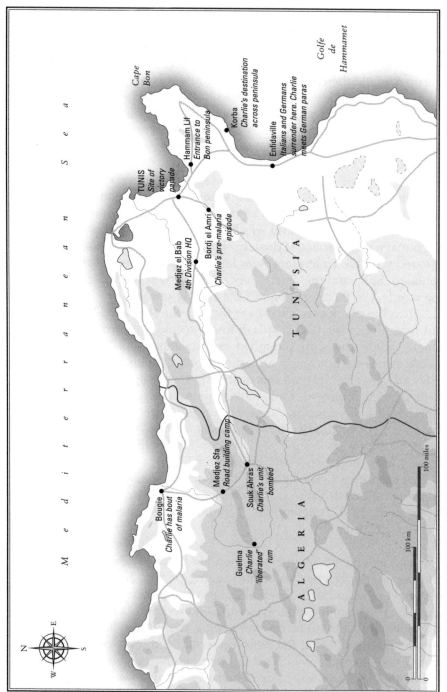

Map 2. Charlie's tour of Algeria and Tunisia.

Mediterranean Sea

Cape Bon

Golfe de Hammamet

Korba
Charlie's destination across peninsula

Enfidaville
Italians and Germans surrender here. Charlie meets German paras

Hammam Lif
Entrance to Bon peninsula

TUNIS
Site of victory parade

Bordj el Amri
Charlie's pre-malaria episode

Medjez el Bab
4th Division HQ

TUNISIA

Medjez Sfa
Road building camp

Souk Ahras
Charlie's unit bombed

Bougie
Charlie has bout of malaria

Guelma
Charlie 'liberated' rum

ALGERIA

N E S W

100 km

100 miles

24

nearer we heard for the first time the muezzin's call to prayer and began to smell the unique odour of French North Africa, a compound of fermenting wine, burning charcoal and Gauloise cigarettes. *Strathmore* was quickly moored alongside and the familiar vibration of the ship's engines ceased for the first time in ten days.

We fell-in on the quayside, then marched uphill to the Botanical Gardens to bivouac for the night. Here we met 'stand on the footprints' lavatories, which caused much ribald comment. We had to use these as we did not want to upset the locals by digging latrines in their elegant *jardin botanique*.

After a stint of guard duty I returned to my platoon for a brew-up, using the newly issued 'Compo' (Composite) ration dried tea-milk powder, which came in a small, flat tin. A mess tin half of water was boiled over a Tommy cooker and spoonfuls of the mixture stirred in. Sadly, the consensus amongst the lads was that it tasted like gnats' piss. However, the Tommy cooker was given the seal of approval: it was light, handy to carry and held tablets of solid paraffin ready to use, and they were welcome as they did not produce any smoke. 'Compo' came in stout cardboard boxes, each holding rations for seven men for one day. Everything was tinned except a packet of four cigarettes and toilet paper, otherwise 'Army Form Blank'.

That first night in Algiers I was unhappy at being cooped up after ten days at sea. As there was no light at all in the gardens I figured my absence could not easily be detected, and persuaded a friend to come with me to a bar we'd seen across the street. Without further ado we climbed the railings and scurried across to the bar, which was crowded with French colonists jabbering away noisily – that is, until we entered. We walked to the bar in silence, all eyes in the room on us, and I asked the barman, in my best schoolboy French, for two beers. 'Pas bierre,' I was told, so we settled for *vin rouge*. I proffered a BNAF note in payment, which caused murmurs of interest among the clientele. It was passed from hand to hand and finally returned to the barman. He reluctantly accepted it in payment, and even more reluctantly gave me some real francs as change. This transaction broke the ice, for these Frenchmen were keen to hear our views on the war, and how life was in wartime Britain. At first my schoolboy French was barely adequate to cope with the barrage of questions but after a glass or two of *rouge* it quickly improved. Then, having flouted authority long enough to get a drink and to satisfy our curiosity, we returned to base. No one had noticed our absence.

25

Next day we marched to the main station to join a train bound for the front line. Each eight-man compartment had to take ten sappers, squashed onto wooden-slatted seats. They were excruciatingly uncomfortable. As there were no corridors one had to be rather careful when leaning out the window in case someone was urinating from another window further along. So started my tour of Algeria, and, although I did not know it at the time, Tunisia.

The engine was a huge, powerful-looking machine, emitting vast clouds of steam accompanied by menacing hissing sounds. The journey was long and slow, with frequent stops at small stations. At each of these, hungry-looking, tattered Algerians begged for cigarettes and biscuits. They got no cigarettes but we were quite generous with the tasteless Compo biscuits, with which we were well supplied. The typical local male costume was a long, thick, woollen ankle-length robe with a deep hood; when wet they gave off a powerful goat-like odour. At most stops we made a quick dash to the engine to draw boiling water for a quick brew-up, a useful technique picked up on exercises in Britain.

As darkness fell the train pulled into a station at Guelma and into a siding and stopped to allow another one to pass in the opposite direction. Alongside us was an unguarded goods train. One tarpaulin-covered open wagon looked interesting, and not having anything else to occupy us, and being full of curiosity, in seconds a corner of the tarpaulin was untied and pulled back. There, protected by a ring of crates and boxes, were several dozen earthenware jars of genuine army-issue rum. We seized one, retied the tarpaulin and dived back into our compartment, where we filled our mess tins with beautiful rich, strong, red, red rum.

Until the train moved off again we were in danger of being caught red-handed by some nosey officer or NCO. So, having rid ourselves of the jar, we swiftly slurped down the rum. The result was inevitable and within minutes we were all as drunk as lords. Being the youngest and unused to spirits, I was the first to pass out. I was also the last to regain consciousness, helped by hefty slaps across the face from the others, who thought I might be dead. A long drink from my water bottle made me feel much better and I soon sobered up, which was fortunate, as shortly afterwards the train stopped and we were ordered to dismount.

It was very dark and orders were given in whispers and one of them was that there was to be no smoking and no lights of any sort to be shown. Apparently, no one knew where the enemy forces were as the front had not stabilized and both sides were mounting deep recce probes with some vigour. We were in a completely blacked-out town, Souk Ahras, but there was no movement whatsoever of people or vehicles. We were ordered to stay put, but could lie down on the pavement with our equipment on and rifles to hand. There was not much left of the night, but most of us got a couple of hours of sleep, the rum being a help in that respect. At least it was not raining.

As soon as dawn broke we fell-in on the street and marched to a large two-storey school, which was to be our billet for a few days. After settling in we enjoyed a breakfast of powdered egg, fat bacon rashers and Compo biscuits before spending the day unloading stores at the railway station, then before nightfall were deployed at various points in the town as guards.

That night there was a successful air raid on the railway station, which held two trains, one of petrol tankers, the other carrying ammunition. The tankers went up in huge balls of flame and some of the ammunition exploded. The raid continued for the best part of an hour without any defensive action, as no AA units had arrived in the area. Shortly after the aircraft left, one of our sergeants appeared and told us to get to the railway station at once. We found a terrible mess – burning buildings revealed derailed wagons, twisted rails and masses of hot unexploded ammunition scattered everywhere. We were told that the line had to be cleared as soon as possible since it was the only one feeding the front and so vital for the passage of troops and supplies.

The first job was to remove the unexploded ammunition, a task done very quickly indeed! Then the overturned wagons were dragged clear of the rails, and by noon the line was open again for trains in both directions. We had one casualty: a sergeant killed by a bomb splinter while standing outside our school billet.

A few days later our MT arrived from Algiers and we motored north to Medjez Sfa, a small Berber village in the foothills of the Atlas Mountains. As a Line of Communication unit our job was to keep one section of the road in reasonable repair. Our billet was an empty cargo shed beside the railway line, a couple of hundred yards from the station, and big enough to accommodate the whole company. It had an earthen floor, but luckily this was covered by a slightly raised wooden floor.

The section of road had deteriorated and was full of potholes. Lacking any earth-moving equipment, we worked with pick, shovel and sledgehammer. And as there was no hardcore to hand, earth and stones were dug out of nearby banks and thrown into the potholes, hardly a satisfactory method of repair. However, PP soon located a quarry, which we ran jointly with the French, with us making several

27

major improvements. We found they were extracting stone by creating a series of horizontal ledges in the rock face. Arab workmen would stand along them, making vertical holes for explosive charges. The way they made these holes can only be described as primitive. Every workman had a crowbar, which he would lift for about a foot, then drop so that the chisel-end hit the bottom of the hole. This was repeated hundreds of times, occasionally with some water poured into the hole. It would take one man several hours to make a hole deep enough to take an explosive charge.

We used a Tilly-mounted air compressor to power four rock hammer drills, which cut holes horizontally in a few minutes. We soon had an adequate and continuous supply of hardcore for road repairs and, as amongst our number were miners and a quarryman, the quarry was soon being worked professionally.

As we spent our days out on the road we had the opportunity to observe the customs of our Berber neighbours. Their mode of transport was invariably on the back of the ubiquitous donkey, which they encouraged to keep moving by making a 'brrr-brrr' sound. The docile little beasts were so small that the rider had to hold his legs out at an angle to prevent his feet dragging on the ground. Usually, the rider carried a short, pointed stick with which to prod the neck of the poor little donkey to keep it moving. This treatment produced sores on its neck, which incurred our wrath – we would curse the offender, much to his astonishment.

The poorer Berbers lived in dome-shaped mud-brick houses with roughly thatched roofs, a rickety door and no windows. Smoke from the central fire simply oozed out through the thatch from lack of a proper chimney. The Berbers lived a hard and frugal existence, so it was not surprising they seemed dour and uncommunicative when we spoke to them. The usual response to a greeting was to hold two spread fingers to his mouth, as a sign to ask for a cigarette.

The Berber women were subdued and seemed resigned to their lot as beasts of burden, just like the donkeys. They all bore blue-coloured tattoos on their foreheads and sometimes also on their cheeks. Their hard way of life probably aged them prematurely, and the younger ones were probably kept at home to perform household chores away from the covetous eyes of others.

There was no mosque in Medjez Sfa but it was a common sight to see a lone Berber praying at the side of the road. There was a village café, more accurately a tea shop, since that is what they mainly drank there. It came in small glasses, not cups, sometimes with herbs added to it.

By arrangement with the French authorities, some Berbers were sent to us to help with the roadwork. They did not prove to be much of an asset since they lacked energy and enthusiasm. They brought their own food with them, just a piece or two of flat unleavened bread and nothing to go with it, so it was not surprising that they had no energy. They were paid by the French, who, I imagine, did not pay them much. There was a French overseer who occasionally paid them a visit. They were very scared of him, and with good reason. He was a big brute who always carried a heavy stick and shouted abuse at them in the Berber dialect.

The battlefront in Tunisia had now stabilized, as the Germans and Italians had brought in their reinforcements more quickly, and in greater quantity, than could the British and Americans. This was due to their very much shorter lines of communication, theirs from nearby Sicily and ours from the distant UK and USA. The enemy also had air superiority as they operated from all-weather airfields at Tunis and Bizerta, close to the front. Our nearest all-weather airfield was at Maison Blanche, near Algiers, too far away to provide constant air cover for our troops, and too small to handle many aircraft.

In mid-December we were joined by a company of French sappers. As I spoke French I was detailed to provide their air cover, using a tripod-mounted Bren with 100-round AA magazines. This was an extremely boring job, just standing there, waiting all day for enemy aircraft that never appeared. A further annoyance was that every morning every one of about 150 Frenchmen came up, shook my hand and wished me 'Bonjour.' On the credit side they always invited me to share their midday *soupe*, a delicious treat in winter, and were generous with their *rouge*, both much better than Compo. After a week or two of that undemanding task, I was not sorry when PP decided it was unnecessary and I returned to roadwork.

Apart from a small estaminet, amenities for recreation at Medjez Sfa were non-existent, and there was no opportunity for leave to Algiers or any other civilized place. Christmas Day brought little change except that we only worked in the morning. There was no special fare: Christmas dinner was Compo tinned steak and kidney pudding. That night a crowd of us went to the estaminet and got drunk on *rouge* with our French sapper colleagues. It was enjoyable while it lasted, but the next day I felt like death, and some peculiar chap told me I had had seventeen drinks. It certainly felt like it, working on the road the next day, and it was two days before I felt well again. At least we had had a good Christmas compared to 2nd Battalion Coldstream Guards, who had spent three days in a fierce battle at Longstop Hill, in Tunisia. It was taken and retaken several times and casualties had been heavy on both sides.

In January 1943 we and the French sappers were ordered to make a new section of road strong enough to take the passage of a full armoured division. We did not have the luxury of tipper trucks, so our 3-tonners had to be loaded with large stones by hand and offloaded in the same way, piece by piece. Neither did we have bulldozers, or other road-making plant. The whole job was done using only picks, shovels and sledgehammers. The French Public Works Department provided drums of bitumen, which had to be heated over a fire before it could be poured from buckets, a messy job. Nevertheless, the job was completed on time, and the British 6th Armoured Division passed through on its way to the battlefront, equipped with Churchill tanks armed with 2-pounder guns.

By this time I had had more than enough of this 'chain-gang-without-the-chain' existence and decided to apply for a transfer to an RE Field Company to see something of the real war. A stupid attitude to take, perhaps, but, as a career soldier I felt that I was wasting my time with my present unit. I had been turning these thoughts over in my mind for some time, and it was an incident that had occurred the previous day that tipped the balance. A party of us had been working in the quarry and at about noon we had lit the fuses to some blasting charges. A convoy of ambulances approached and we stopped them, telling the drivers to wait until after the charges detonated as sometimes boulders flew onto the road. While they were waiting we went round to the backs of the ambulances to chat with the wounded lads and give them cigarettes. One badly wounded chap said to me, 'What are you lot doing here? Are you on manoeuvres?' That was enough! Fortunately, next day PP sent for me and appointed me to drive his Tilly. He had been posted to Tunisia as CO of a Field Company. The next day we left to find our new unit.

Chapter 5

Tunisia

After entering the British Zone of Tunisia we headed for the town of Medjez-el-Bab, until recently on the front line. It had obviously seen heavy fighting, with many shattered buildings and burnt-out trucks and tanks. Not far beyond the town we found 4th Infantry Division HQ where we would be given the location of our new unit. As we approached the HQ, really just a cluster of trucks and tents on a knoll, I saw someone going through the motions of bowling a cricket ball, albeit without a ball. This looked familiar and, as I drew nearer, I saw it was my sports-mad brother, Arthur, now a staff sergeant in the HQ. We had a quick chat while PP reported in, then we were off again to find 225 Field Company RE, somewhere in the divisional sector of the front line.

We found 225 on the floor of a wadi (a dry riverbed); a few vehicles were scattered about, with little groups of sappers chatting or singing in a relaxed manner. I reported to the Company Sergeant Major who directed me to my new platoon where the Sergeant welcomed me, then told me to dig a slit-trench as Jerry was in the habit of disturbing the peace with an occasional *stonk*, a sudden very heavy artillery or mortar bombardment. By the time I had dug my trench it was getting dark, so after lining up for, then eating, a tin of M&V rations, there was nothing else to do but get into the trench and go to sleep.

Apart from the odd rifle shot in the distance, it was a night without incident. At crack of dawn I got up, feeling cold and stiff, and made my way to the latrine. This was simply a tree trunk mounted over a pit. Then I strolled over to the cook's truck to fill one half of my mess tin with tea and receive a soya sausage and a packet of biscuits in the other half.

Our platoon had three fifteen-man sections, each with a Morris CDF six-wheeled 30-cwt lorry. Their backs contained built-in lockers that doubled as seats and held our tools, including mine detectors. CDFs had a canvas roof, rolled back in hot weather, something that had saved our driver's life when he detonated a mine that blew him clean out of the cab – he was without injury apart from minor cuts and bruises. Fortunately there had been no passengers in the truck at the time. These trucks became our mobile homes in Tunisia, although they were too cramped for us to sleep in.

That morning I was amused to see an upright piano in the wadi, which some of the sappers had liberated from a wrecked house. Our pianist was the unit Don-R (Motorcycle Dispatch Rider), a dapper little man with a pencil-line moustache who always wore riding breeches and carried a revolver on his waist-belt. For singers, we had the two Linforth brothers – they had pleasant voices and seemed to know the words of all the popular songs.

Like 102, 225 was a TA unit, originally raised in Birmingham from employees of the Dunlop Tyre Factory. It had been in Tunisia for just a month but already the OC had been injured, hence the arrival of PP. Nothing much happened that day, giving me a good opportunity to get acquainted with my new comrades, who were a pretty friendly crowd.

Next day we were detailed to go to out to an iron bridge in No Man's Land, which the enemy had failed to destroy during their retreat. Our job was to search for, and then remove, any explosive charges and this took some time as the enemy mortared us, so we frequently had to take cover. Luckily there were no casualties, and the sergeant in charge was awarded a Distinguished Conduct Medal. It was my first time under fire, except for air raids, which are rather impersonal.

Our unit was part of 12th Infantry Brigade, along with Black Watch, Royal Fusiliers and Royal West Kent infantry battalions. Our principal task was mine clearance. If, for example, the infantry wanted to do a night patrol for reconnaissance purposes, two or three sappers with a mine detector would accompany them. The Germans were very adept at mining and whenever they stayed in a position for any time they laid minefields. Sometimes they would be surrounded by a strand of wire, two or three inches above the ground, strung at intervals with little metal signs painted with skull and crossbones and the words 'Achtung – Minen'. At times they would lay wire and markers but no mines; in other places mines would be laid with no warning signs whatever.

The main German types were the anti-tank *Tellermine* and the anti-personnel *Schrapnellmine*, or 'Bouncing Betty', mines. These, when detonated, rose into the air to explode at chest height, spewing 360 steel balls in all directions. Lastly, there was the nasty, sneaky anti-personnel *Schumine*, a small wooden box containing plastic explosive that did not register on a mine detector and had just sufficient explosive to blow off a man's foot or lower leg, hence its name (from the German for shoe). A minefield might contain only *Tellermines*, relatively easy to pull up, although some had anti-handling devices. But frequently mine-fields would have both anti-tank and anti-personnel mines. As for the *Schumine*, unless it was possible to prod every inch of the ground with a bayonet, one could only pray that there weren't any there.

The only equipment we had to detect mines was the 'Polish' mine detector, invented in England after Dunkirk by a Polish Army officer, Lieutenant Józef Kosacki. It had a long wooden handle, at the end of which was a plywood disc containing coils of wire connected to a pair of headphones worn by the sweeper. It was used by sweeping the disc in arcs in front of oneself, keeping it just an inch or two clear of the ground. In theory, if any metal was detected, a high-pitched squeak would be heard. In that event the detector man would stop, at the same time marking the spot where the squeak was loudest. The man behind him would then place a marker cone on this spot for a third man to find and lift the mine. It sounds simple enough, but on any battlefield there are usually countless shards of metal from shells and mortar bombs that have exploded and these will all give readings on the mine detector. Owing to the rough treatment to which they were subjected, bumped around in the backs of trucks on rough roads, these far-from-robust instruments were often defective and would give false readings, or even no readings at all. In such cases we would have to resort to prodding the ground with bayonets; a slow, laborious process.

A further difficulty encountered was trying to clear mines from a cornfield. The Medjez-el-Bab area had been almost static for some weeks, giving the enemy ample time to sow minefields when the corn was an inch or two high. Now it was waist high, and to swing a mine detector was almost impossible. Trip wires were also a serious hazard as they were hard to see even in daylight, and would be attached, under tension, to an igniter on a mine, and if one should increase or decrease the tension by tripping over the wire, the mine would detonate instantly. Add to this the fact that much mine clearance was carried out at night and no light could be shown, it was a dangerous, nerve-wracking job, so it is not surprising that so many sappers are lying in Tunisian CWGC cemeteries.

We were in an area known to the British as Peter's Corner, where there had been fierce fighting against the *Kampfgruppe Schmid*, formed from elements of what was to have been the *Hermann Goering Fallschirm* (Parachute) Division. The area was littered with burnt-out tanks, many of them Churchills from the 6th Armoured Division, which passed over 102's road. One particularly poignant grave was marked by a piece of

33

wood on which was written, in German, 'Here lie the bodies of nineteen British tank men.'

With the drier weather there came a marked increase in air activity at practically all hours: enemy aircraft were becoming a rare sight. Several times a day we watched waves of medium bombers attacking enemy targets in the outskirts of Tunis. Lots of flak was going up against them, but their course was always unwavering.

One afternoon 225 assembled to be addressed by PP. He told us that there was going to be a massive bombardment that night against the enemy lines followed at first light by an advance. This news provoked some mixed reactions among the lads, and that evening many could be seen scribbling letters, which no doubt they fervently hoped would not be their last. The normal larking about and bursts of singing seemed half-hearted and rather forced. As for me, I had accumulated about 400 cigarettes as I preferred a pipe, so I shared them out amongst my section, thinking that if I was killed I wouldn't need them, and if I wasn't I could always get some more.

It was an incredible bombardment, the biggest since El Alamein it was said, and no one slept very much. Just before we left we were each issued with one tin of bully beef and a packet of biscuits, then shortly after dawn our vehicles started to move. Another division had the task of breaking through the enemy line and its minefields. Our division was to pass through their positions, skirt Tunis and round up the enemy in the Cap Bon peninsula.

We moved slowly forward amidst thick clouds of dust, while the barrage continued and our shells whined overhead. We were on rough tracks that were ankle deep in dust. Now and then we passed dead enemy soldiers, many with their hands clasped on their heads. At first the prisoners were Italian, but soon after, Germans began to appear.

At one of the frequent stops we made, out of the dense dust appeared a young German soldier, alone. He was bare-headed, and from his glaring eyes and foam-flecked mouth seemed to be badly shell-shocked. He shouted what sounded like gibberish at us as he approached. We waved him to the rear, and, still shouting, he was swallowed up by the dust.

That night we halted in a cornfield somewhere near the town of Massicault, now known as Bordj El Amri, south west of Tunis. There was some enemy resistance ahead and we could hear small arms and mortar fire. Over in one corner of the field a burial party was burying some of our infantry who had been killed that day; a padre was reading prayers over them. Overhead, and unseen, an aircraft was slowly

34

flying around and dropping flares, which cast a ghostly light over everything. My section was sitting in the back of our CDF, waiting for orders to move. Suddenly my body started to shake uncontrollably, much to the consternation of the other lads as well as my own. This continued for perhaps an hour, and I had no idea what was causing it. I was to discover later that it was the first signs of malaria, but after the shaking stopped I felt quite normal again.

As soon as it got light we were ordered out of the truck to sweep the road ahead. While we were thus employed a Jeep drew up with two brass hats in it – a brigadier and a major general. I imagine that it was the divisional commander with one of his brigadiers, but could not be sure as I had never seen either of them before. They wanted to know how far the road had been cleared and were told by us that it was clear up to the point where we were now standing. They told us to get cracking as they wanted to get the tanks through. We all said 'Yes sir' very loudly and saluted, but carried on at the usual methodical pace. Mine clearers in a hurry do not live long. Then a few mortar bombs fell and the Jeep took off speedily in a cloud of dust.

We began to notice Indian troops in our area. They were from the famous 4th Indian Division, which had been victorious in Eritrea, Italian Somaliland, Egypt, Libya, Tripolitania and now Tunisia. They had been loaned to First Army for this battle from Eighth Army, together with the equally famous, if re-born, 51st (Highland) Division. I wondered what the Indian troops' thoughts were about being so involved in this war between Europeans.

Next day the advance was held up at Hamman Lif, on the north side of the entrance to the Cap Bon peninsula. Dominating the town was the narrow, crescent-shaped Jebel er Rorouf ridge, heavily fortified by the enemy. It was captured by direct assault by the Guards Brigade at the cost of twenty-four men killed and fifty wounded. After the town was attacked by our Brigade's infantry and tanks and there was bitter house-to-house fighting. The Germans had sited 88mm anti-tank guns very carefully so by the time the town was taken twenty-two Sherman tanks had been knocked out. But the way was now open for the pursuit around the peninsula and as we passed through Hamman Lif French colonists lined the streets and gave us a cheer, but we weren't allowed to stop.

Once clear of the town we were able to drive a little faster as there was little likelihood of there being any mines since the enemy was in rapid retreat. At rare intervals we encountered a makeshift obstruction such as a large Fiat lorry left crosswise across the road. Within four hours we had crossed the foot of the peninsula to the small town of Korba, on the eastern shore. The peninsula was now sealed off and the other two brigades in the division were circling the western side and would shortly meet up with us again. Then the enemy troops in the peninsula would be completely encircled and unable to evacuate by sea, which was just as well for them because Royal Navy destroyers were patrolling offshore with orders to sink any craft trying to escape. There had been attempts by the enemy to evacuate troops in Junkers Ju52 transport aircraft, but they had been shot down into the sea in their dozens by the RAF and US fighters in the Cap Bon Turkey Shoot.

Korba was a dusty little town that had been heavily bombed and there were a few dead Germans lying around. We in the ranks were not really aware of the military situation, though we began to feel that we were winning. But, to be on the safe side, we manned foxholes dug by the enemy and after an hour or two we were happy to see the appearance of our Black Watch battalion, who took over from us.

Next day was one to remember. The crack DAK started to surrender in hundreds, then thousands, and finally in tens of thousands, as did the Italian First Army. They came in *Kübelsitzwagen* ('bucket-seat' cars, like Jeeps but designed by Porsche and built by Volkswagen), vans, petrol-bowsers, buses, lorries, half-tracks towing 88mm guns and even a *Gulasche-kanonen* ('Stew-gun', so called for its fold-flat chimney) and a mobile field kitchen/bakery. No tanks – they had been demolished. But the majority came in on foot. They were so numerous that to fence them in behind barbed wire was just impossible, so they were directed to an open area until PoW camps could be organized.

Our unit was driving in convoy through this vast horde and halted to brew up and lunch on bully beef and biscuits. This seemed like a good opportunity to meet the enemy without having to kill each other. I walked over to a group wearing *Hermann Goering* sleeve-bands and offered one of them a cigarette, but he immediately pulled from his pocket a flat tin of his own and insisted I take one. He was an officer and spoke quite good English. I asked his opinion of how the war was going, to which he replied that although we had beaten them in Africa, we would never, ever beat them in Europe. I then asked him what he thought of their Italian allies. He answered with a wry smile, 'You have the Americans: we have the Italians.'

His group had a jerrycan of *rouge*, and they poured some into my enamel mug, toasting me by saying 'chin chin', which they seemed to think Englishmen said when taking a drink. They must have been reading P.G. Wodehouse.

I saw that my section was making signs of moving out, and as I turned to go one of the Germans said something that I shall never forget. 'War is good, young men should fight!' Up until this point I had been favourably impressed with these men: they had good physiques, looked intelligent and had a pleasing manner, but after hearing that remark I thought, *What a stupid bastard, what about the killed and maimed?*, wondering how many of them felt that way.

I got back into the section's CDF, and just before we moved off a US P-39 Airacobra fighter roared overhead, very low. As it passed us it suddenly fired a burst with its cannon and machine-guns. We did not stay around to see if any casualties had been caused, but there must have been some since the area was packed with German and Italian PoWs. It seemed that the pilot had not been told that here, at least, the war was over.

We moved out and soon stopped by a long, sandy beach. Word was passed that anyone who wanted a dip in the sea was free to do so. Within minutes 3,000 naked men were whooping, hollering and splashing in the deliciously cool sea – a great way to celebrate! It was a significant victory, yielding approximately 250,000 German and Italian PoWs. That was more than Stalingrad, where only 91,000 were made prisoner. The cost had not been cheap, at just over 70,000 casualties on the Allied side, including killed, wounded and missing.

We halted that evening near the former joint German–Italian HQ. The whole area was covered with twisted telephone wires, and discarded weapons, equipment and helmets were scattered around, as were soldiers' letters and postcards. Adding colour to the scene were dozens of Italian Mod.35 grenades, which we called 'Red Devils'. They were cheap-looking things, round in shape and made of thin sheet metal. We kept well away from these as they could have been booby trapped and were dangerous to handle anyway.

I did a bit of selective looting there, including a complete Italian field medical kit in a Red Cross satchel. It included a set of beautifully made surgeon's instruments, which I later passed on to our MO. For myself I picked up an Italian Beretta 9mm SMG and two sets of German and Italian illustrated propaganda postcards. The German ones showed various military units in action and were most professional. The Italian ones tended to be dramatic, with overtones of religion, such as the Pope blessing the soldiers going off to war. I also picked up a German camouflage groundsheet, much superior to ours. Two could be buttoned together to make a tent. I also acquired a

German pull-through for my rifle and a German Army leather belt, with *Gott Mit Uns* written on the buckle.

I then went into a small dugout to see if there was anything worth looting. Immediately I felt a strange tickling rising up my bare legs and quickly dashed outside, where I saw to my horror and disgust that there were hundreds of what I took to be lice climbing up my legs. I quickly brushed them off, hoping that I had got rid of all of them. Even so, I felt itchy for quite a time afterwards.

Soon after this we were told that our past endeavours were to be rewarded by forty-eight hours in a leave camp. There, they said, discipline would be completely relaxed – we would not even have to salute officers. This was not much of a bonus, considering that all officers had departed for the fleshpots of Tunis! Anyone who had imagined he was going to a sort of military Butlin's Holiday Camp had his hopes dashed. The camp was pitched on the beach and apart from the tents there was absolutely nothing. We were to sleep ten to a tent and there were no beds, so we slept on the sand, which was no hardship to us. The sea bathing was great, but there were no showers to wash the salt off after a swim. The food was the usual Compo, with no beer to be had for love or money, only rough *rouge* at 5 francs a mugfull.

On our second, and last, night there a film show was put on for our entertainment, and what an amazing choice of film! It was an Army Film Unit documentary, *Tunisian Victory*. Betty Grable would have been much preferred. Even Laurel and Hardy would have done. Probably later these camps improved and better amenities were provided, but at that particular time there were more pressing problems to deal with, for instance, feeding 250,000 prisoners: that was why First Army was on half rations for a few days after the surrender.

After our rest the company moved back to the old battlefield area near Peter's Corner and took up residence at a place called Cactus Farm. The officers were billeted in the farmhouse and the ORs were issued with small two-man tents. These stood about thirty inches high and were only for sleeping in. One had to get down on the knees to get in and out of them and they were very hot in the North African summer.

Our job was to clear all minefields in the area, a gargantuan but necessary task. First priority was to clear those with dead soldiers in them so that burial parties could carry out their grisly business. The smell of dead bodies decomposing under a hot sun is something not to be forgotten. This was further exacerbated by the stink of animal carcasses: cows, donkeys and goats had also fallen victim to mines. The weather was really hot now and flies were becoming a plague. The only bonus to this job was that it could now be carried out in daylight, and, of course, no one was shooting at us while we did it. Even so, we had one serious casualty. A mine detector malfunctioned and a mine was overlooked. The truck following behind the sweepers to collect cleared mines ran over it, causing it to explode. The driver was unhurt, but Corporal Metcalfe, who had been standing nearby, was badly wounded in the leg, which had to be amputated. He was a very popular chap and we all felt badly about it.

During this period one of our sappers, Jimmy Doe, rejoined my section. He had been taken prisoner a month before while on a night patrol with the infantry. They had been ambushed and although unwounded he lost his sense of direction. He sheltered in a small concrete hut but soon after Germans entered and captured him. He went to sleep on the floor of the hut and one of the Germans gave him a blanket. The next morning he and other prisoners were escorted through the street of Tunis. They passed a street cigarette seller who jeered at them, but without further ado one of the German escorts grabbed his goods and gave them to the prisoners. The vendor protested furiously, but the German gave him a contemptuous shove and they proceeded on their way.

Their destination was the docks, where they boarded an Italian cargo ship, already holding many other prisoners. The ship made three attempts to leave for Sicily but each time was attacked by Allied aircraft and returned to port. On the third attempt the rudder was damaged by a near miss and the prisoners were put ashore. The next day Tunis fell and they were all released. It must have been a scary experience, being bombed by our own aircraft, but Jimmy didn't appear any the worse for it. He and I became good friends as we were of the same age and temperament.

On 20 May we were taken by trucks to the outskirts of Tunis to take part in a grand Victory Parade, a march past of some of the Allied troops who had taken part in the campaign. On the reviewing stand would be the British Generals Alexander and Anderson, American Generals Patton and Allen, and the French Generals Juin and Girard. There were a few politicians present, including Harold Macmillan.

Although I was part of this parade I only saw our small section of it and a brief glimpse of the top brass as we were given 'Eyes Right' as we marched past the reviewing stand. For political reasons French colonial troops were in front and made a good showing with their colourful uniforms. There were *Spahis* (cavalry) in their cloaks, followed by infantry – *Zouaves, Tirailleurs, Goumiers* wearing burnouses – and, lastly, a Foreign Legion detachment. Next came two regiments of Americans in neatly pressed uniforms and headed by a brass band, but their impact was somewhat reduced as their rubber-soled boots caused them to pass in silence. Finally the British came past, headed by the impeccable Scots Guards with their pipers and the massed pipers of other Scots regiments, followed by the Grenadier Guards and then regiments of the line, all putting on a good show. By the time we sappers got to the reviewing stand the bands were almost out of earshot and someone mumbled, 'After the Lord Mayor comes the dust cart.' However, we held our heads high and were pleased that we had been given the opportunity to see the brass hats.

A few days later we were taken to a long, straight stretch of road outside Medjez-el-Bab and kept standing in the hot sun for more than two hours. Both to the left and the right of us, as far as the eye could see, stood ranks of soldiers. While we waited we were told that the King would be passing by at some time. Eventually a group of cars was seen approaching and we were brought to attention, but when within 100 yards of us, the small convoy stopped and the occupants got out. They entered a German military cemetery at the roadside and for a minute or two walked around the graves. We were able to identify the two unmistakable leading figures as the King and none other than Winston Churchill. They then got back into their vehicles and drove slowly past us, giving us the opportunity to get a good look at them. At the same time PP raised his hat and called for three cheers. I have to say that the response to the first 'Hurrah' was not much more than a mumble and to the second and third it was non-existent. It was not lack of patriotism, as these men would prove their worth over and over again before the war ended – rather it was that they were a different generation from that of the Great War and they had no use for jingoism.

Our day out over, it was back to the minefields, but in my own case not for long, as I came down with a dose of dysentery. This was very prevalent at the time in the old battlefield areas owing to the flies. Our usual lunch was two sandwiches each, usually one of cheese and one of jam, occasionally varied with tinned pilchards or corned beef. Hundreds of sandwiches would be laid out by the cooks on trestle tables and covered over with strips of cheesecloth. This did not deter the flies and they clustered on the cheesecloth until the tables appeared to be draped in black.

They were so many cases of dysentery in the area that only those on the point of collapse could expect to be hospitalized. For those who have never had the misfortune to experience this undignified illness, I should explain that one's bowels turn to water, one constantly needs to go to the toilet and suffers excruciating stomach gripes and dehydration. I held out for as long as I could but eventually had no option but to report sick.

The MO's tent was only a mile away, but our truck had to stop three times en route for men to relieve themselves at the roadside. On arrival we sufferers formed a single line in front of the MO's desk. The chap in front of me had a thin stream of excrement, just like water, running down the backs of his legs and he collapsed while talking to the MO. That made it my turn. I was given about 100 Sulfaguanidine tablets and told to take six every two hours.

Back at the camp again, some genius decided I was fit enough to do a wireless operator's course, to be held within the company. I was getting progressively weaker, and visiting the latrine about twenty times a day. My last visit was made on my hands and knees, so I decided to remain there with my water bottle and tablets until they started to take effect. I stayed there for the next twenty-four hours.

The latrine was typical of those used in North Africa. It was a large wooden box-like structure with holes cut in its upper surface and mounted over a deep pit. The holes should have had hinged lids but quite often did not. Our eight-holer was surrounded by a high cactus hedge, which gave privacy from passers-by. I had plenty of company there, but conversation was minimal as no one was in a state or mood for casual banter.

The tablets worked, and although I had lost a lot of weight I was soon back on the wireless operator's course. We were using the bulky No. 19 set – 225 had four; one in PP's Tilly and operated by his driver, the other three in each Section HQ's Tilly.

Towards the end of June we moved to the Algerian coastal town of Bougie. Almost as soon as we arrived I was taken ill with malaria. In theory, no one should have caught this since we had to take a daily Mepacrine tablet, but in practice, apart from turning the taker's skin yellow, those tablets were far from 100 per cent efficacious.

I was admitted to hospital, which was overflowing with malaria patients. It was fine to have a proper bed to sleep in, but unless one was in a coma it was not permitted to lie in during daylight hours. This restriction did not apply for the first couple of days whilst one was still in a high fever or if one suffered a relapse.

The lad in the next bed, a Black Watch private about my age, had been there for two days so knew the ropes. I asked him how to summon a medical orderly to bring me a bottle as I needed to urinate. He said the orderlies were overworked so only came for emergencies, and to hand out pills. He said that I would have to go to the urinals at the other end of the ward, and he would help me to get there and back. So, leaning on his shoulder, and taking it slowly, we reached the lavatories just as my legs gave way. I could not get up again, even with the help of the wee Jock, who probably was not much stronger than I was. He went for help and two other 'up' patients assisted me back to my bed, remarking, 'It doesn't seem right; somehow, exposing kids like these to diseases like malaria.'

I got a message to my brother Arthur at Div HQ and he visited me next day, bringing a copy of the British Army newspaper, *Union Jack*. He could not stay long, but we agreed to meet in Bougie for a drink when I was out and about again.

After three days I was judged fit enough to transfer to the tented convalescent camp, from which, after a few days' rest, patients returned to their units. There were no parades other than the daily morning inspection by the MO, which consisted of being asked how was one feeling and having one's temperature taken. There was not a lot to do, but that was never a problem to soldiers, and as there were no officers around there was a nice, relaxed atmosphere. Our beds were simply three long boards resting on pieces of 4×4 timber, one at each end, with a 'donkey's breakfast' (palliasse) on top. They were no hardship.

It was accepted intelligence by the patients that if one's temperature was checked as normal for three consecutive days, then one was RTU. Therefore the majority of us indulged in a bit of lead-swinging by maintaining our temperatures at a high level. It was a common sight to see men running up and down outside the MO's tent to increase their pulse rate, while others would be sipping hot tea to raise their mouth temperature. Some swore that toothpaste under the tongue had the same effect, but I used the hot tea method. By these stratagems most of us managed an extra two or three days in the camp. I think that the MO knew what was going on, but being a decent chap he did not do anything about it.

On my last night someone organised a bit of a concert in the ward. There were the usual two or three volunteers who thought they were a budding Bing Crosby or Caruso, and they were given a big hand, irrespective of whether they sang well or badly. The MC was an old, long-service warrant officer. There was a Vietnamese soldier in the ward, from the French Army, who was persuaded to sing in his own language. To our ears it sounded like a cat in the mating season, and it seemed to go on endlessly. When it finished, the old MC, who had trouble with his aspirates, stood up and said 'Hin hall my twenty-five hexperience years has a hinfantry sergeant major, this hoccasion 'as been unikwoo [unique].'

Back at 225, and on light duties, I was approached by Sapper 'Doc' Downing with an unusual proposition. Doc, as his nickname implies, had done a medical orderly course and been ordered to act in a temporary capacity as the usual one was in hospital for a few days. Doc did not want to fill in and asked if I would take his place. My first reaction was to question his sanity and to tell him that I didn't know a bedpan from a syringe, and how the hell did he think that I was going to fool the MO? But Doc was a very persuasive chap. He reminded me later of the famous TV star Sergeant Bilko as they both wore glasses and could charm the birds from the trees. They even looked alike. So, foolishly perhaps, but tempted by Doc's offer of fifty cigarettes, I suc-cumbed to his blandishments.

Our MO, known throughout the Brigade as the 'snake charmer', owing to his collection of snakes, which he kept in glass jars, and was something of an eccentric. Next morning I approached his tent with more than a little trepidation, expecting soon to be revealed as an imposter. I stopped outside the tent when I heard a soft voice mur-muring what sounded like endearments inside. Thinking that he might have a nurse in there with him, I took a peep through the tent flap. Anticlimax. He was just having a cosy chat with a praying mantis on the wall of the tent.

I introduced myself, not mentioning my complete lack of qualifica-tions. I would keep that card up my sleeve for the time being. He said that shortly a company of Royal Fusiliers would be arriving for typhus inoculations, and enquired if I had ever administered one. I replied that I had a good idea of the process but had never actually done one. Without further ado he gave me one, then, to check that I had been paying attention, told me to give him one, which I successfully did. The Royal Fusiliers duly arrived and, working in tandem, we soon polished them off. Only about twenty per cent of them fainted, but I put that down to their faintheartedness, not to my ineptitude. That seemed to be about it for the day and the MO dismissed me and told me to come back the next morning.

The following day I was in attendance for a normal morning sick parade, held, in army parlance, for the 'sick, lame and lazy'. There were clients from different corps and regiments, but on this particular morning the majority were Black Watch, distinguished by a red hackle on their floppy bonnets, or 'Tam o' Shanters' as they called them. Many were suffering from desert sores on their arms and legs and the MO told me that I could deal with them and that he would deal with all the other complaints. He provided me with a pair of tweezers, a large wad of cotton wool and a bottle of antiseptic solution, called Eusol. He instructed me to gently remove the scabs of the sores with the tweezers and then to dab on the solution.

I sat my first client down on a chair, knelt down in front of him and began my very first surgical operation on his legs. He was a big, sandy-haired Scotsman, tough looking, and with legs like tree trunks. I had only been working on him for a few seconds when he suddenly fell on top of me in a dead faint. Feeling rather nonplussed, I poured some water on his head and he soon came round. I got him back into his chair again, handed him the tweezers and told him that he had better remove the scabs himself. He gave me back the tweezers, muttered some strange Gaelic oath and departed at speed back to his unit.

All this had taken place outside the tent and in full view of the line of potential clients. When I had finished my ministrations to the hairy Jock I looked up and to my surprise the line had virtually disappeared. They obviously did not approve of my bedside manner. After about half an hour the MO came out of the tent and observing the lack of clients remarked, 'That was quick, you must be experienced!' Next day the proper medical orderly returned to duty and I was able to return to the unit, thus cutting short my brief but eventful medical career.

Because of my ability to speak French, which had become more fluent after working with the Berbers and the French sappers, I was often given tasks where local labour was involved. So it came about, shortly after my session with the MO, that I was put in charge of a huge stone-crushing machine that produced hardcore material for road works. I was supplied with a string of twenty donkeys, supposedly under the supervision of four Arab boys. These ragged urchins understood French, but not English, hence my being there. The donkeys were each equipped with a basket on either side. The idea was that they should all go in convoy to a nearby wadi. There the boys would load the baskets with large stones and lead the donkeys back to the crusher. The complete cycle should have taken about twenty minutes and did so for the first two round trips. But then there was a lull, lasting about three-quarters of an hour, and I began to feel anxious and annoyed. I decided that I must take a walk to the wadi and find out the cause of the delay. When I got there I witnessed the Arab kids assisting the donkeys to perform a mass copulation by lifting the males on to the females. They considered that I was quite a spoilsport when I broke up this animal orgy.

Of course, even if the kids and donkeys had worked flat out, their efforts would have been completely inadequate to keep the stone crusher supplied efficiently. I reported this to 225 and the project was changed so that a lorry was used in preference to donkeys. Returning to the company, I was soon sent off on another detached duty at another coastal town called Djidjelli. This time I was provided with one wheel-barrow, twelve picks, twelve shovels and thirteen adult Arabs. The odd man out was the gang boss to whom I would give my orders in French and he would pass on to the men in Arabic. Initially I was employed at the camp of an RAF Signals unit, carrying out main-tenance work such as drainage or any other odd jobs they wanted done. I used to return to 225 at night but at midday took my lunch in the Airmen's Mess. I found them to be a rather stuffy lot with a superior attitude to a mere soldier. Fortunately, I did not stay long at their camp as I was moved, with my Arabs, to do a job at the nearby airfield.

The airfield runway, taxi tracks and lay-bys where stationary aircraft were dispersed were constructed of PSP – pierced steel planks. The planks had lugs down each side so that they could be connected with each other. The task we had to perform was to remove thousands of these planks and fit them at the far end of the runway in order to lengthen it. My men would each pick up one of those planks and walk with it to the far end of the runway, drop it and walk back again for another. Slow, laborious and inefficient. There were three American engineers employed on the same job, and of course they were using a truck. I got friendly with these guys and reached an arrangement with them whereby my men loaded and offloaded their truck. The work was easier, quicker and everyone was happy.

We often had to act with caution as the runway became very busy at times. There were three nationalities using the airfield: British, American and French. There seemed to be some confusion at times, especially when they were scrambled, and I once saw aircraft taking off at opposite ends of the runway. On another occasion I was standing near an aircraft lay-by, chatting to an RAF erk who was making a brew of tea. Some time before a lot of aircraft had taken off in a hurry because an Allied convoy off the coast was being attacked by German aircraft. Suddenly an American P-38 Lightning fighter landed, taxied down the runway and did an abrupt turn into the lay-by, thus giving us the full benefit of his slipstream and covering us with dust. That was bad enough, but even worse, as far as the erk was concerned, was that his Primus stove and pot of water were blown several yards away. The American pilot cut his engine and quickly pulled back the Perspex cockpit canopy and yelled to us excitedly, 'Hey you guys, I've just been shooting shit out of a kraut JU88!' to which the erk indignantly replied, 'Fuck you and fuck your JU88, look at my tea!' So much for Anglo-US relations ...

One evening, having nothing better to do, I took a stroll around to look at the various aircraft and while I was looking at an RAF two-engined Beaufighter I was approached by an RAF officer. He asked me what I was doing there and, being satisfied with my reply, he asked me if I would like to see the controls of the aircraft. So I followed him up the little ladder into the cockpit and he patiently answered all my questions about the various instruments and the aircraft's armament. I was most impressed with his friendliness as not many of his equivalent rank in the army would have acted in such a manner. I enquired about him and discovered that he was Wing Commander Boyd and that he had been an ace in the Battle of Britain.

Probably the most spectacular incident I saw while I was at this air-field was an emergency wheels-up landing by a US Airacobra. It was just getting dusk and as it hit the runway everyone held their breath, expecting it to burst into a fireball. Instead it sped along the steel run-way, emitting a huge shower of sparks, like a comet, finally coming to rest at the extreme end of the runway. The pilot got out unharmed, and a very lucky man!

With my job at the airfield finished, I returned to 225 to hear that PP had left us. No one knew to where, but later a rumour circulated that he was in charge of a petrol-issuing point in southern Italy as, by this time, the Allied armies had taken Sicily and were well established in Naples. It began to look as if the war had passed us by. The other divisions that had been with us in the Tunisian campaign, 6th Armoured, 46th and 78th Infantry, were all in action on the Italian Front, but our 4th was still hanging about in Algeria. Furthermore, the Italians had asked for an armistice in September 1943, and some had now changed sides and were part of the Allied forces.

There was a lot of speculation in 225 about our future movements and the general consensus was that we would soon be going back to England to train for the invasion of France. There was also the current topic of conversation, the new OC, Major G. In the event he turned out to be a very decent man and no one had cause for complaint.

The company at this time, autumn 1943, was engaged in building Nissen huts and once again I was put in charge of half a dozen Arab labourers. These were younger men and at times a bit cheeky. The tallest of them, who appeared to be their leader, kept challenging me to *'le box'.* As he was several inches taller than I was, and for all I knew might have been the champion of Algeria, I put him off with excuses. However, he persisted so often that I finally agreed as I felt that British honour was at stake.

So at the midday meal break, with the other Arabs gathered around, I said to my opponent *'En avant.'* As we had no gloves it had to be a bare-fist affair. He started prancing around in what he probably presumed to be the correct boxing posture, but I could see that he was not protecting his face properly. Deciding that the best form of defence was attack, I charged straight in with no finesse and belted him hard on his nose, quickly following with a punch to his right ear. That was enough. Complaining that it was not boxing and it was not fair, he walked away from me. I had no further offers for *'le box'* after that, much to my relief

A few weeks before there had appeared on Daily Orders an item soliciting volunteers for the paratroops. There were only two volunteers, Ned Parker, who I had known at Darland, and me. PP had interviewed us individually and had asked me if I was aware what I was letting myself in for. I had replied that I was well aware, but in fact I did not have the foggiest notion. Since then neither of us had heard anything about our applications and we assumed that we probably would not hear.

Suddenly, in mid-December, we were told that the unit was on forty-eight hours' notice to move to a transit camp in Algiers, which meant a move by ship to somewhere. As usual, we were not told our ultimate destination.

Months earlier we had a whip-round and purchased two piglets with the intention of fattening them up for consumption at Christmas. Obviously we couldn't take them with us, so we would have to eat them as soon as possible. The Don-R, the only one of us with a revolver, was delegated to shoot them. The first one was executed successfully, but his mate, seeing what was happening, tried to bolt. The dispatch rider hurriedly pulled the trigger again and the bullet passed through the head of the pig but also continued on into his foot. He squealed louder that the pigs, though fortunately the damage was slight, as the bullet passed between his toes. Not having time to hang the carcasses and drain off the blood, they were cooked almost immediately, and the pigs took their revenge! The next morning the whole unit had the squitters and there were long queues at the latrines.

We were not sorry to be leaving Algeria, although it had been pleasant enough, except for the shortage of beer. I think that in the fourteen months I had been in French North Africa I had only been able to get hold of three or four bottles of beer, and they had been Australian. British soldiers do not really take to wine and tend to drink the sweet fortified stuff, like Marsala or Vermouth, which makes them sick. Apart from the beer problem, it was generally felt it was time to move on – perhaps to the UK?

We moved to Algiers by rail in forty *hommes*–eight *chevaux* trucks, arriving in pouring rain. 225 was accommodated in two large marquees and not allowed to leave the camp, so visits to Algiers City were ruled out. Christmas Day started with gale-force winds and torrential rains. There was a shallow gully down the centre of our marquee, which soon turned into a stream, and ran all day.

Christmas dinner was literally a washout. There was some tinned chicken, which we ate sitting in our tent on the damp ground, but that was the only concession that the Army made toward the festive season. We were all glad when the dismal day was over. Only one thing brightened it. The officers' latrine was not far away, set in splendid isolation on a knoll. We were outside our tent, trying to divert the water flowing through it. Suddenly there was a furious gust of wind and the flimsy hessian and bamboo construction that was the officers' toilet went flying down the hill like a demented bat. There, exposed to the gaze of all the world, with his trousers round his ankles, sat our Major G. Taking his pipe out of his mouth he gave us a nonchalant wave and a grin. In return we gave him a cheer and wished him a Merry Christmas.

The next morning we went to the docks and boarded our troopship.

Chapter 6

Egypt, Gibraltar and UK

The convoy started to move just before dark and most of us were on deck to see which direction it would head in after clearing Algiers Bay. If west, then we would be going to the UK, but if it turned to the east then we could be going anywhere from Libya to Burma. It was east, and next morning we found we were going to Egypt to train for an amphibious assault on Italy.

It took six days to reach Egypt, and although it was winter the sea was reasonably placid and the voyage uneventful. We hove-to for a few hours at Port Said, waiting our turn to enter the Suez Canal, and giving us the opportunity to get acquainted with the famous 'bum-boats'. These were skiffs manned by Egyptian vendors who came alongside to offer goods for sale to troops gazing down from the high sides of the troopships. Their goods were mostly leather, such as wallets, pouffes, suitcases, belts and so on, much of it gaudy but of poor quality. Most of it was useless for soldiers on active service but some of the lads bought smaller items as souvenirs, and one or two even purchased dubious-looking wrist-watches. The vendors could speak English of a sort, and to everyone's amusements claimed to be of Scottish origin, calling out 'Me Jock MacGregor' or similar names.

The transactions between vendors and troops were based on mutual trust. The vendors were not allowed onboard the troopship, and the soldiers could not leave it, therefore the vendor would throw up a line and whatever the prospective buyer was interested in would be tied on the other end. He could then haul it up and examine it, and if he was happy with it he should throw down the money. There was a lot of bargaining over the price and the vendor would invariably reduce his price to a certain point but then would stick at that. There were a lot of good-humoured exchanges between buyers and sellers and it was fine entertainment after six days at sea.

We were anchored quite close to the impressive Australian and New Zealand War Memorial. It commemorated men, women and animals (horses, donkeys and camels) that lost their lives in Egypt and what were to be Palestine and Syria between 1916 and 1918. They were from the Australian Light Horse, New Zealand Mounted Rifles, Australian Flying Corps, the Imperial Camel Corps and various nursing corps. The memorial was destroyed in December 1956 by Egyptian rioters during the Suez conflict.

Soon we were moving through the canal and entranced with the new sights of camels and date palms and occasional fellahin on the banks. Groups of little boys would stand and make derisive and obscene gestures as the ship slowly passed. Some of the old hands on board who had served in Egypt before would shout '*Shufti zubrick*' and the kids would respond by lifting up their gelabiehs and showing their all!

Within three hours we reached the Bitter Lakes, the junction of the two halves of the Suez Canal. We were told to be ready to disembark and shortly after we were taken ashore in flat-bottomed lighters. From there we travelled by MT to a tented camp. It was a dusty, fly-blown place and stretched as far as the eye could see along a road that ran parallel to the canal. The whole division was encamped in this area and, when the wind was not raising the dust, it was being raised by the constant stream of motor traffic. It soon became evident that amenities such as a canteen or camp cinema were non-existent. Anyone who grumbled was told that we had come here to train and not to rest.

Training started in earnest in the following evening when we got our first taste of a night amphibious assault landing. This took place on the eastern shore of the Great Bitter Lake, using landing craft from HMS *Saunders*, a 'stone frigate' or naval shore establishment. It housed the Middle East Combined Operations School, and was on the west bank of the lake. The 'enemy' shoreline was protected with dense thickets of barbed wire and anti-tank obstacles including 'dragons' teeth', conical pillars of reinforced concrete set closely together.

Our job was to make a path through these obstacles so that the infantry and tanks could go through. To deal with the barbed wire we used Bangalore torpedoes, formed from lengths of two-inch piping packed with explosives. The lengths had threaded ends so could be screwed together to form the appropriate length to cross the barbed-wire barrier. The pipes were pushed through the barrier manually and if the ground ahead was perfectly flat there would be no problem. Sometimes, however, the leading end would be obstructed by a rock or a small mound, in which case a lot of wiggling and waggling would be required, usually accompanied by *sotto voce* cursing. When the torpedo was in place it was detonated by slow-burning safety fuse or an electric charge, but in either case it was prudent to seek cover of some sort because a lot of bits of metal would be flying about. If no cover was available the only thing one could do was to lie very flat and hope for the best. In addition to clearing a gap through the barbed wire the torpedo would also detonate any mine that may have been near, thus making it safe for the infantry to go through.

To destroy the dragons' teeth we used the 'Beehive' demolition charge, so named because it looked like old-fashioned cone-shaped beehives. This charge had three metal legs and was stood on top of the concrete obstacle; its 'hollow-charge' explosion was directed downwards, reducing it to rubble. Because of its irregular shape the Beehive was an awkward thing to carry, until someone came up with the idea of employing the Yukon pack for it and for any other difficult items. The Yukon pack was simply a flat board, which could be worn like a rucksack. Down each side of the board were a series of cup-hooks and a cord was woven over the top of the article being carried and criss-crossed from side to side through the hooks. Quite simple, but effective.

These night exercises were very good training and gave us confidence that we should be able to carry out what lay ahead. At the end we were given an opportunity to go into Ismailia town for a few hours. There was not a lot to see or to do there. We were constantly pestered by street vendors who wanted to sell us the usual junk, or sometimes even their sisters. One amusing character kept saying 'My sister very sweet, very clean, white inside, all same Queen Victoria.' Obviously, this advertising come-on had been handed down through many generations since the time of the Mahdi and Gordon of Khartoum.

Also in attendance was the ubiquitous *gulli-gulli* man, who did conjuring tricks, such as producing a day-old live chick from his mouth, or so it seemed. He would also tell fortunes for a piastre or two. I remember being displeased with mine, as he told me that after the war I would go back to England and get a good job in a factory, which was about the last thing I wanted to hear, but he probably told everyone the same thing. Ismailia also had several street photographers with ancient box-type cameras on wooden tripod legs. They operated with plates rather than film and the photographer got behind it with a hood over his head to take the picture. The results were surprisingly good and I still have a photograph taken there sixty years ago.

The transport in Ismailia, as in all towns in Egypt at that time, was mainly horse-drawn, and the poor horses looked weary and half-starved as there was no succulent grass anywhere for them to crop. Instead of taxis there were dilapidated carriages, each pulled by a single horse and known as *gharries*. Inevitably British military vehicles in Egypt became *'gharries'*. The English language as spoken in UK in those days was much influenced by words brought home by servicemen coming from the Middle East and, even more so, from India. Usually these words became anglicized and were only used in informal speech; for example, the Hindustani word *bilati*, 'foreign', became corrupted into Blighty, which was what the old soldiers called Britain. With the British Army no longer serving in Egypt or India most of these words have died out, but a few have survived, such as the word *cushy*, from the Urdu word *khush*, meaning easy or comfortable.

The food we were supplied with in Egypt was more varied than that we had been accustomed to in Algeria, probably because the British Army had been in Egypt a long time, so had long-established sources. There was a good supply of fresh bread and meat, and sometimes even fresh vegetables. At times we were given sweet potatoes, which I liked but most of the lads did not – anything new or different from their normal diet was viewed with deep suspicion.

As part of our training in Egypt we had to attend courses of instruction at the 'mines school'. We thought that we already knew all that was to be known about mines but we soon found that we were mistaken. The stress on this course was laid on booby traps and these had become more and more ingenious and dangerous. Anything and everything could be used, and was used, by the enemy to kill the unwary: moving a dead body, lifting a toilet seat, opening a door or picking up some desirable article such as a pair of binnoculars or a Luger pistol. It was a salutary warning not to be tempted to look for souvenirs. It was also a reminder that this was one more dangerous task for us sappers.

Ned Parker and I had almost forgotten we had applied to join the paratroops until one morning, about six weeks after we had arrived in Egypt, we were told to report for a medical examination at Divisional HQ. We both passed with flying colours – in fact, the MO said to me 'You're just the sort of chap we are looking for.' A few days later we were ordered to Abassia Barracks in Cairo, where we would wait until called forward for air passage to Britain.

So once again it meant saying goodbye to close friends and a good bunch of lads generally, with genuine feelings of regret, knowing that I probably would never meet any of them again. I should also be giving up my lance corporal's stripe because King's Rules and Regulations stated that a 'lance' rank could not be carried forward on posting. This did not bother me at all.

Abassia Barracks was a pleasant surprise after living in a tent in the desert. It was a permanent pre-war building, three storeys high and built round a spacious yard. The rooms were cool and airy with high ceilings and had verandas running along the front of them. They also had proper beds, an unaccustomed luxury.

On the rooftops of the barracks were permanently perched a gathering of kite hawks, known to the troops, of course, as shite hawks. In the corner of the building, on the ground floor, was a canteen, which sold 'char and wads', soldier's slang for tea and buns. On the far side of the yard, which was in the shade most of the day, were some chairs and tables where one could consume one's tea and buns in comfort. On my first day at Abassia I purchased a mug of tea and two buns and was walking across the yard towards the chairs and tables, taking care not to spill my precious tea. Suddenly there was a swoosh of wings, and to my surprise there was now only one bun on my plate. The shite hawks had struck again, much to the merriment of watching old hands. I was told that those wily birds could always spot a newcomer. Thereafter, I always kept my hand firmly on the buns!

We were only in Abassia a few days but that gave us ample time to get haircuts, clean up our uniforms, darn our socks and generally improve our scruffy appearance. The Egyptian barber was quite dis-mayed at the state of my hair and had to wash it twice to remove all the sand and dust, making disapproving tut-tutting noises as he did so. Not long afterwards we were ordered to get our kit together and then were taken by truck to Cairo West airfield. On the drive there we saw the Pyramids in the distance, the first time that I had seen them.

On arrival at the airfield we were handed Kapok-filled flying suits and three blankets as the transport aircraft, a converted US B-24 Liberator, was unpressurised and therefore unheated. It was getting dark as we boarded the aircraft, and we found that the only other passengers were an RAF pilot, blinded in an air crash, escorted by an RAF medical assistant. The pilot was lying on a stretcher in the forward part of the fuselage, and we were told not to disturb him. Ned and I sat in seats at the rear, and the rest of the hold was occupied by odd bits of cargo, firmly lashed down to the deck. There were no machine guns in the turrets, perhaps to reduce the weight, so we were completely unarmed. But as our course would take us across North Africa until we reached Gibraltar there would be little chance of interception by enemy night fighters.

One by one the engines started up and the plane began to tremble. It was soon rumbling down the runway and then suddenly everything felt smoother as it left the ground, a familiar experience to nearly everyone nowadays, but this was our first time flying, and we grinned at each other nervously. One of the aircrew fitted us with oxygen masks plugged into the aircraft's oxygen supply and told us to keep them on until just before we landed at Gibraltar. Apart from the flight deck and the empty gun turrets, there were no windows in the aircraft, and as it was too dark to read and we were not allowed to smoke, like good soldiers we went to sleep. But we soon became bitterly cold, especially our feet, as we only wore army boots, not fur-lined aircrew ones. Ice started to form on our oxygen masks from condensation, and we wrapped our three blankets round us as tightly as we could and huddled together.

The night seemed long, and although the Liberator is quite a slow aircraft by modern standards, I don't suppose we were airborne for more than six hours. Dawn was just breaking as we landed at Gibraltar. Ned and I were taken to a house in the town and shown a room containing nothing but four beds. One other man, dressed in civilian clothes, was already there. He did not speak to us, and we were told not to speak to him. This struck me as rather mysterious, but I imagine he was either some sort of secret agent or an evader or escapee who had arrived from France via Spain. We were told that our time was our own until 1900 hours, when we would re-board the B-24 for the flight to the UK.

At that time Gibraltar was teeming with servicemen, mainly sailors. Because of petrol rationing there were few cars in the narrow streets and the drivers were not allowed to sound their horns. Instead they hung their right arms out of the window and banged the door loudly to warn pedestrians to get out of the way. We enjoyed visiting the little bars, restaurants and shops where everyone spoke English and by the time we reported back to the airfield we had a few drinks inside us so were feeling quite happy. We donned our flying suits and settled into our seats. The engines started up and seemed to run for a long time before takeoff, so long that, helped by the drinks, we fell asleep. The next thing I knew one of the aircrew was shaking me by the shoulder and saying that the aircraft was very near the end of the runway as on takeoff one of the engines had failed, and we were very lucky indeed not to have gone into the sea. At that time the Gibraltar runway was very short and had the harbour at one end and open sea at the other. There had been many accidents there, including one where General Sikorski, the Polish commander, was drowned. Another saw the deaths of nineteen fighter pilots returning home as passengers after surviving dogfights during the siege of Malta.

54

So Ned and I returned to our room again to await another aircraft going to the UK. No one seemed to know when that would be. We found that the 'mystery man' had gone, so for the rest of our stay on the Rock we had the room to ourselves. The delights of Gibraltar soon palled and we began to feel the claustrophobia that affects most people who stay there for long. We had no duties to perform and time hung heavily on us. As it was wartime the border with Spain was tightly closed, so no relief there. One night we went to a large NAAFI canteen, which was full of garrison troops. Some started to make derogatory remarks about the Africa Star ribbon we were wearing. We were both somewhat upset about this as we felt we had earned the medal and could do without remarks from people who had never seen any action, but there were too many of them for us to cope with and, discretion being the better part of valour, we got up and left.

Happily, after a week we found we would leave the next day, but in a Douglas Dakota. This was the Second World War's workhorse, carrying cargo and passengers, dropping paratroops and supplies, and towing gliders. We did some last-minute shopping in Gibraltar but as we had spent most of our money this consisted of a large bunch of bananas each. These were cheap, and had been completely unattainable in Britain since the outbreak of the war.

Boarding the Dakota very early the next morning we found it to be jam-packed with mail sacks. They covered the bench seats down each side of the aircraft's interior and the entire space between them. Ned and I were the only passengers, and were told by the crewman that we would have to make ourselves as comfortable as we could on top of the sacks. This time we were not given flying suits or blankets because, according to the crewman, we would not be flying at any great altitude. He was the third member of the crew, the other two being the pilot and co-pilot.

The first hour of the flight was not too bad, and there were even small windows to look out of, though the only thing to see was a grey choppy-looking sea, far below. Then we ran into dense cloud and the flight became a nightmare. The turbulence was so bad that it felt as though the aircraft was a butterfly in a hurricane and, as we had no seatbelts, we had to hang on to whatever we could to avoid being bodily thrown around. We had not been provided with sick bags so had to use the toilet at the rear of the fuselage, reached by walking along the top of the sacks. There were no exceptions to these vomiting expeditions, and even the pilots were affected – in fact, one of them remarked that he had never had such a rough flight before. After a time the rain turned to hail, then to snow. The turbulence never let up; some periods were more violent than others. We were hugely relieved when we finally broke through low clouds and saw the green fields of England not far below.

We landed at a small airfield a few miles outside Bristol, where we were subjected to a very thorough search by RMP security men. All our kit had to be turned out, even the contents of our pockets, and everything examined minutely. To this day I don't know why they were so suspicious, but I suppose they had their reasons.

We had anticipated going on leave as soon as we arrived in the UK, but it was not to be. We were told that first we were to report to the Army's Airborne Forces Training Battalion at Chesterfield in Derbyshire, where we would be given leave. We received a railway warrant and were taken by MT to Bristol Temple Meads railway station. By the time we reached Chesterfield, after a three-hour wait in London where we changed trains, it was time for breakfast. We reported to the ATB and were each given a seven-day leave pass, an advance of pay, ration cards and return railway warrants, and dire warnings about being late in returning! Then we headed south again, feeling more than a little fatigued, so decided to break our journeys in London, at the Union Jack Club near Waterloo Station, where beds were available for 1/6d a night.

The wartime club was very different from what it is today, with its quiet, comfortable bedrooms, many en-suite, lifts, well-stocked and welcoming bar, and good restaurant. In those days the rooms were basic, with only iron bedsteads and a washbasin, and paper-thin walls. There were no elevators, bar or restaurant. It was, in fact, a military doss-house. But it was cheap, clean and convenient, and thousands of servicemen were glad it was there.

After checking in our kit at the club lock-up we headed out to find a decent pub. Attracted by the sound of singing we found one, which, although completely blacked out on the outside, was bright, cheerful and thronged with happy drinkers on the inside. Before long, with the aid of a pint or two, we forgot our tiredness and were deep in conversation with a couple of pretty ladies. They matched us drink-for-drink and we really enjoyed their feminine company after being without it for so long. At closing time it was mutually accepted that we should spend the night with them. As they lived in different streets Ned and I agreed meet at the club next morning. My girl lived in a ground-floor flat close by, so it was not long before we were in bed together. I had great expectations, but sad to relate our union was not consummated, as we lacked contraceptives. She told me her husband was in the Navy and she did not know where he was. She added that she could not go 'all the way' as she was afraid of getting pregnant. This didn't prevent her from rubbing herself against me and bouncing up and down on me all night until I felt like a misused trampoline. In the middle of this performance the air raid sirens sounded and a battery of AA guns started banging away, apparently just outside the window. My bed-mate seemed quite unperturbed and did not want to go to the air raid shelter. She said that the real Blitz was long past and that this was just a nuisance raid, where the Germans sent over a few planes to disturb people's sleep. So a disappointing night ended, and I was still a virgin.

Next morning my ladyfriend insisted on coming to the club, where we found Ned and his girl waiting. The girls wanted us to stay on in London for a few days and just to shut them up we agreed. However, as soon as we got inside the club, which was out of bounds to them, we agreed to give them the slip. We retrieved our kit from the lock-up, left by a back door and took the Tube to Paddington station. Ned was going to Weymouth and me to Yeovil in Somerset, so we caught different trains. My parents had moved to Yeovil because Father had been promoted to District Manager of the numerous NAAFI canteens in that area.

On the journey my bunch of bananas were conspicuous, being loosely tied to the top of my kitbag to prevent them being crushed. They had been green when I bought them but now they were ripening to a nice yellow. I was twice approached by young mothers, pleading to be given a few, since their kids had never seen a banana, so by the time I got home the bunch was much smaller!

My arrival at 36 Coronation Avenue, Yeovil, was not entirely unexpected, as I had written from Cairo to say that I hoped to be back in the UK soon. Both parents were there, also Kathleen, now a WRNS telegraphist in Plymouth.

The town was surrounded by military camps, mostly American. There was also a Fleet Air Arm airfield nearby, and an aircraft factory in the town itself. This meant Yeovil was a hive of activity in those days prior to D-Day. There were signs of it everywhere: stacks of shells stored along the side of country roads, continual military convoys on the main roads, and everywhere men and women in uniform.

As a market town, Yeovil's pubs were allowed to stay open in the afternoon on the twice-weekly market days, a bonus for servicemen on leave. After more than four years of war there were shortages of many things, including the most basic articles. A familiar morning sight in Yeovil was long queues of US soldiers outside pubs waiting for them to open at 11.00am, each man holding an empty jam jar due to the chronic shortage of glasses. At times the beer ran out and customers had the choice of doing without or of drinking cider, a freely available local product. It came in two categories, sweet and rough, both stronger than wartime beer. However, if too much rough was imbibed, it had the immediate effect of a violent laxative.

In pubs Americans could usually get a shot of whisky, which was very scarce, some hotels illegally put up signs restricting entry to US officers only. Others, while reluctantly serving British soldiers, would make the prices so high that UK personnel would soon leave. This gave rise to the British taunt to Americans 'You're overpaid, over-sexed and over here!' The American riposted 'You're underpaid, under-sexed and under Eisenhower!' The latter was true, of course, because General Eisenhower was the Supreme Allied Commander, European Theatre of Operations.

The US soldiers always referred to themselves as GIs, meaning 'Government Issue'. There was some bad feeling between them and British soldiers, partly because the GIs were better paid. Other factors were their much nicer uniforms, on which they all wore two medal ribbons as soon as they arrived in Britain. However, the principal reason was the attitude of British females, young, middle-aged and, yes, older, which amounted almost to adoration of the Yanks. The Americans would often hire dance halls, or even town halls, and give dances with their own bands. All females could enter free, but British males were excluded.

With the arrival of US forces the music of American 'Big Bands', like that of Glenn Miller, Benny Goodman and Count Basie, became extremely popular. Their music, 'swing jazz', or just 'swing', using swing, shuffle or even lilting notes, was completely different from that of British bands, having more rhythm, much syncopation and a wider variety of instruments. With it came 'jitterbugging', energetic dancing where the male subjected his female partner to all manner of contortions in time with the music

The white GIs' attitude to their black comrades was seen by the British as racist and unnecessarily harsh. Generally, white soldiers from the southern states were the most extreme in their actions toward the blacks. Once, during this leave, I was in a quiet country pub where the only other customers were four black soldiers, peacefully minding their own business and enjoying a leisurely drink. Half a dozen white GIs entered and, seeing the black soldiers, one said in a southern drawl, 'You niggah boys bettah get outta heah raht now or y'all be in big trouble.' It looked as if there was going to be a fight because the black soldiers made no sign of moving, but the landlord told the white soldiers he wasn't going to serve them, and that they had better get out before he called the police, adding that they had better not show their faces in his pub again. Exit the white Yanks to big grins from the black ones.

After the US retreat from the Kasserine Pass in Tunisia, British troops used to singing the following jingle to the tune of 'Yankee Doodle':

Yankee Doodle built a tank
He called it General Sherman
And took it to the Kasserine
Then gave it to a German.

This did not do much for Anglo-US relations, and God knows was unfair, since we British had had more than our share of retreats and military disasters.

Chapter 7

Airborne Soldier

After a short but enjoyable leave I reported to the Airborne Forces Depot at Hardwick Hall, near Chesterfield, Derbyshire. The Hall was one of the stately homes of England and belonged to some duke who had put it at the disposal of the Army for the duration of the war. It was a magnificent building but we never got to see inside as it was used as the School's Officers' Mess, and to house some admin offices.

Before setting foot in an aircraft we had to be toughened up to paratroop standards. Every morning we went for a road run, distance and speed being increased exponentially. After that everything was done at the double, the idea being to increase our stamina. After the morning run the rest of the day was spent lifting heavy poles, pulling on ropes or running the obstacle course. Another useful exercise, performed in full battle order, was to lift a similarly dressed man from the ground and carry him in a fireman's lift for 200 yards – not easy if you are small and he is big. Probably the most important part of ground training was learning how to land. This was practised dozens of times, first by jumping out of a mock fuselage onto a mat, then by descending from a tower attached to a rope running through a pulley.

On the final day of ground training we did an early ten-mile speed march in full battle order, to be completed in two hours or under. The method used was to run a hundred paces then double-march for another hundred and so on until the route was completed. There were no halts, and the route was very hilly; even so, we had a couple of minutes in hand at the end. We later speed marched to RAF Ringway, home of No. 1 Parachute Training School, to carry out more ground training before making our first descents.

After several days of ground training, one afternoon we were taken up in an old Armstrong Whitworth Whitley bomber, converted for parachuting, for twenty minutes' 'air experience'. Ned winked at me and we laughed at how much experience we already had. A Whitley usually carried eight parachutists, four fore and aft of the Joe-hole in the middle of the fuselage floor. To reach the hole one had to slide along

60

on one's bottom, then put one's legs into the hole while maintaining a sitting position. The RAF PJI (Parachute Jump Instructor) acting as dispatcher would scream 'Go!' and the parachutist would push off with both hands and disappear straight down through the hole. The man on the other side of the hole would repeat the process, and so on alternately until the plane was empty of paratroops. After the flight we were informed that our group would be doing its first parachute on the following morning. There was a lot of chatter in the billet that night and half-hearted jokes about 'ringing the bell' and 'Roman candles'. The first referred to pushing off too hard from one side of the hole in the aircraft and thus banging one's nose on the opposite side of the hole; the second to improperly formed canopies after they left the back-pack, which were always fatal.

The US paratroopers jumped wearing two parachutes, a static liner on their backs and a hand-activated reserve on their chests, to be used if his main 'chute failed to open. The British Army only had one static-chute. This parachute was operated by a thirty-two-foot canvas strop, one end of which was anchored to a steel wire running the length of the aircraft's fuselage. The other end of the strop was attached to the outer bag of the parachute pack by a string tie, which would break by the weight of the falling body, thus releasing the silk canopy automatically. The strop and outer bag of the parachute would remain dangling outside the aircraft until pulled inside by the dispatcher. Supposedly, we British only had one parachute for reasons of economy. Now, of course, British paratroopers have two parachutes when they jump.

Morning came, bringing with it a bounteous supply of butterflies in the stomach. Happily, as soon as breakfast was over we were kept too busy for moments of gloomy contemplation to unnerve us. Wearing our loose-fitting overalls and cloth hats with an outer ring of sponge rubber we were marched to the parachute packing shed with immensely long wooden tables where WAAFs carefully packed the parachutes.

We were each given a parachute from a long line of them and assisted by our PJI in putting them on correctly. Each parachute had four stout canvas straps with a metal attachment at the end. Two straps were passed over the shoulders and the other two up between the legs. The four ends were then inserted into a round metal lock known as 'the box'. The four straps were then tightened by their individual buckles until a really snug fit was achieved. Thus equipped, the first eight men were ordered to waddle over to the nearest Whitley aircraft, parked not far away.

The aircraft had a short metal ladder leading to the door halfway along the fuselage. We entered on hands and knees, four to the right and four to the left, and sat down on the floor of the fuselage. Our dispatcher/PJI boarded last and closed the door. He just had time for a quick final briefing and to order us to hook up to the fixed wire before the engines roared into life and further conversation became impossible. There was a very short flight to Tatton Park DZ, which gave the dispatcher just enough time to crawl around and inspect that our chute hooks were properly secured. As an added safety precaution, each hook was further secured by a detachable pin, and it was the responsibility of each parachutist to make sure that the pin was secure in the hook of the man next to him, but the dispatcher also always checked.

On this occasion, it being our first jump, the aircraft would only drop one pair at a time. Later on, the whole stick of eight would exit as fast as possible. Arriving over the DZ, the dispatcher crouched near the hole, connected by intercom to the pilot, and facing two signal lights, one green and one red. When the red lit up he signaled to the first jumper to put his legs into the hole; when green showed screamed 'Go!' and No. 1 vanished, followed by me, as No. 2.

I had a wild a rush of exhilaration as the parachute snapped open and I saw the park spread out below. What fun! What a glorious feeling! Suddenly I saw the ground approaching at an alarming rate and heard someone bawling through a loud hailer 'Close yer legs!' and suddenly realized he meant me. I complied just in time, as a couple of seconds later I hit the ground with a solid bump and rolled over in the prescribed manner. So far, so good, but I still had to stop the parachute, which was dragging me along the ground. I rolled over on to my back, gave the box a hefty clout to release the harness straps, stood up and rolled the canopy and harness into an untidy bundle. I walked over to the WVS tea wagon, feeling very confident and cocky, to swap boringly similar stories with my mates.

That afternoon our section did its first balloon jump, a very different experience. The fat barrage balloon was tethered to a winch lorry and suspended below it was a large wicker basket, just like those used for artillery observation in the First World War. They probably were the same baskets – the Army doesn't like to throw things away – except that a large hole had been cut in the floor for the departure of parachutists.

I was amongst the first four detailed to board the basket by a small door in one side. The dispatcher was already aboard, and after checking our parachutes he called to the corporal in command to winch 'up 600,

4 down', meaning the dropping height and number of bodies to descend.

The balloon quickly reached 600 feet and stopped. It was a still day and there was no movement of the basket, and it was very quiet. The view was quite breathtaking but the dispatcher did not allow us time to admire it. We were ordered to hook up to strong points in the basket, with No. 1 sitting with his legs in the hole. In seconds he was gone and in quick succession we followed suit. This drop was different as there was no slipstream and everything was so quiet, but the exhilaration was the same. A pull on the lift-webs just before my feet touched down gave me quite a gentle landing. It could easily have been a stand-up landing, but this was frowned on by the PJIs, who insisted that all landings were completed with a sideways roll on the ground. So, like a good soldier, that is what I did. On successive days we made five more descents from a Whitley, dropping as a stick of eight and exiting as fast as possible. All went well and there were no unfortunate incidents or accidents. One more jump remained to complete the course – a night balloon one.

The night was dry but really dark, with unbroken cloud and no moon. We boarded the balloon in fours and hooked up by the light of the dispatcher's torch. Seconds later the balloon was up and away to the usual 600 feet. It was abnormally quiet and the darkness absolute; it all felt quite eerie. The dispatcher's voice was matter of fact as he ordered No. 1, me, to sit on the edge of the hole with No. 2 on the other side. On the command 'No. 1, *Go!*' I shot down into blackness. It was so quiet that I heard him yell 'No. 2, *Go!*'

My chute had opened but I could not yet see the ground when suddenly something touched my face. I put my hand up and to my horror felt a boot, which quickly disappeared and was then moment-arily followed by some sort of material, which also quickly passed me. A few seconds later I made a normal landing. No. 2, nearly twice my weight, had descended more rapidly than I had, and passed me in mid-air. This can happen with balloon jumps as there is no slipstream to enhance the separation of parachutes. We were lucky as our parachutes could have easily become entangled, with disastrous results.

Next day when we received our wings and maroon beret we were bursting with pride. All that remained to do now was to 'wet the wings' and Ned and I went into Manchester that night with this purpose in mind. We tried a couple of very dull and quiet pubs that didn't seem to fill the bill, and so, in desperation, we asked a bobby on the beat to direct us to somewhere with a bit of life. He mentioned the 'The Hole in the Wall' but admonished us to be careful, as it was a rough place. We found it be a noisy, smoke-filled room with a deep alcove in one wall in which a band was performing, hence the name. As there were plenty of unattached young women, we felt we had found the right place. Soon we were chatting up two pretty girls and, of course, paying for their drinks. By closing time we were all feeling convivial and happy as the girls had agreed to take us home for the night. They were both married, of course, with husbands in the armed forces somewhere, but this was wartime Britain and morals had gone out the window long ago.

I walked through the blacked-out streets of working-class Manchester with my girl until finally we stopped at a door of one of hundreds of dreary terraced houses. Instead of entering, she knocked on the door, and was obviously expected, for her knock was immediately answered by an elderly woman. After a quick whispered conversation, a wrapped bundle was passed to the girl. It turned out to be her baby daughter, only a few months old. It appeared that the elderly woman was a relative who looked after the child while she worked at the factory or when she was in the pub. Soon after this we reached her house and went inside. She took the still-sleeping child upstairs and put her into the only bed and whispered to me to be quiet so as not to wake the baby. I looked around the room and observed that there was very little furniture and the place badly needed cleaning. In one corner was a sink, chock-full of dirty dishes and utensils. This was just one of thousands of terraced houses, one up and one down, with a privy in the tiny yard, built by the prosperous mill owners of Victorian times for their employees.

For lack of a bed we made love on a dirty rug on the floor in front of the gas fire. She was so tired that she would not even remove her working overalls, just unbuttoned them. Considering that it was my first real experience of sex I found it profoundly disappointing. After an uncomfortable night, I awoke with a dry mouth and a thumping headache. She supplied me with two aspirin and water in a dirty glass in lieu of breakfast and, after ascertaining from her the correct bus number to get me back to camp, I bade her farewell.

Next day, our group traveled by MT to the Airborne Forces Transit Camp, at Clay Cross, Derbyshire. There exists a feeling of impermanence and restlessness about such places and no one is really happy there, except possibly the permanent staff. It was now March 1944 and most airborne units were up to strength and did not require reinforcements. One seemed to spend one's time there just hanging about waiting for a posting that never came.

Then came word that a Special Air Service Regiment recruiting party would visit very shortly, seeking volunteers. I put my name forward as I knew it was an elite unit and I had a good feeling about it. Two days later I stood outside a hut with a handful of others, waiting to be interviewed by the SAS party. When my turn came, I marched smartly up to the table, halted and gave my best salute. Behind the table sat a captain and a squadron sergeant major, both wearing sand-coloured berets. I was told to stand easy, then quizzed about my service. This included asking if I had been under shellfire, and my reaction to it. I decided to be truthful, saying that at first I was scared but that in time got used to it, but never liked it. I told them that I had a good grounding in the use of explosives, and that my French was quite fluent. They seemed quite satisfied with my answers and told me to stand by for a posting to the regiment in Scotland. I left that hut a happy man.

Chapter 8

SAS Trooper

I travelled by train to Ayr and arrived with two other volunteers from the transit camp, and we reported to the 2nd Special Air Service Regiment, or 2SAS, at Monckton, Ayrshire. The unit had just arrived in Britain from Philippeville in Algeria, and was actively recruiting and developing a training programme with help from the 'originals' of 1SAS, who regarded us as upstarts.

I was allocated to G Squadron, which later was re-titled 3 Squadron. I was immediately impressed by the informality – there were no squads marching hither and thither, controlled by bawling NCOs. Instead, there was an air of quiet confidence in everyone I met. But the informality did not permit scruffiness or 'hands in pockets' behaviour, as everyone was properly, and smartly, dressed. I witnessed a body of men who had no need of discipline imposed from outside simply because they possessed self-discipline. This was a hallmark of the regiment, as it was, and is, always called, and I soon found that the only punishment was the dreaded RTU. On my second day I was told to go to the Armoury, really just a Nissen hut, and try out some weapons. There was quite a large variety to choose from: American, British, German, and Italian. I chose a German Schmiesser SMG, and was given a spare magazine and a couple of boxes of 9mm ammunition. On asking where the shooting range was I was told there wasn't one but that I should go to the nearby beach and pop away at anything to familiarize myself with the weapon, which is exactly what I did, quite taken aback at the apparent disregard of the usual strict army range discipline. This was my first taste of the SAS attitude to training and I was very happy with it. Obviously they had trust in their men not to do anything bloody silly.

2SAS was at that time commanded by Lieutenant Colonel Bill Stirling, brother of the famous David Stirling who created the SAS at Kabrit, my old training base in Egypt. David had been on many raids in the desert war before being taken prisoner in Tunisia in March 1943. The SAS was intended to be used strategically, not tactically. This involved small well-armed parties infiltrating deep behind enemy lines by parachute, amphibious landings or Jeeps moving through gaps in enemy defences. The unit had been very effective in the desert war and it intended to operate in similar manner in the forthcoming European campaign. In North Africa the SAS had wreaked havoc on enemy airfields and supply dumps, and it was envisaged there would be an abundance of strategic targets to be attacked in France.

Once the regiment had established its credentials in North Africa it had been pretty much allowed complete freedom of planning and selection of targets. This did not happen in Europe, where a different war was being planned. The 'planners' intended forming an SAS Brigade, comprising 1 and 2 (British), 3 and 4 (French) Regiments and a Belgian squadron, later 5 (Belgian) SAS Regiment. At one stage 6 (US) SAS Regiment was proposed, but nothing came of the idea. The Brigadier appointed to command this formation had no previous experience with Special Forces, but then neither had any other senior officer at that time! This would be corrected later when Brigadier 'Mad Mike' Calvert, of Chindit fame, was appointed to the post, but in the meantime our man did his best.

Then it was ordered that the sand-coloured beret would be replaced by the maroon Airborne Forces beret. Sand-coloured berets were not available in the UK apparently, and no one would order small quantities when factories everywhere were working flat out ahead of the invasion. This seemingly petty interference annoyed the old desert hands, and some did not comply with this order. More importantly, it became known that the planners intended to change the strategic role of the regiment and use it as shock troops in tactical situations.

Bill Stirling was adamant this should not happen, and protested vigorously against it. Eventually he won the day and it was agreed that our deep-penetration role should remain, but because of his disagreement with the higher echelons he felt he had no option but to give up command of 2SAS. He informed us of this at a gathering of the unit outside RHQ, the Manor Hotel, Monckton, where he explained what had happened and introduced his successor, Lieutenant Colonel Brian Franks. We were sorry to see the departure of a good man who had sacrificed his career for the benefit of the regiment – it seemed unnecessary and unfair. On the credit side, we acquired a good, experienced CO, a pre-war Territorial and early Commando, and felt we were in a safe pair of hands.

In preparation for Operation OVERLORD we were issued with all kinds of new equipment. This included loose-fitting camouflaged

Denison smocks, worn over BD, and special trousers. Among other features these had a large, suede-lined external map pocket on one leg and metal fly-buttons, one of which was also an escaper's compass. We also received string vests and a good-quality thick khaki woollen pull-over with a drawstring at the high neck, and reinforced elbow and shoulder pads. Lastly, we exchanged our old metal-studded boots for rubber-soled ones. They were more durable, and, more importantly for our kind of work, quieter. However, the cleated soles let distinctive footprints, later to betray SAS men's presence to the enemy on the Continent.

We also exchanged our 1937 Pattern large and small packs for what became the SAS hallmark, Bergan rucksacks. They were voluminous, waterproof and comfortable to carry. They had numerous internal and external pockets, handy straps and buckles for attaching kit, and were mounted on a strong steel frame. Bergans became our constant companions in everything we did, and everywhere we went, in the coming months. They held many things: spare boots and clothing, rations, mess tins, hussif, ammunition and explosives, so they were usually very heavy. The best new thing they carried was, luxury of luxuries, a down-filled sleeping bag with a full-length zip-fastener so that one could get out of it very quickly in the event of a surprise attack.

Everyone was also issued with two knives. The first was a double-edged Fairbairn-Sykes Fighting Knife, shaped like a stiletto and intended to kill a sentry quietly, demonstrated to us as follows. Creep up behind the sentry, put your left arm round his mouth to prevent him crying out, pull him off balance, insert the knife below the bottom ribs and strike upwards into the heart. This did not appeal to most of us; we regarded it as Hollywood-style drama, or, in the vernacular of the troops, 'a load of old bollocks'. Few of us carried this useless bit of kit. On the other hand, the second knife, a US Army-issue one, was really useful. It had a leather-bound handle, a strong broad blade and a robust sheath with a button-fastened loop. It could be used for chopping wood, prodding for mines and had miscellaneous camping uses; it could even be used for sticking into an enemy. I have mine, more than sixty years later, and still find it useful.

We were introduced to PE2, a new explosive that was beautifully malleable, just like plasticine, and, unlike 808, did not give one a head-ache. It was very safe to handle and would burn fiercely without detonating and was frequently used for brewing up. We became familiar with other 'funnies' that the boffins dreamed up, though their intent was anything but funny! Probably the nastiest of these was the 'de-bollocker'. It consisted of a hollow tube, about six inches long, with a pointed end. This tube could be pushed into the ground until only its rim was visible. A bullet was then gently placed into the tube, and when an unwary and unfortunate person stepped on the bullet it would depress a catch in the tube, which released a striker pin that would act as a firing pin on the bullet. The bullet would then hit the victim's testicles. Clusters of these could be put on paths frequently in use by the enemy, such as to their latrines. Not really cricket, was it? I would not give much for the chances of anyone who was caught setting them.

More useful were mines made to look like dried cow-pats. These could be scattered on the roads and enemy vehicles could not hesitate to drive over them because they looked so natural. They were strong enough to destroy the front wheel of a truck, therefore ideal for ambushes. Even more innocuous were 'caltrops' tyre-busters. They were designed so that no matter which way they were thrown on the ground there would always be a sharp point sticking upwards. They had the advantage of being light, so that many could be carried.

Every man was issued with a prismatic compass, carried in a pouch on the waist-belt, also a Colt .45-inch pistol. They were carried in a canvas holster and came with a lanyard, which was either looped round the neck or one shoulder. There was a choice of personal weapons, including the US M1 carbine, with a magazine holding fifteen rounds of .300-inch ammunition. Ours was the paratrooper's version with a collapsible stock, which could be clipped to the parachute harness chest straps, making it available for instant use on landing.

We not only fired all our weapons on the beach, but also on proper classification ranges, and on new field-firing ones with pop-up and moving targets. We also trained with heavier weapons such as the Vickers .303, and Browning .5-inch, machine-guns, 2- and 3-inch mortars, the US Bazooka, and explosive, smoke and phosphorous grenades. We also trained with two special weapons. The Lewes Bomb, a mixture of explosive and oil, was invented by Jock Lewes, an SAS 'Original', for use against aircraft. The other was known as the 'Gammon Bomb', named after the inventor, Captain R.S. Gammon MC , Parachute Regiment, but officially it was the No. 85 Grenade. It had an elasticated skirt into which PE was placed, then moulded into a nice round shape. It was the custom to press bits of iron, or if that was not available .45-inch bullets, into the PE, like raisins in a plum pudding. On top was a Bakelite cap, which, when unscrewed, revealed tape wound around the neck of the bomb. This tape had a small lead weight attached to it and when the bomb was thrown the tape would unwind and so release the firing pin, which detonated the bomb on impact. It was meant as an anti-personnel weapon, but if thrown into the back of an enemy truck would completely wreck it.

We also received training in the best methods of wrecking a train by cutting the rails with small charges. These 'cutting charges' were made beforehand and several could be carried in a Bergan. It was stressed that the venue chosen for the derailment was important in that a train wrecked in a tunnel would take a long time to remove. The Germans knew this and guarded or patrolled tunnels. The next best site was a sharp curve, preferably above a steep embankment, down which, hopefully, the whole train would tumble.

An essential adjunct to demolition work was the time pencil. These were detonators in the form of copper tubes about the size of pencils. The spring-loaded firing pin was held back by a copper wire and beside a glass phial of acid. When the pencil was squeezed the phial was broken and the acid released. The acid then got to work on the copper wire until it was eaten through and the firing pin was released, striking the detonator, which initiated the explosive charge. The length of time it took the acid to do this was dictated by the thickness of the copper wire in the pencil and consequently there were half-hour time pencils and others of two or three hours. The use of these time pencils was essential in order to give the demolition party time to get well away from the scene of the crime, especially if they were on foot.

Alternatively, if a demolition party had transport and carried heavier weapons, it could carry out an ambush after the derailment. In that case the charge on the line could be initiated by a modified railway fog signal. It was connected to the charge but instead of lying on the side of the rail it was laid on top of it. When the train passed over it exploded and ignited the charge immediately.

Interspersed with all this weapon and demolition training were parachute jumps, orienteering and map-reading exercises, learning to select and prepare LUPs, all combined with cross-country marches to build up our stamina. The hills, forests and moors of Scotland were ideal for this purpose and we became confident in our ability to cover long distances on foot and to live off the land if need be.

We normally trained in twelve-man 'sticks', an Airborne Forces term for a number of paratroops who are to jump together from a plane. In 1944 an SAS stick had a lieutenant, a sergeant, a corporal and nine troopers. If necessary, sticks could be formed into 'half sticks' or even pairs, depending on the number and variety of tasks that had to be accomplished. My stick, No. 7, was commanded by mustachioed Lieutenant J.E. Cameron, Queen's Own Cameron Highlanders. In 1940, while in France with the 51st (Highland) Division, he was captured after being badly wounded in the head. The Germans put him into a civilian hospital where a steel plate was inserted into his skull. When nearly recovered he realized he would soon be sent to a PoW camp in Germany so escaped to the unoccupied South of France, where he had many friends from a pre-war days. However, in late 1942 the Germans occupied the whole of France and Loopy, as he became known, convinced them that because of his head wound he was no longer sane. This made him eligible for repatriation under the terms of the Geneva Convention and after some weeks he arrived in Britain on a Red Cross ship. He then persuaded the medical authorities that he was not insane, and ever after claimed that he was the only man in the British Army who could prove that he was sane. He was certainly a bit eccentric, hence the nickname.

Our sergeant, Bill Rigden, was a great big former Royal Artilleryman, as was Corporal Robbo Robinson, who had served with Bill in Malta and North Africa. Robbo was a very good man, always pleasant and helpful, a popular member of the stick and a good friend. He had had a troubled childhood, ending up in borstal, but that had not embittered him at all. We still correspond with each other nearly sixty years later. Bob Loud and Eric de Gay, also ex-gunners, were inseparable and good friends of mine but unfortunately I lost touch with them completely after the war. Mick Meager was another close friend. A pre-war Regular Army man, he had served throughout the North African campaign as a tank crewman in the 8th King's Royal Irish Hussars. Despite being short of stature he was a great Casanova and his Irish blarney could charm the birds out of the trees. He kept us amused with tales of pre-war army life in Egypt, such as one St Patrick's Day, when many Irishmen take a drink or two, when the orderly officer decided to make a snap inspection of the guard. One somewhat fuddled trooper couldn't find his rifle, but picked up a mop, sloped arms with it, and fell in with the rest of the guard, in the rear rank. The officer, who was also 'with drink taken', walked past the front of the guard without comment, then, having passed along the rear, said to the Guard Commander, 'Corporal, make sure that last man gets a haircut.'

Also in our stick, attached from the French SAS as an interpreter, was Jean Canonici, a young Corsican whose parents kept the Les Voyaguers Hotel in Bonifacio. He was quite short and cared a lot about his personal appearance; his comb seemed to be as important to him as his carbine. When we were in a small camp near Keir House, Bill and David Stirling's family home outside the small town of Dunblane, near Stirling, he located a house where some ATS girls were billeted. It was out of bounds to men, but that didn't deter Jean. He climbed an oak tree that graced the building and serenaded the girls, accompanying himself on his guitar. He, Mick Meager and me palled up and were referred to as 'the Three Musketeers'.

Lastly there was 'Tommo' Tomkins, older than most of us, always calm and unexcitable, but with a dry humour. His fitness was not up our standard so sometimes on a long march he lagged behind. This earned him the name of Tortoise, which did not seem to bother him in the least. I often wondered how he got into the SAS.

We nine formed the nucleus of the stick. Others came to make up the numbers and because of leave, sickness, courses and postings to other squadrons, their stay was often of a temporary nature.

When 3 Squadron were in Dunblane we spent much time on mountain training. Here we were learned how to abseil down cliff faces, starting with descents down the front of a requisitioned mansion, Inverardoch House, outside the nearby village of Doune. Afterwards we did more advanced rope work in the mountains around Kinlochrannoch, deep in the Highlands, as well as patrolling in what seemed to many to be really wild and lonely country.

On one occasion the entire squadron, in groups of three, went off on a three-day orienteering exercise. On the second day my group was working our way through deep woods near Loch Tay, well south of Kinlochrannoch village, when in a clearing we found a log cabin. We peered into the two small windows and saw that it was empty but bore the signs of habitation. There were three small bunks with neatly made-up beds, and a kitchenette. Behind the cabin was a corrugated iron lean-to full of hay. Taking off our Bergans, we made ourselves comfortable in the hay and prepared to await events.

Just before dusk we heard voices approaching and to our great, and very pleasant, surprise saw three girls, dressed in what looked like Women's Land Army uniform, carrying axes on their shoulders. We made ourselves known and found they were from the Scottish Women's Timber Corps, part of the Women's Land Army, and were felling trees nearby. During the week they stayed in the cabin but returned to their homes in Glasgow at weekends. They were really handsome, buxom lassies, absolutely glowing with health because their outdoor work kept them fit. They invited us into the cabin where we handed over what Compo we had left. Before long we all sat down to a splendid meal cooked by one of the girls, and afterwards listened to records played on their wind-up portable gramophone. It was the kind of domestic harmony that we lads had not experienced for a long time and we really appreciated it. The girls said we were welcome to sleep in the lean-to, but we declined, as we had an RV to make that night. But we arranged to meet them in Glasgow on the following Sunday before setting off through the dark forest.*

The girls were as good as their word and we met them in Sauchiehall Street. They wore their SWTC dress uniforms, which I thought were quite attractive, with rakish broad green berets, green woollen pullovers that accentuated the breasts and tan twill breeches. Fawn woollen knee socks and stout brown leather shoes completed the ensemble.

I paired off with the youngest girl, Jeannie, who had a wonderful complexion, with a slight dusting of freckles and a figure to dream about. For the first date the six of us kept together and as the weather was good we spent most of the day in Blythswood Square Park. While there, I had a slight recurrence of malaria, broke into a bout of shivering and sweating and had to lie down for a while. After an hour or so I felt better and was able to walk normally. Being a Scottish Sunday, the pubs were closed, but we were told we could get a free tea in the Sauchiehall Street YMCA. We found the place packed with servicemen and a hymn singing session in progress. This was followed by prayers, and an invitation to anyone who felt like it to come forward to the platform and be 'saved' – whatever that meant! Certainly no one was killed in the rush. We stoically endured these religious blandishments and were rewarded with a slap-up tea; I suppose we could have been regarded as 'rice Christians'. Afterwards we arranged to meet the girls the following weekend, although I privately arranged with Jeannie to meet her alone, if I could make it.

Luck was with me and I got a lift into Glasgow and spent a happy day with Jeannie, mostly in the park. We had a meal at a café and then went on to a pub for a drink but did not stay long. In those days the typical Scottish pub had a circular bar around which the drinkers stood, drinking 'hawf-n-hawfs', a dram of whisky with a half-pint of heavy beer as a chaser, as fast as possible in order to get drunk as quickly as they could. Women were not exactly welcome in these places. There were few chairs and tables and not much conversation, unlike English pubs, so the atmosphere was joyless. I imagine things are very different today, but that was Glasgow in 1944.

We walked the streets for a while until we eventually arrived at Jeannie's home. We kissed and embraced for an hour or two in the dark

* Editors' note: a nice memory, but Rosemary Elder, now of Vancouver but a wartime member of the SWTC, informed me that under no circumstances were girls allowed to sleep in the woods. They were confined at night in hutted, fenced camps and were guarded – whether to keep men out or the girls in is not recorded!

of the stairwell – 'canoodling up the close' as she called it, a 'close' being the tunnel-like entrance to Scottish tenement buildings. I did not want to leave her, as she was a very sweet girl. However, she told me that she would be in trouble with her parents if she got in late, and so I had to let her go. I never saw her again.

When I got back to camp I was told that all leave was stopped and that we were off on another training exercise. It was the end of May and though we did not know the date of the invasion of France it was obvious to all that it would be soon.

A few days later our stick was passing a remote country pub when the landlord came out and said 'Have you heard the news, boys? They've landed in France.' We went in and heard the news of the invasion on the pub radio and the landlord treated us to a beer. This did little to mollify our resentment at the fact that we were not over there in France but instead were training hundreds of miles away in Scotland. The landlord, a Great War veteran, told us not to be in a hurry as our time would come. He was right, of course, but that did not make it any easier.

A few days later the regiment was on a troop train bound for southern England. Our first destination was a large tented camp on Salisbury Plain, somewhere near Bulford. There we were 'sealed in' – no one could leave for any reason, at any time. This did not prevent someone bringing in vast quantities of draft beer, how or from where it was better not to ask. It arrived in our tents in large cookhouse tea dixies, and although lukewarm was very welcome.

We were told that our role in France would be cutting railway lines and damaging associated equipment in order to paralyze the movement of German troops, equipment and supplies. Later, individual sticks would be given detailed briefings and maps of their operational areas.

Adjacent to our camp was a US one, also part of the confined area. One evening, hearing music and laughter coming from the US area, some of us strolled over there. On a stage, surrounded by literally thousands of Yanks, stood none other than Bob Hope, with his audience really enjoying his jokes and patter. Moments later he must have spotted us because he shouted out 'Any British here?'

I shouted back, 'Yes, Bob, and don't forget you are a Limey too!'

He smiled; but did not reply. I doubt if many in that audience knew he was born in Britain.

The days went by and we were still stuck in the camp and beginning to get impatient and disillusioned. Some of the regiment had been over there since D-Day and more than a few had been killed. To counteract this decline in morale and restore our physical condition, 3 Squadron mounted a day-long cross-country march in full kit, followed by a night exercise. It was probably the toughest thing any of us had ever undertaken. We marched across fields, over streams and through woods, without stopping. Finally, in the late afternoon, we halted in some woods and were allowed fifteen minutes to brew up. Here every man was given a Benzedrine tablet and told it would 'keep us going'. The squadron then split up into sticks, which were then briefed on their tasks and given the appropriate map references; all were several miles from the woods. My stick was told to set up an ambush position on a country road.

It took us most of that short summer night to reach our ambush site as it was very dark and navigating through trackless woods is far from easy even in daylight. We took up our ambush positions along an embankment above the road and awaited the enemy, probably another stick, but we could not be sure about that. The effects of the Benzedrine were wearing off and we were rubbing our eyes in an attempt to stay alert. Just before dawn we saw in the half-light a figure darting across the road from side to side in a furtive manner. It was wearing a voluminous gas-cape, which ballooned out like wings each time it flopped to the ground. It was Loopy. We could not figure out what he was doing, but put it down to Benzedrine. He reminded me of a film I had seen about Count Dracula.

Hardly had we stopped tittering over this incident when a Jeep driven by an officer roared into view and pulled up with a screech of brakes. 'Gather round, you lot,' he shouted. 'There'll be a 3-tonner along in a minute to take you back to camp. You're going to France tonight.' On the journey there were a few moans and groans about how typical of the British Army to get us absolutely knackered and then send us off to do a job. Inevitably there was going to be a lot to do in the way of preparation before we took off that night and it was doubtful if there would be much opportunity to catch up on lost sleep.

Immediately after breakfast there was a squadron briefing by our Intelligence Officer, Major Bill Barkworth, on Operation RUPERT, in the Haute-Marne department. It was to involve fifty-eight men, mainly from 3 Squadron, with some signallers from F Squadron, GHQ Liaison Regiment, better known as 'Phantom'. We would be dropped in our operational sticks of twelve men. He showed us on a large-scale map exactly where our DZs would be and told us what enemy units were in each area, including Cossacks, White Russian cavalry units serving with the Germans. He also told us that the RAF would raid St Dizier airfield at the time of our drop to divert attention from us. He added that our operational area was in parts densely wooded. We were each given a set of maps of our area and of adjacent ones in case we should have to go into them. He then confirmed something we had heard rumoured – that we should have gone in late July, but the advance party's aircraft had crashed in France on 23 July, killing nearly everyone on board. They are buried in the CWGC plot of the Graffigny-Chemin, Haute-Marne, civil cemetery. Another advance party, eight men under Lieutenant DV Laws and including two Phantom operators, was assembled, briefed by Major Barkworth, and dropped in to act as reception party for the main force.

That day we were issued with further items of equipment, the most impressive of which was a personal radio receiver, worn on the waist-belt in two 37 Pattern Bren magazine pouches. The frequency had already been set and to receive messages all one had to do was to switch on twice a day at pre-arranged times to receive orders and information from base. We were also issued with felt-soled boots, presumably to be used if one wanted to walk near the enemy without alerting him. As our normal rubber-soled ones already fulfilled this purpose there seemed to be no point in carrying this extra weight and so the rope ones were left behind. Another item issued that day was a khaki peaked cap similar to those worn by the Afrika Korps. These, too, were viewed as superfluous and left behind; we were proud of our SAS berets with their cloth 'winged-dagger' badge, and wore them all the time. Escape kits, issued individually, contained useful items such as a fishing line, a small compass, a silk map of France and a plastic-bag water bottle, all packed into a small Perspex box. We each received a bundle of franc notes, and six gold sovereigns to be sewn into the lining of our uniforms.

So that day, 11 August, passed, and we were too busy making last-minute preparations to give much thought to what lay ahead. We had a meal at 5.00pm and an hour later mustered at the side of the road with our kit. The heavy Bergans were packed into leg bags, also called Parachutist's Kitbags, which could be opened from the side as well as the top. After the Bergan was inserted, the leg bag side opening was secured with a quick-release device. Once on the ground one pulled the quick-release and the Bergan could be easily removed. On the opposite side of the kitbag was coiled a fifteen-foot length of rope. The purpose of this was that once the parachute was open the paratrooper would lower the kitbag below him to the full extent of the rope. It hit the ground first and the sudden reduction of weight on the parachute would cause it to slow its rate of descent a little. We had practised this on two training jumps and it seemed to work OK except in one or two cases where men had just let the kitbag drop to the full length of the rope, which had broken, sending their kitbags plummeting to the ground.

Just before dusk we traveled by truck to RAF Fairford. We drew parachutes from a hut and helped each other to put them on and secure all the straps. We then donned our newly issued rimless parachutist's steel helmets, and were taken by truck to the dispersal area. Our aircraft was a large Short Stirling bomber, adapted for dropping paratroops and their supplies. We lay on the grass for a while, having a last smoke, until ordered to board the aircraft, where we were directed to get as far forward as possible for takeoff. After the engines had been warmed up for a few minutes the plane started to taxi toward the runway, halted, then, after an accelerated roar of the engines, rumbled down the flight path and suddenly was airborne.

The dispatcher told us that we could spread out a bit and make ourselves as comfortable as we could but as there were no seats we sat on the floor. As the aircraft was not pressurized it was very noisy. The only way to communicate was to shout loudly and directly into someone's ear, or by sign language. This ensured that there was practically no conversation between us. For an hour or so the flight was smooth and then suddenly the aircraft manoeuvred violently for a minute or two, which prompted the dispatcher to bawl 'OK! Just a bit of flak.' He then told us to stand and hook up, meaning clip our parachute straps onto the overhead wire. Satisfied that this had been done properly, he then went to the rear of the aircraft and lifted the shutters that covered the Joe-hole. Immediately a blast of fresh air was felt in the fuselage and the noise of the engines increased considerably. The hole was bath-shaped; about seven feet long and wide enough for wicker supply panniers to be pushed through it. The drill was that panniers, each of which had a parachute, were pushed out first, quickly followed by us. We would jump from a standing position, just walk up to the hole and step into it.

We stood there waiting for the word to go for what seemed an interminable time but was probably no more than fifteen minutes. Suddenly the dispatcher replaced the shutters, and bawled 'Returning to base!' without further explanation. After landing it was explained that no signal had been received from the DZ. The return journey was uneventful and dawn was breaking when we landed. Our feelings were mixed: part relief and part anti-climax. We had now gone two nights without sleep and were feeling rather jaded, but a good breakfast bucked us up again. Loopy told us we were going to try again that night, but we were free to go where we pleased until 1800 hrs.

Chapter 9

Operation RUPERT

Fairford was not far from Cheltenham, Bob Loud's home town, so he invited Eric de Gay and me to visit his parents. We hitched a ride there, but before going to Bob's home had a few beers at a nearby pub. We attracted some curious glances from the locals, but no one asked questions. The British public was well imbued with the idea that careless talk cost lives. If anyone had asked, we should have told them that we were on exercise in the area.

Bob's home was on the edge of town, practically in the country. We had lunch with his mum and dad and then tried to grab a couple of hours' sleep, without much success ... we were too wound up to be able to relax. Before long we decided to take a walk. We wandered aimlessly round the local lanes, occasionally taking a kick at any stone that was lying about just to give vent to our frustration. We came up to a greenhouse at the bottom of a garden and Eric deliberately kicked in a pane of its glass. Almost at once a middle-aged man came out to investigate. He didn't say anything, just stared at us. Eric mumbled an apology and the man, he must have been psychic, softly said: 'Don't worry about it lads, I know how you feel. I was over there in the last war.' Feeling embarrassed and foolish, we apologized again, and moved on. It was a relief when the time came round for us to get back to the airfield at Fairford.

After a meal in the Airmen's Mess, served by pretty, smiling WAAFs, we drew and fitted our chutes and were taken by truck to our aircraft just as dusk eased into night. Either we were too early or there was some other reason for delay because we waited for almost an hour before boarding. While we waited we were accosted by an erk who persisted in telling us how many aircraft of his squadron had failed to return from operations in the past week. I could have cheerfully murdered him.

When we finally got on board we found that we had a different aircrew. They kindly presented each one of us with twenty Players cigarettes, much appreciated in view of the chronic shortage of cigarettes in wartime Britain.

The flight across was pretty much the same except that there seemed to be more violent evasive action against upcoming flak, so much so that two of the lads vomited. This time, when the hole was opened, we only had to wait for a couple of minutes before we got word from the dispatcher to push out our wicker pannier. Out it went, quickly followed by us. As my parachute opened there came a loud explosion from the ground below. It was very dark, and I could not make out the ground until I hit it, making a bad landing and falling backwards. My helmet struck a rock, which put quite a dent in it. As I gathered up my chute a figure appeared out of the blackness and told me to pick up my gear and to go in the direction he pointed out, where he said the rest of the stick would be assembling. Sure enough, I found them all there, and we got busy burying our chutes; helmets and kitbags. The aim was to leave no evidence of the drop, but in the pitch dark that was almost impossible. Perhaps the DZ party would tidy up when daylight came.

I asked about the explosion and was told it had been our pannier – presumably the detonators had been packed in with the PE and that the landing had caused them to detonate. Not exactly what should happen on what was supposed to be a clandestine landing. We could only hope that the enemy would take it to be a stray bomb from the RAF raid on St Dizier airfield. What was even worse was that all our rations and other supplies had been blown to smithereens – a really bad start. One small problem remained: a stout rectangular box, dropped with some other items. When opened it was found to contain a .303 sniper's rifle, with telescope. Who was going to carry it? Apart from heavy rucksacks and personal weapons, we also had a Bren, with a spare parts wallet and several boxes of loaded magazines, which we would take turns to carry. We solved the sniper's rifle problem by burying it, box and all. We reasoned that we could always come back for it if it was needed – which it wasn't.

There were still four hours of darkness left so we took off through the woods as fast as we could to put as much distance as possible between ourselves and the DZ before daylight. Loopy went in front, compass in hand, and we followed in single file, heading southwards. Occasionally he would halt and we would freeze, listening. Nothing seemed to disturb the deep silence except the odd chirp of a cricket. We walked as quietly as we possibly could, but ten heavily laden men walking through a forest in the dark were bound to make some noise. As it started to get light we began to look for an LUP for the day. This was not difficult as there were several areas of thick secondary growth, and we soon found a good site in a depression surrounded by thick bushes.

Our thoughts now turned to food, which was going to be our biggest problem. All we had was a twenty-four-hour ration pack each, to last several days. Loopy insisted that we would not approach farmhouses or the like until we reached our operational area and contacted the Resistance. The ration packs consisted of small tins of meat and cheese, 'Biscuits, Hard', oatmeal blocks, sweets and tea. We ate everything cold as it was too dangerous to cook or brew up. The day passed very slowly and in some discomfort as any movement, other than that which was absolutely necessary, such as relieving ourselves, risked disclosing our hideout. Once during the day we heard voices but they never came near enough for us to identify them as either German or French. Because of lack of sleep on the preceding two nights we slept, or, really, catnapped. One chap started to snore and had to be quickly dug in the ribs. We were tensed up and alert. We were deep in enemy territory and for all we knew half the German Army might be scouring the country for us. This feeling was to pass and we became blasé, and a little careless.

When it got dark we set off again, sometimes walking on timber-extraction roads providing they were going in our southward direction. There was a violent thunderstorm and torrential rain. We were soon wet through but the frequent lightning flashes helped us find our way. By the time dawn came we were almost dry again and the sun soon completed the job.

That day was a carbon copy of the previous one and apart from oiling our weapons after the rain, there was nothing to do. We checked our maps together, attempting to locate our position, and where we were heading for. It seemed to be an awful long way off yet. Loopy reckoned another three days would see us there.

At night there seemed to be a lot of unseen ditches across our line of march and woods were thinning, so now and then we had to walk through open pasture. While passing through one Mick Meager collapsed with an epileptic fit, and by the time we recognized what was wrong he had severely bitten his tongue. We wondered what was to be done with him as he obviously could not continue with us. Jean Canonici volunteered to find a farmhouse that would shelter Mick, and said he would stay with him until he recovered. Loopy assented, as there seemed to be no alternative. However, he told Jean not to approach any farmhouse for five or six hours in order to give the rest of us time to get well clear of the area.

Mick had no history of epilepsy, but had fought in many battles with the Desert Rats. Four times he had been in tanks knocked out by enemy fire, so perhaps delayed reaction had brought the fit on. The family Jean found sheltered Mick until the Germans withdrew. He then spent a few days in a US hospital before being repatriated to the UK. We never saw Jean again – on his return to the UK he rejoined his French SAS unit. Jean was not indispensable, as both Loopy and I spoke French.

We continued our trek, and by this time we were really hungry, so we gnawed raw turnips from the fields. They did little to assuage our hunger but did give us stomach cramps. We lay up in the woods as usual during daylight, dreaming of food. Fortunately the weather stayed fine and dry. Even so, we were beginning to feel pretty weary.

That night we had a real fright while crossing a field when suddenly there was the thunder of hooves behind us. Thinking it was a Cossack patrol and I automatically brought my carbine up to the firing position, but, when almost upon us, they stopped dead. It was a herd of curious cows, coming to see who was passing through their field!

Next day we must have become careless in our LUP discipline because suddenly we were confronted by a Frenchman, complete with Gauloise in mouth. He was Emile Hormonsey, a farmer from the nearby village of Sommeville sur Marne, where he had contacts with the Resistance. He obviously recognized us as British parachutists. We impressed on him the importance of keeping our presence secret except to the head of the local Resistance, and he concurred with this. An hour or two later he returned with some food. He apologized for the small quantity, explaining that there were Germans in the village and if stopped by them while carrying a substantial quantity of food they would start to ask awkward questions. But he said he would try to bring more the next day. As you may imagine, half a loaf and half a salami sausage did not go far between eight men! To our relief, Loopy decided that as we were now within our operational area we would remain in the wood and make it our base.

True to his word, our French friend arrived just after dawn, bringing more bread and salami. He had a companion, a tall man in his mid-twenties, wearing a grey–blue uniform with silver buttons and a dark floppy beret with a small round silver-coloured badge. He introduced himself as Maurice, and said he would be our go-between with the Resistance. He added that we should go with him to a place in the woods that was both safe and weatherproof. He led us deep into the woods to a disused woodman's hut, approached by a track overgrown with brambles. It was a good place to store our explosives, and made a good base.

...arlie, Cecina, January 1945, before Operation COLD COMFORT, wearing Africa Star ribbon. (*CR*)

Scottish Women's Timber Corps uniform, 1944. (*Margaret Brown*)

Memorials to Operation LOYTON personnel executed near La Grande-Fosse, Vosges, 15 October 1944. (*CR*)

LE G.M.A. VOSGES
EN HOMMAGE AUX GLORIEUX COMBATTANTS
S.A.S. FUSILLES ICI PAR LA GESTAPO
LE 15 OCTOBRE 1944
SGT. PATT NEVILL | PCT. MC GOVERN
SGT. HAY | PCT. WEAVER
PCT. BENNET | L.CPL. ROBINSON
PCT. CHURCH | L.CPL. AUSTIN
ILS SONT MORTS POUR LA FRANCE
ET LA LIBERTE
REMEMBER!

Partisan hut used by 7 Stick showing 'polenta' pot and spoon, late winter 194[ ]
(*CR*)

Operation ZOMBIE: 7 Stick,
Iago, spring 1945. Charlie,
part hidden, third from right,
behind Sergeant Rigden.
Sergeant Lipscombe is far
left, the rest are unknown.
(CR)

Charlie with Shannon
c.1978. (CR)

Custodian 'Roberto', CWGC Padua War Cemetery, October 1995. (*FM*)

Grave of Major Ross Robertson Littlejohn MC, October 1995. (*FM*)

Grave of Corporal Joseph Patrick Crowley, October 1995. (FM)

Charlie with Rejane, June 2003. (CR)

Charlie about to lay the wreath at the execution site. SAS Pilgrimage, September 2004. (*CR*)

Moussey ceremony. British SAS veterans foreground; French 'Anciens' top right. September 2004. (*CR*)

ussey: SAS Graves and plaque. (CR)

ICI REPOSENT LES CORPS
DES OFFICIERS SOUS-OFFICIERS ET
SOLDATS DU 2E RÉGIMENT DU SERVICE
AÉRIEN SPÉCIAL QUI SAUF TROIS EXCEPTIONS FURENT MARTYRISÉS ET
FUSILLÉS PAR LES ALLEMANDS EN 1944 APRÈS AVOIR ÉTÉ FAITS PRISONNIERS

LIEUT CASTELLAIN TOMBÉ EN COMBAT PRÈS DE RAON-L'ÉTAPE LE 11 OCTOBRE
LIEUT SILLY FUSILLÉ À SAINT-PRAYEL LE 22 OCTOBRE
SERGENT LODGE TUÉ D'UNE BALLE À LA TÊTE À MOUSSEY LE 19 AOUT
SERGENT FITZPATRICK FUSILLÉ À PEXONNE AVEC LES
SOLDATS CONWAY ET ELLIOTT LE 16 SEPTEMBRE
SERGENT DAVIES FUSILLÉ DANS LES BOIS DE MOUSSEY VERS LE 19 AOUT
LES SOLDATS BROWN ET LEWIS FUSILLÉS AVEC UN FRANÇAIS INCONNU
AU HARCHOLET LE 16 OCTOBRE
SOLDAT GASPAROVITCH TUÉ ACCIDENTELLEMENT À MOUSSEY LE 28 SEPTEMBRE
SOLDAT JOHNSTON TOMBÉ EN COMBAT PRÈS DE
FONTENOY-LA-JOUTE LE 11 OCTOBRE
— R. I. P. —

ussey: close-up of plaque. (CR)

Asiago Plateau: Val d'Ass (V), Val Portule (P), Partisan camp area (X), Camporovere (C). (FM)

Charlie outside the former German HQ, Asiago. (CR)

During our trek we had regular one-way contact with base via our small radio receivers. Up to now there had been no specific orders addressed to our call sign. But that evening we got a coded message giving map references for places where railway lines should be cut on the following night. They were on the line that followed the Marne Canal from Joinville through St Dizier then on to the north.

The next day was spent preparing PE charges for the night's work. Two parties of three went out to blow the line at different places; both returned before dawn with no incidents to report. Bill Rigden and Robbo went out the following night but hid in bushes for hours because the line was patrolled by uniformed horsemen, probably the Cossacks we had been warned about. However, they eventually succeeded in laying their charge and got away. Whether or not their charge was discovered by the patrols we had no means of knowing.

I felt suspicious about Maurice for some reason, and asked Loopy what uniform Maurice wore. I almost had a fit when told it was that of the *Milice Francaise*, a Vichy paramilitary force used by the Germans against the Resistance. France, like all occupied countries, had a goodly share of traitors, turncoats, collaborators, call them what you will. It looked as if Maurice had gone over to the service of the Germans and now they were losing had changed sides again. He appeared to be accepted by Emile, who was quietly spoken, with an honest face. He kept us regularly supplied with food, and one felt he could be trusted. He had served in the French Army during the Great War, winning the *Medaille Militaire* at Verdun in 1916.

News came through from HQ that the Americans had broken out of the Normandy bridgehead and were heading for Paris, and that at Falaise, in the north, a large part of the German Army were trapped and suffering heavy casualties. A week or so later we heard Paris had fallen to the Allies. By this time I had found a good friend in Emile and to celebrate the good news he invited me dine that night with his family. Loopy agreed, admonishing me to be careful, and at dusk I set off with Emile. I was surprised to find we were the only about a mile and a half from the village, and as his house was on the edge of it we did not have to walk through its streets. He introduced me to his wife Marie, daughter Rejane (age sixteen), and son Jacques (fifteen). Also present was a family friend, Monsieur Jean-Jean; tall, cadaverous and with a conspiratorial air. Later two more male guests turned up, both claiming to be members of the Resistance. The food was excellent – I had not had such a good meal for years, and the company most convivial.

It was a typical French farmhouse, with one large kitchen-dining-living room downstairs and bedrooms upstairs. Apart from a long table and its chairs there was little other furniture except a large cupboard. An alcove housed a huge black cast-iron range, with an open fire in the centre. Suspended over it by a chain was a large black stockpot, which seemed to be perpetually steaming. We finished our dessert, a really scrumptious fruit flan, and Emile got his children to sing. The wine was flowing steadily and I started to feel very relaxed and comfortable. Suddenly there came a hard knocking at the outer door and conversation stopped dead. Quickly Emile stood up and opened the cupboard door, beckoning me to get inside it. I did not need telling twice. I quietly drew and cocked my Colt .45, leaving the safety catch off. If a German opened the cupboard, then too bad for him, because I was determined to shoot my way out. I could hear a distant conversation, which tailed off to silence after about five minutes. Then came Emile's reassuring voice, telling me to come out as 'they' had gone. He meant German soldiers from the local garrison, come to buy eggs, which apparently they often did.

Their visit put a damper on the celebrations and it was decided we should all turn in. As there was a curfew in force I had to stay until morning, sleeping in Jacques' bedroom. Before getting into bed I asked Jacques where I could pee. 'Out the window,' he replied, and did just that. I quickly followed suit. Now I really knew I was in France!

Before falling asleep I reviewed the night's events and resolved never to visit that house again until the Germans had gone for good. If I had been discovered the Germans would have shot the family and burned the farm to the ground. Early next morning, after Emile made sure the coast was clear, I made my way back to the lads.

Maurice came by later and told Loopy that there was to be an important meeting of the local Resistance at a farmhouse three miles away and suggested he attend it. Loopy agreed and took Robbo Robinson and me with him. The meeting was held in a barn, with about thirty Frenchmen, so there was a great deal of shouting and gesticulating. The purpose was to agree on the action that could be taken against the retreating Germans. I formed the impression they preferred to act independently of we British, which was quite OK by us.

The Germans were now retreating in earnest; the trickle had become a flood. One day I went with a couple of Maquisards to a vantage point where the main road passed through the woods to observe the exodus. The road was choked with soldiers on foot, on bicycle or horseback, and in horse-drawn carts. An occasional car full of officers forced its way through the throng. There was no sense of panic, and every man had his weapon with him. It was an orderly retreat, not a rout, and though dusty and weary, they still looked determined. They made a tempting target, and no doubt we could have sent a few of them to their maker, but it would have been a folly as they would probably have burnt down the nearest village and killed many civilians in reprisal. Nor was there a good escape route for us, essential in an ambush.

That night Monsieur Jean-Jean arrived, wearing a Great War helmet and carrying an equally old rifle. He imparted some news to us in a dramatic whisper. The Sommeville garrison, some 200 poor-quality Luftwaffe troops, would be leaving the following morning, heading east. He added that they were of such poor quality that after the first shots they would surrender. The local Resistance wanted to ambush them, with our participation. An RV was agreed on, and it was arranged that we should be in position before dawn. Monsieur Jean-Jean then disappeared into the darkness to confirm the plans with the local Resistance. In later years, when watching the TV comedy *Allo, Allo*, I was reminded very much of him.

We were in position well before dawn and arranged ourselves so that we had a clear field of fire. When it got light it was clear that it was a poor position for a successful ambush as it was flat as a pancake, and the roadside bushes gave concealment but no protection from return fire. Our weapons were seven carbines and the Bren, which was in my charge. Bearing in mind that we were on foot, and that if the enemy troops had any tactical training at all, then it would be only a matter of time before they first outflanked, then put paid to, us! To add to our precarious position, no Resistance men appeared, not even Monsieur Jean-Jean.

Fortunately for us the garrison troops did not turn up either. After about three hours Loopy decided it was time to move on. As soon as we abandoned our positions and stood up, we came under rifle fire, apparently an upstairs window of a house about 200 yards away. We were in an exposed position and after dropping to the ground we started to crawl towards the cover of some hedges. 'Tortoise' Tomkins, deciding crawling was too slow, rolled down the road. Always an individualist, Tommo. I put a couple of bursts of Bren through the window, which seemed to do the trick, as there was no further fire.

Soon after this we spotted a line of German soldiers crossing a field in single file. They were about 400 yards away, and we all opened fire, but I don't know whether we hit any as they immediately dived for cover. We were too few to stick around for a pitched battle and so moved back into the nearest woods and took up position on the edge, where we had a clear view of the open ground. After five minutes two German soldiers came into view, wearing helmets, carrying rifles and with stick-grenades stuffed into their belts. When they were no more than thirty yards away I stood up, aimed my carbine at the nearest and pulled the trigger. Nothing happened! Miraculously, the Germans had not seen me as they were passing parallel to our position. I threw down the carbine, picked up the Bren and fired a long burst from the hip, making them hit the ground. I heard Loopy shout 'Boche!' Turning, I saw everyone dashing headlong into the woods. 'Shoot and scoot' was definitely the name of the game, and I soon caught up with them. Loopy told me that when I had fired at the two Germans he spotted a lot more coming from a different direction.

As we continued to warily patrol the area we came across two more men in German Army uniform. They were bare-headed and unarmed, and as soon as they saw us raised their hands. One explained that they were Poles conscripted by the Germans and they were trying to get home. We examined their identity discs and pay books, and found they certainly had Polish names. They were very frightened, seemingly thinking we might shoot them, for they produced snapshots of their wives and children. They seemed pretty harmless and so we let them proceed on their way.

By now, various French civilians began to appear, most wearing armbands with the letters FFI (*Forces Francaises de L'Interieur*). They carried a variety of arms, including Stens and old French Army rifles, while some carried No. 36 grenades on their belts. The majority thought the German rearguard had passed through and that the area was now liberated. Being of the same opinion ourselves, we walked into the village of Sommeville, where everyone was out in the streets and gave us an undeserved heroes' welcome. Emile escorted us back to his house and insisted that we make it our base until ordered elsewhere. We had no sooner got there when we heard the roar of a convoy passing through the village. It was American infantry in GMC trucks. Some appeared bemused; others looked bored. The scene must have been repeated many times as they advanced across France. Just for the hell of it, we pelted them with wild flowers, just like the French.

That night we had a magnificent dinner at the Hormonseys, and Rejane sat very close to me the whole time. She was only sixteen but pretty and well developed, and I was flattered by her attention. There was plenty of wine, and it loosened our British inhibitions, so that we were able to sing for our supper.

We were given the barn to sleep in, and that night slept very well. It was to be our home for the next two weeks and we soon made ourselves comfortable. During that period we became well known in the village and got to know many of the villagers. One old chap, who must have been in his eighties, would come out whenever we passed his garden gate and beckon us inside, saying, 'Schnapps, schnapps, très bon. Long way to Tipperary.' He would then pour generous tots of Calvados. Once he proudly showed us a very small pearl-handled pistol, a real ladies' handbag gun. We persuaded him to fire it, but the ammunition must have been very old as the bullet remained stuck at the end of the barrel, much to his chagrin.

On another day three of us were taken to the bedside of an old lady. She was dying, and had expressed a wish to see the English soldiers so that she would have living proof that her country was again free. She took each one of us by the hand and gave a weak smile. It was quite an emotional episode.

Shortly after the German withdrawal a celebration banquet was arranged by several villages in the area. The venue was a very large barn and it was attended by around 200 people. The guests of honour were the local Resistance and us. Course followed course, seemingly without end, each accompanied by a different wine. It was soon more than our shrunken wartime stomachs could cope with, and we reverted to sipping our wine, while the French tucked in with gusto. Prior to D-Day the British public had been told that the French were starving because the Germans had taken all their produce. It was partly true of the cities, because lack of transport prevented produce reaching them, but even in Paris there was no shortage for those who could afford to pay black marketeers. The French countryside presented a completely different picture as their agriculture produced enough for both the French and the Germans. I went into one farmhouse kitchen and found row on row of cured hams hanging from the beams of its ceiling.

My romance with Rejane matured rapidly and reached its consummation one hot, lazy afternoon. Unfortunately it was soon to end because the regiment had plans for us. We were to be supplied with Jeeps, each armed with no less than three Vickers 'K' machine guns, or 'Gun, Machine, Vickers Gas-Operated, .303-inch'. These guns had originally been used by the RAF and had a rapid rate of fire, 950 or so rounds per minute. The ammunition was contained in 60- and 100-round drums mounted on top of the guns. They were arranged on the Jeep with a twin-mounting for the right-hand front seat passenger and a single one for the driver, which he could fire with his left hand while driving with his right. Special mountings had been welded onto the Jeeps for these guns.

Heavily armed Jeeps had been used by the SAS in the desert war with great success, and were to do so again in France and Germany, providing the two great advantages of mobility and firepower. In comparison, the 'on foot' type of operation we had just carried out had severe limitations. It involved a lot of exhausting marches to avoid attacking targets near to one's base. It also restricted the amount of explosives and weaponry that could be carried. Most importantly, a foot party, owing to its lack of mobility, was very vulnerable to attack by superior forces. So it was with great satisfaction that I was appointed third man in Loopy's Jeep, with Robbo as driver. I was to sit in the back where it was very cramped because two long-range petrol tanks were fitted, one each side of me. Furthermore our Bergans, spare kit, boxes of Compo and ammunition was also stowed there, so eventually I was not in the Jeep, but on top of it. Sadly for them, Bob Loud, Eric de Gay and Tortoise Tomkins had to return to base as there were not enough Jeeps to take all of us. There were six Jeeps; the other five crewed by men who had been operating in other parts of France. Bill Rigden joined the crew of one of the other Jeeps as Troop Sergeant.

Our last night in Sommeville, for me at least, was one of mixed emotions. I felt rather like one of the *Bounty*'s mutineers when they had to leave Tahiti. I had become very fond of Rejane and had made friends with many of the villagers. Tomorrow we were going back to the war and to an uncertain future. Rejane was looking very subdued as she knew that there was no way that she could get away to be alone with me – her family kept a close watch on her.

I went back to Sommeville while on a car tour of France in May 2002, and asked if any of the Hormonsey family still lived in there. I was told there was one, a widow, and pointed out her house. I called on the lady who told me she had been married to Emile's brother and that both brothers were dead. I enquired about Rejane and was told that she lived in the nearby town of Joinville. I found her address in the telephone directory and called on her unannounced. When she opened the door I was confronted by a sprightly lady of seventy-five. She did not know me from Adam until I produced a photo of her and another of me, taken in 1944. She was delighted to see me, and invited my friend and me into the house where she opened a bottle of champagne in our honour. She was separated from her husband, and living with another man – fortunately he was at work at the time. We chatted about the old days for a couple of hours and she told me that my visit had made her very happy, as had seeing the photo of us together again! She said that a relative had some photographs of us lads, taken the day we left the village. I asked her if she would send me copies and she did so a month later. They are the only photographs I have of us in France and they are remarkably clear. But back to 1944.

Before we left Sommeville we were addressed by the mayor, who was accompanied by most of the village population. He made a short speech of thanks and presented Loopy with a bunch of flowers. Loopy looked embarrassed and passed them on to me. I had a flash of inspiration and marched smartly to the nearby village war memorial, laid the flowers at the foot of it and gave a snappy salute. The mayor then surreptitiously passed Loopy a sheet of paper, which he later told me was a bill for food supplied to us by the village during our sojourn there. Apparently this was a custom dating back to Napoleonic times. I imagined Loopy passed it to whoever dealt with these matters, but as to whether or not it was ever paid, I have no idea. So, with the formalities over, we revved up the Jeeps and moved out, waving goodbye as we went.

We soon joined the *Voie Sacree*, the 'Sacred Way', the Great War French supply route during the Battle of Verdun. We reached Verdun in the afternoon and found it full of American troops. The town was little damaged as the Germans had made no attempt to hold it. Leaving our Jeeps under guard we went in search of a drink and a meal. We found a place that looked promising, as it was crowded with soldiers and women, but when we saw couples going upstairs we realized it was a brothel. The food was as plain as the women.

That evening Robbo decided to take our Jeep on a road test as he had been working on the engine. Before leaving we removed our kit and the machine-guns. We headed out into the country, going quite fast because there was no traffic on the minor roads. Suddenly, something white flew out from the roadside and hit the front of the Jeep with a loud thump. We stopped abruptly and found a dead goose lying in the road. Taking the unfortunate bird on board we thought it would be a good idea to find someone to cook it. We soon came across a dingy-looking country tavern and presented the less-than-enthusiastic patron with the bird. He grudgingly agreed to cook it but said it would take some time. While waiting we consumed a couple of bottles of wine. By the time our roasted goose was put on the table we were in a happy mood and tucked into it heartily. After concluding our repast with a brandy and a smoke, we paid the patron and went out into the night.

Horror of horrors … the Jeep had disappeared! We went back into the tavern and quizzed the patron, but all we got from him was an indifferent shrug of the shoulders. No doubt he knew something, but there was no way we could prove it. Whoever had stolen it had probably pushed it away until the noise of the engine starting was out of earshot. We were to blame as we had not immobilized the vehicle by removing the rotor-arm from the distributor before entering the tavern.

There was nothing to do now but walk back to Verdun, which was not far away. I suggested that in the morning we tell Loopy that we had had a bad accident and that the Jeep was a complete write-off and that the Yanks had towed away the wreckage. But Robbo had an even more ingenious idea. He had noticed that at a nearby US airfield a lot of Jeeps were being flown in. So early in the morning we got a lift to the airfield and were delighted to find that there were plenty of Jeeps lined up and they all had their ignition keys in them. We took one and just drove away, as simple as that. Next stop was a French civilian garage that quickly welded on the pipe mountings for the machine-guns. All that remained to do then was to remove the windscreen and dump it. Our Jeeps had no windscreens because they would interfere with the traverse of the guns.

That day our little column of vehicles drove to Nancy, which had just been occupied by the US Third Army. The Germans must have pulled out without a fight as the city appeared to be undamaged. As we passed through its streets I was astonished to see a tall turbaned Sikh soldier, complete with beard, walking in the opposite direction. We did not stop, which I thought was a pity, as I was curious to know how he had got there. There were no Indian troops in France; the nearest unit was on the Italian Front. Perhaps he was a former PoW, or maybe he had gone over to the Germans after being captured, joining the *Legion Freies Indien*.

We stopped for a brew-up in the large, well-known and quite elegant Place Stanislas while our three officers went to confer with the US HQ. The Germans must have been just outside the city because shells from US artillery sites were still wailing overhead. When our officers returned they told us that we would spend the night in Nancy and go forward to the Front on the following day. After leaving our vehicles in a guarded area, Robbo and I decided to take a walk round. We returned to the Place Stanislas where I struck up a conversation with a really attractive girl. She was beautifully dressed and smelt like heaven. She wanted me to go home with her and I was more than willing. But Robbo thought it was a bad idea as we might have to move out in the middle of the night. So it did not happen, something I have regretted all my life because she was absolutely gorgeous. I guess she was a pro, but for all that I think she genuinely liked me because I told her that I had no money and yet she still insisted I go home with her. In fact, the next morning early when we rendezvoused with the Jeeps in Place Stanislas, she was there to say goodbye to me.

The object of our patrol was to infiltrate through the German lines in order to reinforce a party from 1 Squadron, 2SAS, which was conducting Operation LOYTON. They had been operating in the Vosges foothills for some weeks but HQ had not received any signals from them. We drove out just past Luneville until we came to the US forward position. Their commander informed us that the enemy defences were strong at that point, and there would be no chance of infiltrating them. There was nothing else to do but try some other point. To infiltrate deep into enemy territory when they are in full retreat, as they had been a month before, is relatively easy. But once the enemy halts and forms a solid defensive line it becomes a very hazardous business indeed. The best method is by parachute, but we had to make the attempt by Jeep. We did so at several points and were fired on from all of them, luckily without sustaining any casualties. On one occasion our Jeep caught fire and I baled out in a flash as I was sitting between the long-range petrol tanks. Robbo stopped the Jeep and we managed to beat out the flames.
We reported all our enemy contacts to the US 4th Armored Division who were quite happy for us to stick our necks out for their benefit. Personally, I could not see much future in it for us. We had no rations of our own as we were a long way from the British Sector, so had to rely on the generosity of the Americans. We used to queue up at their cook houses with the GIs and were impressed at the quality of the food so near to the front line. We particularly enjoyed breakfast with the Americans as they invariably had waffles, or pancakes, with a generous dollop of syrup poured over them. In addition there were fried eggs and fried spam washed down with excellent coffee. Also, their facilities for washing of mess tins and cutlery after eating were much superior to British ones. The Americans provided copious amounts of boiling water, frequently changed. The British, on the other hand, would use two cut-down oil drums, full of lukewarm water, which, by the time the

last man dipped his dirty mess tins into it, was cold and greasy. On such occasions we usually scoured out our mess tins with sand or even earth.

The US Third Army sector was commanded by General George Patton, who had a strong antipathy towards the British Army in general, and to Field Marshal Montgomery in particular. Though we did not know about it at the time, the US Third Army was then at a standstill, which was anathema to General Patton as he was a hell-for-leather go-for-broke cavalryman. The Supreme Allied Commander, General Eisenhower, had been persuaded by Monty to allow him to mount Operation MARKET GARDEN, using two US and one British Airborne divisions to seize two bridges over the Rhine and hold them until relieved by the British XXX Corps. To achieve this it was necessary that supplies such as ammunition, and in particular petrol, would have to be diverted from the other Allied armies and given to the British effort. This exacerbated the already virulent antipathy that Patton felt towards the British and it must have reached boiling point when the airborne offensive failed at Arnhem.

One day we were at a town called Saint-Dié, which had been completely razed to the ground by the Germans as a reprisal for Resistance operations, when we received a call to report to the nearest US Divisional HQ. On arrival we were informed that General Patton had ordered that we were to be escorted out of his area next day. This came as a surprise to us, as at that time we were completely unaware of the bad feeling that existed between the British and US top brass. So after that little contretemps we got into our sleeping bags, on the bare ground, as usual, and pondered on what the next day would bring.

Not long after dawn two US Jeeps arrived with four MPs in each. They were immaculately dressed and wore white helmets with the letters MP prominently displayed on them. One of the Jeeps took up position at the head of our little convoy and the other at the rear of it. Engines were started, and without further ado we moved off. The MPs escorted us for what must have been thirty miles in a westerly direction and then abruptly left us.

Since we could no longer find a suitable role in France, our officers contacted base. Lieutenant Laws, OC of our detachment, sent this message, No. 390 in the base signal log, the original of which is in The National Archives: '16 Sept 1944 2050 hrs *161400hrs from Rupert 503 Henderson* injured evacuated one zero one hospital. FIVE men from CAMERONS stick cannot be employed here returning UK, LAWS.'

Loopy decided that we would make our way back to the UK in a leisurely fashion. The town of Epernay, in the heart of the Champagne region, was quite near and so we headed for it. We were well received there and given a guided tour round some of the miles of caves where the wine is stored and matured. At the end of our visit we were given several cases of top-quality Champagne, marked *Reservé pour le Wehrmacht*. After this pleasant interlude Loopy decided to visit his old battalion of the Cameron Highlanders, still serving in 51st (Highland) Division, which was conducting Operation ASTONIA, the siege of the German garrison in the port of Le Havre. And so we swanned off, just Loopy, Robbo and me.

We went by way of Paris. We drove along a wide boulevard until we reached the huge and splendid Arc de Triomphe. Then, on the road that surrounds it, we stopped and brewed up under the gaze of a crowd of curious onlookers. I was impressed by the beauty of the city, which had survived the war with minimal damage, and would like to have spent some days there. But it was not to be, as Loopy wanted to press on to Le Havre. But we made a detour through what had recently been the battlefield of Normandy.

Some clearance had started, but so far had made little impression on the frightful scene of devastation. Some villages, like Troam, Tilly and Villers-Bocage, had practically disappeared, and the fields around them were churned up by tanks and other vehicles. Power and telephone lines were festooned at the roadsides and dead cattle still lay in the fields. Army Graves Registration units were still disinterring and identifying bodies and the whole area stunk of death.

No wonder the Norman peasants looked so glum: they had been liberated, but at what price. We passed the city of Caen, which had been very badly damaged in the battle for it, and where thousands of French citizens had been killed. It was a relief to get to Bayeux, of the famous Tapestry, and find it almost undamaged. It had fallen without a fight on the first days of the invasion, unlike most other towns in Normandy.

Our next stop was at the Yvetot monastery, where the famous liqueur Benedictine is made. Loopy purchased a few bottles to take home with him, but Robbo and I refrained as it was not our kind of tipple. From there we carried on to the outskirts of Le Havre where we met up with the Highland Division. In 1940 the division had made a fighting retreat in the face of superior German forces until it stood with its back to the sea at St Valery-en-Caux, on the Normandy coast. As the Royal Navy was unable to evacuate them due to being overwhelmingly engaged off the beaches of Dunkirk, the division it had no alternative but to surrender to General Erwin Rommel's 7th Panzer Division. A new

51st Division was formed by re-naming the 9th (Highland) Division, a second-line TA formation raised in 1939. This new 51st gained its retribution in October 1942 when it played a major part in the defeat of Rommel's *Panzergruppe Afrika* at the Second Battle of El Alamein. Subsequently the division took part in the pursuit of the Axis forces in North Africa until their defeat in Tunisia in May 1943. Thereafter it was engaged in the invasion of Sicily and Italy before returning to Britain, at Monty's special request, for D-Day.

When we arrived at the open field where the Camerons were bivouacked it was late afternoon and the weather was gloomy and wet. Some pipers were counter-marching as they performed the daily ritual, when out of the line, of Beating Retreat. Near to them was a small barbed wire enclosure, open to the skies, in which sat two bedraggled and miserable-looking Scottish soldiers. Apparently they were undergoing detention as a punishment for some lapse of discipline. Seeing them made me very glad that I was in the SAS.

While Loopy went off to the officers' mess Robbo and I had a meal arranged by a CQMS, who had been with the division since before Alamein. He arranged for us to sleep in the back of a 3-tonner, for which we were grateful, as it was a cold and wet night. On our way to Dieppe the next morning we made a brief stop on the high white cliffs to look down on the beach below. Loopy was lost in thought as he gazed down, for it was here that he had been wounded and captured. Finally, he roused himself and fired a long burst out to sea from the Vickers guns, to commemorate the occasion, I imagine. Then we made our way to Dieppe to rendezvous with another group of 2SAS men.

Dieppe was rather battered, but there were still plenty of intact empty houses for us to settle into for the two days we spent there. One of the boys gave me driving lessons in our Jeep in a quiet back street during our stay; it helped pass the time. Eventually we went down to the docks and drove our vehicles through the gaping jaws of a Landing Ship, Tank. We sailed that night and arrived at Portsmouth early next morning, driving away quickly before customs arrived.

So ended my first visit to France.

Chapter 10

Sunny Italy

It was a great pleasure to be back in the peaceful, green countryside of England after the grim devastation of Normandy. We stopped at a country pub and enjoyed a pint or two, our first beer for many weeks. Then on to Wivenhoe Park, near Colchester, the new base for the SAS Brigade. There, in typical SAS fashion, we were given a seven-day leave pass, a return railway warrant, pay and ration cards.

On arrival at Yeovil station next day I decided to walk home rather than take a taxi, not for reasons of economy, since I had accrued quite a healthy amount of back pay and as a paratrooper I received 2/6d a day jump pay in addition to my basic pay. I just wanted to see the place and, to be honest, to let the town see me. I thought I looked quite the warrior in my red beret and camouflaged Dennison smock with an automatic pistol on my belt. Along the way a civilian stopped me, shook hands and thanked me for what I had done. He probably assumed I had been at Arnhem and I felt a bit of a fraud. When I arrived at home only my mother was there. Naturally, she was happy to see me, especially since our regimental padre had sent letters to the next of kin of us people who had been on operations in France. The letter warned that there would be no letters for some time, but not to worry, as we were not in such danger as people in the infantry. That was probably true in most cases, but I doubt if most of the recipients believed it. The majority of our chaps did not often write letters anyhow, so it would probably have been better if the padre had held his peace.

My brother Arthur was in Italy with the 4th Division and Kathleen was still at Plymouth. Father, unbeknown to me, had been in the Normandy bridgehead, mobilized as 'Temporary Captain, EFI' (Expeditionary Forces Institute) Radford. He had been taken ill there, but was now recovered and posted to a different part of England, a civilian again.

I enjoyed soaking in the bath, my first for several weeks, and afterwards I sponged and pressed my BDs before sauntering down to the local pub, which was busy as usual. The majority of the drinkers were civilians employed by the local Westlands Aircraft Factory. They were all in reserved occupations and so could not be conscripted into the Forces. Their pay was considerably more than that paid to servicemen but they seldom bought us a drink. Even so, I would not have wanted to change places with them

The pub, the Westfield Arms, was a fairly modern building, but the beer itself, mainly bitter, was drawn from wooden barrels through little brass taps. Because of wartime restrictions the beer was weak, so one had to drink a lot to feel any effect. The locally produced cider was much stronger, and though not popular with urban drinkers was relished by country folk.

During this leave I found a great friend and drinking partner in Phil Hughes, a submariner. He was the epitome of 'Jolly Jack Tar', very intelligent, had a great sense of humour and for some reason addressed everyone, including me, as 'Horse'. We did not talk much about the war but I learned he had operated from Malta, sometimes delivering Special Boat Squadron raiders to the Greek islands. After a night of drinking and playing darts we would end up in his house or mine and consume a whole jar of pickled onions with bread and cheese. What digestions we had in those days! Cheese was rationed but our military ration coupons entitled us to receive more than civilians.

My leave passed quickly, but it was good to get back to the carefree atmosphere of the SAS at Wivenhoe Park. It was a beautiful place with huge spreading horse chestnut trees and lush grass. Our huts were scattered throughout the park in a seemingly haphazard pattern and there was a large, elegant house that served as an officers' mess. I returned in May 2000 for a reunion of wartime SAS men and was pleased to see it had hardly changed at all. Of course, our huts had gone, but the old guard room was still there, and the hotel we stayed in was the old mess. In the foyer of the hotel is a plaque commemorating the wartime presence of 2SAS. The park itself is under the protection of Essex University, so, hopefully, it will remain as beautiful as it now is.

After our relaxing leave we got in some serious training, including a couple of parachute jumps, so were soon back in peak condition. Loopy had departed, presumably back to the Camerons, although we heard later that he had been promoted to Captain and had been 'mentioned in Dispatches'. Our new stick officer was Lieutenant Philip Fell, a pleasant, friendly chap, but who had not yet been in action. Despite that, we were happy enough under his command.

One innovation was what later the SAS called 'The Killing House'. Our version was a cave dug out of an earthen bank; inside were various targets in the shape of people. One had to dash in and quickly fire at targets, barely seen in the very dim light. The targets would then be examined for hits. In practice it would have been more effective to toss in a grenade as we did not have hostage situations in those days, but ours was not to reason why.

In the evening we would walk to a friendly pub in Wivenhoe village, about an hour's walk each way, which was nothing to us fit people. Some of the lads would go into Colchester where the opportunities for female company were greater.

When we were not on operations or training exercises the SAS were very generous about granting leave. I was granted a further seven days in November, spent in Yeovil. Strangely enough, Phil Hughes was also on leave, so we had some good drinking sprees. One morning I was alone in the town and after a bit of shopping entered a rather posh saloon bar for a beer before going home to lunch. There was only one other occupant, a prosperous-looking man drinking whisky. He told me that he was in the meat trade, and I imagine that he was making a good deal of money on the black market, as so many were then. He bought me a whisky and when I had finished that I offered to buy him one. He refused, insisting that he would pay for the next round. By now I was beginning to get a taste for the stuff and made no demur when he bought a further two rounds. Then, as closing time came, he shook my hand and departed.

I started out for home feeling happy, though a little hazy. About half-way there I began to feel very weary, and, spotting a nearby church-yard, entered it and lay down under a convenient tree and promptly fell into a deep sleep. Some hours later I woke in the dark, covered in frost. I must have looked like a snowman as my uniform was frozen stiff as a board. I brushed myself down and walked home as briskly as I could. After a bite to eat and some hot tea I was as right as rain and soon after was off to the pub to meet Phil. We were tough in those days!

My last leave before going overseas again was at Christmas 1944. Father and Kathleen were at home, as was Phil and his brother Jack, also in the Navy. On my first night we all went to a pub and while there we bought raffle tickets for various prizes. This was a common tradition in English pubs at Christmas. Two days later a knock came at our front door. I opened it to reveal a man with a live goose under his arm. He thrust it at me, saying that I had won it in a raffle. The bird seemed very tame and wandered happily about the house, finally settling down on the settee, where my sister fed it with biscuits. By its actions it gave the

97

impression of having been a house pet. Maybe that was why they had delivered it live – perhaps its previous owners hadn't had the heart to kill it.

A little later, Phil and his brother turned up. One of them said that geese were hard to kill and had to be stunned first. So we arranged the murder of the poor bird. Phil was to hold its body, Jack was to stretch out its neck so that the head rested on the edge of the doorstep, and I was to clout its head with the coal shovel. The plan nearly went awry because Jack's hand was to near the head and so sustained a couple of blows from the coal shovel. But he hung on like a hero until the poor bird gave up the struggle. While all this was going on, our pet Golden Retriever was barking furiously and the neighbours thought a murder was being committed, which in a way, it was.

Before New Year I was back in Wivenhoe, where a number of men from 3 Squadron getting ready to leave for Italy to join a detachment commanded by Major Roy Farran DSO MC. We travelled by train to Liverpool, and then by three-tonner to a transit camp, where we were confined for the night. A lot of special kit had travelled along with us and had been deposited overnight in its own stores hut. In the early hours of next morning we were woken by urgent shouts and on going outside saw that the hut containing the special kit was well ablaze. The fire engine arrived too late to salvage anything and the hut was completely gutted. At first light RMP Special Investigation Branch men were at the scene, together with civilian Special Branch officers in plain clothes: apparently they suspected sabotage. In spite of the seriousness of the incident, SAS humour rose to the occasion. One of the lads stuffed a sack with old newspapers and other rubbish. When one of the policemen glanced in his direction he furtively ran behind our hut with the sack over his shoulder. When apprehended by the police and asked what the hell he thought he was doing, he replied that he was the unit's rubbish collector, and opened his sack to prove it.

Another of the lads, a tall guy with a large, beaky nose, had got hold of a Sherlock Holmes outfit from somewhere, Maybe he was an actor in civilian life – we had all kinds of odd people in the SAS. This man was following the police around, wearing a deerstalker hat, smoking a large pipe with a curved stem and peering at everything through an outsize magnifying glass. The police were not at all amused but we onlookers could not restrain our laughter.

We were shocked to hear later that the sabotage had been carried out by one of our own chaps, an Irishman. He had volunteered for the British Army, and until then been a good soldier and a popular one. We could only assume that the IRA had got hold of him and persuaded him to commit this act; perhaps they had threatened to act against his family. Though the Special Branch was well aware of IRA activities, we were not, and it was hard for us to understand why one of our own could do such a thing. We never got to hear what happened to the perpetrator. Presumably he got a long prison sentence.

That afternoon we boarded our troopship and sailed that night. Although it was early January the voyage to Naples was a fairly calm one, and as it was a fast convoy we arrived after only eight days' sailing. During the trip I made friends with three Spaniards who had joined 3 Squadron just before we left Wivenhoe. Two were the brothers Ramos, and all had fought against Franco in the Spanish Civil War. After Franco's victory they fled to France, joined the Foreign Legion and were sent to Syria, at that time a French colony. After the Vichy forces in Syria were defeated they volunteered to serve in the British Army and found their way into the SAS at Kabrit. One of the brothers, Masens Rafael Ramos, was awarded a Military Medal, and the third man, known to us only as 'R. Bruce' was killed in action three months after landing in Italy, and is buried in Milan CWGC Cemetery along with three other SAS men KIA. Our Spanish colleagues were good men, and I often wondered what happened to the other two after the war, as they would have been prohibited for years from returning to their homeland.

Before we reached Naples, Lieutenant Fell asked me if I would be his batman. I refused, telling him I had enough to do looking after myself without having to look after him too. I was surprised at his request, because on operations every man looked after himself, including officers. Perhaps, because he had not yet been on operations, he was unaware of this. He never did get a batman while we were in Italy.

A thunderstorm was rumbling as the convoy slowly crossed the dramatic bay of Naples. Standing at the rail and admiring the view of Vesuvius, which still had a small plume of smoke emerging from its crater, I remember reading in the paper that a few months before it had erupted massively. Suddenly, there was a crack of lightning, almost overhead, and a young soldier standing next to me said, 'Christ! Have they started already?' I was able to reassure him that the front line was a long way north of Naples.

After disembarking at Naples we had no time to see the city as we immediately boarded a train going north, starting what was to be a prolonged tour of Italy. The mode of travel was, as usual, in cattle trucks. The train proceeded very slowly as the condition of the line was still poor; many of the bridges and embankments had been temporarily

Map 3. Charlie's tour of Italy.

repaired after being demolished by the retreating Germans. Their field engineers were masters of demolition and as they slowly retreated northwards they created maximum damage to roads, bridges and all other essential utilities.

The train stopped at Rome in the late afternoon, and we were told that we were free for the night as it would not be leaving until next morning. Mick Meager and I decided that rather than eat in the transit camp we would try and find some authentic Italian food. We had been paid with lire on the ship, so money was not a problem. Neither of us had been to Rome before and we seemed to be a long way from the centre of the city; in fact, by nightfall, the area we were in looked deserted and depressing. We persevered, and kept walking until we came upon a small tavern from which delicious smells were emanating. We had a very good pasta meal there. There was not much meat or cheese in it, for Italy was feeling the pinch of war, but it was tasty and plentiful. The Italian version of *rouge* is *vino rosso*, and it was rough, but drinkable. We called for a second carafe and thereafter *rouge* became *rosso* in our vocabulary. We had plenty of cigarettes, as troopships were always well stocked, and so, feeling pleasantly replete, we lit up again and sauntered out into the dark street. Soon we came upon a piazza that showed more signs of life, with people walking briskly, as it was a chilly night.

Casanova Meager soon spotted a couple of females who were chatting together in a corner of the square. We approached them and they smiled at us. They were not professionals, as they were not heavily made up and flashily dressed. Rather they looked like a pair of happily married, but not affluent, housewives, who would be more at home shopping at their local grocers. In the parlance of the time they would be referred to as 'happy amateurs', out to make a little pin money. Maybe their husbands had been killed or were PoWs – who knew? People's lives were turned upside down in those days, and morality was low on the list of life's priorities. Mick and I knew in the backs of our minds that we had a poor chance of surviving the war: the British SAS had lost more than 300 killed in France alone. We wanted to live a little while we had the chance. So we went with these two ladies to a cheap hotel and spent most of the night with them. Apart from the sex, we all enjoyed each other's company, and there was a great deal of laughter. We parted as friends.

The second stage of our railway journey was even slower than the first, and it was getting dark when we left the train at the town of Cecina, on the north-west coast of Italy. We were taken a few miles in 3-tonners to a large villa on a beach. This was the Villa Sabine and was to be our base. In the morning we saw that our accommodation was spacious, as the villa had many rooms and outbuildings. The villa was completely undamaged, although practically all the furniture had disappeared. This did not present any hardship to us, as we were well accustomed to sleeping on the floor.

Training began immediately, mostly cross-country orienteering exercises carrying full Bergans, and weapon training on the beach. We were also introduced to skis. This was midwinter in Italy, and one did not have to go far to find snow in abundance. Yet, instead of being taken to snow fields, we had our ski lessons on sand dunes. This idiotic kind of training proved absolutely useless when we got to the mountains on operations.

In retrospect, it is obvious that compared to the modern SAS some of our training was woefully inadequate. We could have all benefited from a crash course in Italian, even at very basic level. Similarly, a basic knowledge of first aid could have been invaluable, especially if a small quantity of essential medicaments could have been carried on operations. It must be remembered that unlike ordinary front-line troops SAS troops on operations do not have access to medical facilities. It is also fair to say, however, that the SAS was learning as it went along, and therefore mistakes could be expected. There is no doubt that the modern SAS has learnt, and benefited from, those mistakes.

When not training we were left pretty much to our own devices. That was the joy of being in the SAS – one was treated as an intelligent human being and not constantly harried by officers and NCOs to do this, that and the other. We seldom paraded in the formal manner; instead we gathered round whoever wished to address us.

While we had been relaxing at sea, a squadron advance party of five officers and twenty-eight ORs already been in action behind enemy lines in the mountains north of La Spezia. In spite of the extreme conditions of deep snow and icy tracks, Operation GALIA, led by Major Bob Walker Brown, was a complete success and gave the enemy a great deal of trouble. In addition, Operations TOMBOLA, lead by Major Roy Farran, and CANUCK, under a Canadian officer, Captain Buck McDonald, also caused the Germans and their Italian Fascist allies much harm.

The campaign in Italy was a slow, hard slog against an enemy tenaciously defending every position that lent itself to defence, of which there were very many. The terrain was such that wheeled transport was often more of an encumbrance than an asset. In these situations, there was no alternative but to transport all supplies by manpower or mule.

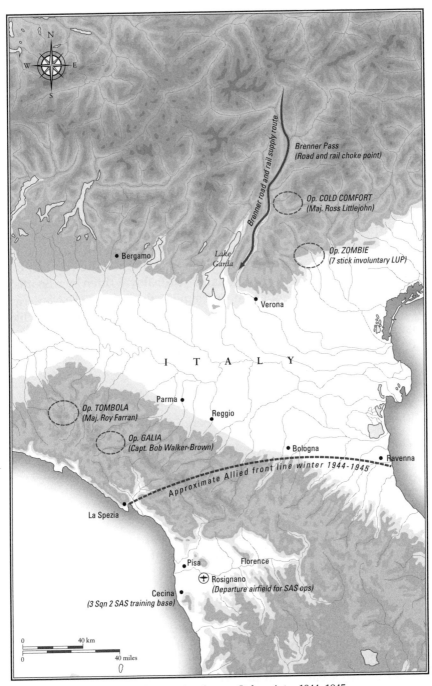

Map 4. No. 3 Squadron 2 SAS, operational areas, Italy, winter 1944–1945.

103

This meant that the wounded also would have to be brought back by the same means. The winter weather in the mountains was usually atrocious and among the infantry deaths by exposure were not uncommon. Because of the close-quarter nature of much of the fighting, casualties were heavy. Allied casualties for Cassino and Anzio alone were about 143,000. The casualty rate for rifle companies was estimated to be thirty-four per cent.

By then Brazilian soldiers were fighting in Italy alongside American, Australian, British, Canadian, Co-belligerent Italians, Cypriot, Free French, Greek, New Zealand, Rhodesian, South African (of all colour) and Yugoslav servicemen; a real hodgepodge of nations and languages. What the fighting troops found hard to bear was that after taking a mountain defence line there was always another one in front. Not surprisingly, after the D-Day landings in France, when all the world's press turned to that campaign, these soldiers felt forgotten by the public at home, which accounts for the bitterness inherent in the British Army song 'The D-Day Dodgers', probably written by a Scottish officer–poet, Hamish Henderson, and sung to the tune of 'Lili Marlene', which was very popular with the troops in Italy. One version goes like this:

> We're the D-Day Dodgers out in Italy –
> Always on the vino, always on the spree
> Eighth Army skivers and their tanks
> We live in Rome – among the Yanks
> We are the D-Day Dodgers, over here in Italy
>
> We landed at Salerno, a holiday with pay
> Jerry brought the band down to cheer us on our way
> Showed us the sights and gave us tea
> We all sang songs, the beer was free
> We are the D-Day Dodgers, way out in Italy
>
> The Volturno and Cassino were taken in our stride
> We didn't have to fight there. We just went for the ride
> Anzio and Sangro were all forlorn
> We did not do a thing from dusk to dawn
> For we are the D-Day Dodgers, over here in Italy
>
> On our way to Florence we had a lovely time
> We ran a bus to Rimini right through the Gothic Line
> On to Bologna we did go
> Then we went bathing in the Po
> For we are the D-Day Dodgers, over here in Italy

When you look 'round the mountains, through the mud and rain
You'll find the scattered crosses, some which bear no name
Heartbreak, and toil and suffering gone
The boys beneath them slumber on
They were the D-Day Dodgers, who'll stay in Italy

So listen all you people, over land and foam
Even though we've parted, our hearts are close to home
When we return we hope you'll say
'You did your little bit, though far away
All of the D-Day Dodgers, way out there in Italy'

The last verse was to be sung with vino on your lips and tears in your eyes.

Chapter 11

Operation COLD COMFORT

Asiago plateau, otherwise the *Altopiano di Sette Comune* (Plateau of the Seven Communities). This lies a few miles north of Venice, and is an enchanting and beautiful place. It is part of a barrier of mountain ranges and deep valleys backing the Venetian Plain from near Trieste in the east to Milan in the west. It starts with an escarpment rising abruptly from the plain to over 4,000 feet, with hills behind well over that in places, forming a formidable barrier to an invader heading north, as in the case of the advancing Allied forces in late 1944.

This mountain wall formed the outer ramparts of the so-called *Alpenfestung*, the semi-mythical Wagnerian redoubt where Nazism was to have made its last stand. There is some truth, and hard evidence, behind the legend, but that story must be told elsewhere … Be that as it may, the Asiago plateau is but one of a series of *massifs* in one section of the mountain barrier lying between Lake Garda and Trieste. Only the four westerly massifs, Monte Baldo, Monte Pasubio, Asiago plateau and Monte Grappa, concern this story. They are divided by deep valleys which in 1945 bore the main road and rail links between the enemy forces in Italy and their arsenals and supply dumps in Germany and occupied areas of the Reich. Baldo and Pasubio tower over the Val (valley) Adige, which carries the main road and rail lines. Pasubio and the Asiago plateau are separated by the Val d'Astico and its poor but, in 1944 and 1945, important road, and in turn the Asiago plateau is separated from Monte Grappa by the Val Brenta, which carried a good road and feeder rail link to the Val Sugana and hence to the Val d'Adige.

However, the apparent weak link in the entire Axis lifeline lay further north, at the Brenner Pass. Here the main north–south road and railway squeezed through a narrow Alpine valley before debouching into the valley of the river Inn, which in turn leads to southern Germany, the Czech armaments centre of Brno and

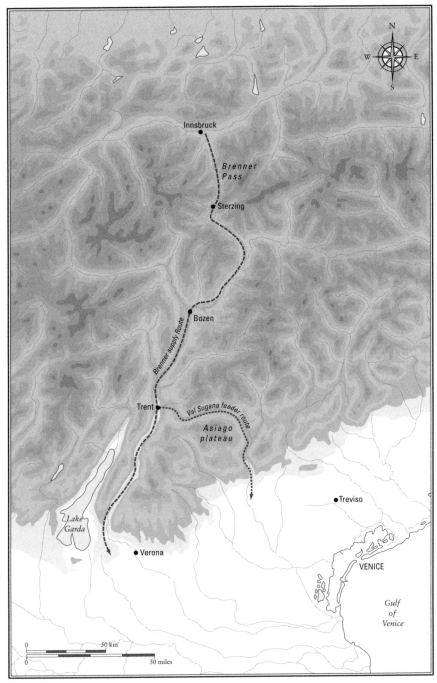

Map 5. Mountain barrier defending southern Germany.

107

other key supply and training areas. Blow the Brenner choke point, and starve the Axis forces in Italy and the outer defences of the Alpenfestung, went Allied thinking. Hence Operation COLD COMFORT.

There is another road linking the Venetian Plain and the Val d'Adige. It climbs, tortuously, the escarpment fronting the Asiago plateau from near Bassano del Grappa, passes through forests covering much of the plateau to Asiago town, then, by way of a long straggling village, Camporovere, and an upland valley, the Val d'Assa, and descends to join the main road through the Val Sugana. In spring 1945, as will be described, this road was much used by German, Italian Fascist and renegade Cossack forces heading for the presumed safety of the Reich. Their passage was hindered by partisans, members of the CLN (*Comitato di Liberazione Nazionale*). This was a huge and well-organized subversive warfare network organized by SOE, the OSS and the Co-belligerent Italian SIM (*Servizio Informazioni Militare*) Military Intelligence Service. Partisan groups were also aided and abetted at times by various Allied Special Forces units. These included the SBS, Popski's Private Army (aka No. 1 Demolition Squadron), Popski's Private Navy (a detachment of 945 Inland Water Transport Company RE), OSS's Operational Groups and its Mediterranean Maritime Unit, and attached US Army units such as Company A 2671st Special Reconnaissance Battalion and the 2677th Office of Strategic Services Regiment, and, of course, 3 Squadron, 2 SAS, sometimes referred to as the Italian Detachment. In return, the Germans and their Fascist allies of the RSI (Repubblica Sociale Italiano) used a variety of special forces units against the partisans, including detachments from the Decima MAS, or *Decima* [10th] *Flottiglia Mezzi d'Assalto*, aka X^a MAS ('10th Assault Vehicle Flotilla'). This was originally a naval commando frogman unit but by late 1944 it was almost a divisional-sized land-based anti-partisan force, some of its members being captured in May 1945 by British troops near the Asiago plateau.

Back at the Villa Sabine it was plain we should soon be off on operations, so most of us had our photographs taken. Someone had the bright idea that before we went to the wars we should organize a dance in Cecina, using the recently repaired town hall. The music was provided by two elderly Italians, a violinist and a player of a rather wheezy piano-accordion. Their repertoire, which hadn't progressed past the 1920s, was played with more enthusiasm than skill. Some young ladies duly arrived, heavily chaperoned. The ratio of soldiers to girls was something like 6:1, so the best-looking girls were monopolized by the few good dancers in the squadron.

Having two left feet, I joined the drinkers at the makeshift bar and got into conversation with the recently arrived Captain Ross Robertson Littlejohn MC, originally from the Black Watch. He joined us after a spell in hospital, having been wounded in Normandy while serving with 4 Commando. He was a short, soft-spoken, self-effacing Australian–Scot, with a noticeable scar on one cheek. As my new troop commander I knew we would shortly be on operations together, so wanted to get to know him. It was not easy as he was basically shy, but I instinctively liked him and felt he would be a good leader.

Long afterwards I discovered how he acquired that scar. During a long two-man recce patrol probing German defences, he had been hit in the right leg by rifle fire and, seriously wounded, could only move with great difficulty. The Germans swept the area with a security patrol, but when they found him he pretended to be dead. One of them poked a bayonet into his cheek to make sure, but with enormous self-control Littlejohn did not flinch. Later, after more trouble, he laboriously dragged himself back to the British front line.

The day after the dance our troop, HQ and three operational sticks some thirty strong, was summoned to the Briefing Room to hear about Operation COLD COMFORT. Captain Littlejohn explained that aerial reconnaissance had revealed a large pinnacle of rock overlooking the River Adige valley, and next to the main road and a railway running from northern Italy to Innsbruck and southern Germany. Behind the pinnacle was a deep crevice, which, if a sufficient quantity of explosives was inserted into it, would when detonated could cause a landslide. This would dam the river and block the road and railway, causing an almost complete interruption to the enemy main supply channel to the Front.

Captain Littlejohn was not specific about the site, and it was not pointed out to us on a map. Possibly this was for security reasons. However, a hint was dropped that it could be near the Brenner Pass. Since then, and after reading SOE reports many years later, I came to the conclusion that this was a red herring. Yet many post-war mentions of COLD COMFORT refer to it as an attempt to 'blow up' the Brenner Pass. What I do know for sure is that the DZ arranged for Captain Littlejohn and his advance party was near Monte Pasubio. This is many miles south of the Brenner and it would have been impossible for a large party to reach there in mid-winter, on foot, without being detected and attacked.

The briefing, which was also attended by Major Farran, concluded with Captain Littlejohn remarking, with a twinkle in his eye, 'We know that Mussolini is living in a villa near Salo, on Lake Garda, and when we have finished the first job, we will go and capture him.' Two days later, on 14 February, the newly promoted Major Littlejohn, together with Corporals Crowley and Clarke and a Phantom signaller, were dropped by mistake into a DZ near Monte Pau, on the Asiago plateau, many miles east of Monte Pasubio. The main party would arrive later, jumping into a DZ arranged by Major Littlejohn. We were to be dropped when the crew of our aircraft saw a pre-arranged Morse signal, by flashlight, from the ground.

During 24 February we were warned that we should be dropped into Major Littlejohn's DZ the following night. On the morning of 25 February I awoke with a temperature and a throat so sore that it was painful to swallow. I was determined not to miss this operation but if I reported sick the MO would stop me. So I spoke to the squadron medical orderly on the quiet, and he gave me a handful of aspirins, telling me to suck them slowly, one by one, throughout the day, and to drink plenty of water. Drastic, but though I was in a daze all day my throat improved and the fever left me. I don't think it did my stomach any good though as I have been unable to tolerate aspirin ever since.

The day was spent cleaning weapons and ammo, packing Bergans and inserting them into quick-release kitbags. We did not pack food as that would be packed into containers to be dropped with us, as would PE, time pencils and so on, and extra ammunition. The only comforts I took was a tin of Oxo cubes, a tiny medicine bottle containing whisky, and, of course, pipe tobacco.

We left the villa in the late afternoon, packed into two 3-tonners. Unlike US trucks, which had bench seats down each side, our trucks were bare in the back, and so we stood all the way to the departure airfield, which was near Livorno, or 'Leghorn'. En route the lads were pretty quiet, each wrapped in his own thoughts. Corporal 'Stanley the Singer' Bolden tried to raise our spirits with a rendition of Wagner's 'Ride of the Valkyries', of all things. The theme is incorporated in the Regimental March of the Parachute Regiment – maybe that is where he got it from. But he didn't get much response and soon gave it up.

In just over an hour we arrived at Rosignano airfield, operated by the American 15th Air Force but also used by Allied units, including RAF Special Duties flights detached from their main base at Brindisi, far to the south. After drawing our parachutes we split up into six-man parties, one per B-24 Liberator, which had already been loaded with our Mark 1 supply containers. They were metal tubes, about six feet

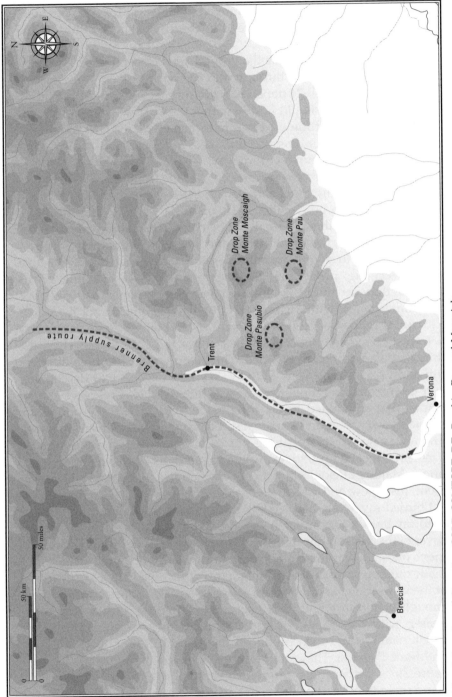

Map 6. Insertion of Operation COLD COMFORT: DZs Pasubio, Pau and Moscaigh.

long and eighteen inches across, hinged along-ways for easy opening. There was a metal buffer at one end to absorb the shock of hitting the ground.

There was a slight delay as the ground crew could not load a sledge into one of the aircraft through the Joe-hole. A compromise was reached whereby the B-24 departed with three feet of sledge protruding from the fuselage. I should add here that the aircrew were Polish and had a 'shit-or-bust' attitude, as was to be demonstrated later that night. When we boarded our aircraft I was pleased to see that the dispatcher was the PJI on our course at Ringway.

Apart from a little flak as we crossed over the front line, the flight was uneventful. The only other thing that struck me as odd was that the aircraft seemed to be circling and banking a lot, and that the flight was taking longer than originally anticipated. Then, suddenly, the dispatcher removed the cover from the Joe-hole, motioning Sergeant Rigden and me to sit on opposite sides of it, facing each other. The hole wasn't very big; in fact, our leg bags were actually touching. I was worried that we might go through the hole together and that our parachutes tangle with each other. But when we quickly got the signal 'Go' Bill disappeared, followed a split second later by me.

I must have been about 3,000 feet above the ground, based on the time that elapsed before I landed. The moon was about three-quarters full and I had a good view of the valley into which I was descending and its surrounding mountains. It was bitterly cold. I released my leg bag so that it dangled on its rope below me. Then the ground was suddenly very close and I made a soft landing up to my waist in snow. There was no wind, so getting out of my parachute harness was no problem. I looked around, expecting to see signs of the reception party under Major Littlejohn, but there was nothing. No sound, no movement, just snow and trees.

I buried my 'chute and leg bag in the snow, and hoisted my Bergan onto my back. I was in open ground and thought it better to get into cover of the forest while figuring out what to do next. Just as I started to move off there was movement, perhaps a quarter of a mile away, and I made out two men on skis coming in my direction. I aimed my carbine at the nearest one and they immediately shouted 'Amici, amici!' I knew enough Italian to know that *amici* meant 'friends', and as they drew nearer, with big smiles, I rightly assumed they were partisans. We shook hands, and I then produced the map of the supposed DZ area on Monte Pasubio. They studied it with the aid of my flashlight, their expressions increasingly puzzled. Eventually they made me understand that my present position, in a valley below Monte Moscaigh, was nowhere on my map. This worried me as it looked as if something had gone seriously wrong with the operation as planned. Where was the advance party?

Over the following two weeks we were able to piece together what had happened. The night we dropped, Major Littlejohn's party left the Monte Pau area heading for the Monte Pasubio DZ. They were accompanied by some partisans who were to assist with moving the supply containers. Shortly after starting off they had been fired on, but without sustaining any casualties, except that most of the partisans dispersed in the resulting confusion. Major Littlejohn decided to press on to the DZ with the reduced party, but about half an hour later they were attacked by a large force of Italian Fascist troops of the *Brigata Nera* (Black Brigade). Littlejohn and Crowley were wounded and captured, but Clarke and the signaller slipped away in the darkness, and helped by the partisans he joined up with us a few days later.

Littlejohn and Crowley were first taken to the nearby city of Trento for interrogation by the Italian Fascist police, and then handed over to the German SS in Bolzano for further interrogation under torture. Statements given at an Allied War Crimes trial some months later revealed that after brutal interrogations, on 19 March 1945, a certain SS *Sturmbahnfuhrer* August Schiffer ordered their execution. He told the two men detailed as the executioners to make it look as if their prisoners were shot while trying to escape. The two victims, together with a shot-down American flyer, Lieutenant Parker, were taken in a car out of the camp. While driving through Bolzano the car had a puncture, and the three victims were ordered out of the car and told to walk down a side-street. As they walked away they were first shot in the back, then given the coup-de-grace of a single shot in the head. Schiffer later pleaded that he was only following the orders, the notorious *Fuerherbefehl* to shoot all commandos. However, he was hanged, and the executioners got long prison sentences.

I have no doubt whatsoever that extreme pressure would have been applied to Littlejohn and Crowley to divulge the DZ signal required for the main party to be dropped. As the officer in charge, particular pressure would have been applied to Littlejohn. Their captors would have been well aware what their purpose was, since parachute drops to partisans were quite common at that time of the war, but not that of uniformed 'commandos'. So I am convinced that we who were dropped later owe our lives to Major Ross Robertson Littlejohn and Corporal Joseph Patrick Crowley, who gave away nothing.

Back on the ground with my new partisan friends I knew nothing of this so decided to go with them to wherever they were going. They put their skis on their shoulders and we headed up into the mountains. The going was slow because of the depth of the snow, the steepness of the climb and travelling through pine forests. I was breathing heavily after a while because my rucksack was weighty, but also because I was not yet acclimatized to the altitude, some 4,500 feet above sea level. After a two-hour climb the ground levelled out to a small plateau, with a log cabin in a tiny clearing. Although I did not know it at the time, we were perched high up on the east side of a deep valley, the Val Portule, and some miles uphill from the nearest village, Camporovere, near Asiago, on the plateau of that name. The Val Portule branches off eastwards from a deeper valley, a ravine, really, the Val d'Assa, which runs south, then west down the middle of the Asiago plateau (see Maps 6 and 7). These, and the general position of the log cabin and of the supposed DZ where I landed, are also marked on Photo 10 as 'General' as I never did find the exact locations on a map!

The solidly built cabin was about 45' × 15', and when we entered I noticed at once how warm it was. The interior vas dimly lit by one smoky hurricane lamp, and as my eyes became more accustomed to the darkness, I saw that nearly the whole length of one side was taken up by a six-foot wide sleeping platform, holding about a dozen partisans, all apparently fast asleep. My rescuers pointed out a vacant place on the platform, indicating that I should make myself at home. I lay down on my sleeping bag as it was too warm to get into it. I was fully clothed and kept my boots on as I noticed that the partisans were in the same condition. The only concession I made to formality was to remove my beret.

What remained of the night was full of disturbances because three SAS lads were brought in at various times. Then, at frequent intervals, someone would put fresh logs into the stove at the end of the hut and rake out the ashes. These were minor interruptions, however, compared to the bites of the bed bugs with which the hut seem to be infested. So I was quite relieved when the first faint light appeared at the small window at one end of the hut. The partisan next to me sat up, and looked surprised to see me there. But not as surprised as I was, for the partisan I had slept next to was a woman, and a good-looking one at that. She was a Yugoslav and the only woman in the partisan group – but more about her later.

Soon, everyone had bestirred themselves, and went off to relieve themselves in the forest. It soon became apparent that there would be no breakfast. The partisans explained that they had no coffee at the moment but that there would be food at midday. We SAS could not help because our rations were in the parachute containers, or so we hoped.

Our first priority was to search the area for our own people, and secondly gather in what supplies that had been dropped with us in their containers. Some of the partisans had already been out very early on their skis and had found some containers and the sledge, plus five more SAS men. We were now nine – Sergeants Rigden and Lipscombe, and Troopers Ayling, de Gay, Loud, Patterson, Sharpe, Tomkins and me. Next day we were joined by a Special Forces signaller, whose name, I regret to say, I cannot recall, and later Corporal Nobby Clarke joined us, but not Lieutenant Fell. We never did get the full story of what happened to Mr Fell and the other men who flew from Rosignano that night.

The search for the containers proved disappointing. A few empty ones, rifled, no doubt, by another band of partisans, were found. Some that had not been pilfered contained a Bren and its magazines ammunition, explosives and a wireless set with its pedal-driven generator, so we were able to contact base. There was also a tent.

After discussing our situation together, we came to the conclusion that only two of the six aircraft involved had dropped their men and supplies into this area. No officer had been dropped in, and we had to assume that the other aircraft had aborted the mission and returned to base. We also all agreed that the Polish aircrew had dropped us in the wrong place, and at too high an altitude, resulting in us and the containers being spread all over a large area. Our first priority on returning to the hut was to make radio contact with base. Our call sign was 'Box Item 18' and all messages were in Morse code. They were also coded by the use of what were known as 'one-time pads'. Each page of the pad was covered in groups of five letters, and the message itself was written under these groups. None of it made any sense until the key, printed on a silk handkerchief, was used to decipher it. It was quite an ingenious system, because every page was different on the pad, and without the silk handkerchief, was impossible to decipher. Our signals were received and many questions were asked by base about our current situation, ending with an order to make contact at 1800 hrs the following day.

While this was going on we agreed between ourselves that rather than endure the bed bugs for another night we would use our tent. A small piece of flat ground was cleared and then covered with small pine branches. The tent was erected on top of this pine mattress in the hope that it would provide some protection from the chill of the ground.

115

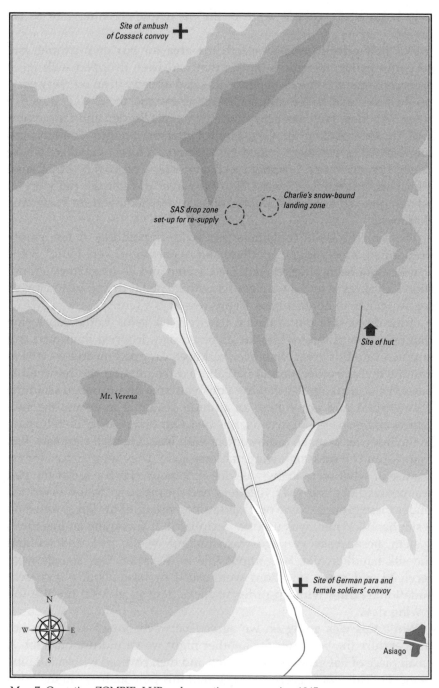

Map 7. Operation ZOMBIE: LUP and operating areas, spring 1945.

116

None of us had seen this type of tent before, and so we were surprised to find that instead of the normal tent flaps to act as a doorway, there was an igloo-style canvas tunnel. To enter or leave the tent one had to get down on hands and knees to pass through it. Not a practical proposition if we were suddenly attacked at night.

The partisans thought we were completely mad to leave a warm hut in order to sleep in this flimsy contraption. They thought we should probably freeze to death. They were not far wrong – it was one of the coldest nights I had ever experienced, even though we were in sleeping bags. After that we all slept in the hut. It was rather overcrowded, but there was a solution to this problem. There was a low attic, reached with the aid of a short ladder. It provided accommodation for half of us British. It was not ideal, since, like the tent, one had to enter or leave on hands and knees. On the other hand it was warm, dry, and relatively free of bed bugs.

Facilities at this partisan camp were practically non-existent. Water was obtained by melting snow in an iron pot over a fire. When spring came, and the snow disappeared, there was a stream not far away. None of the partisans seemed to wash or shave and it was not long before we were forced to follow their example when we ran out of soap and razor blades. There was no proper latrine; instead, an area some 100 yards away was used, but no attempt was made to bury the excrement. It must have stunk to high heaven in the warmer weather, an obvious indication to any enemy patrol that there was a partisan camp nearby.

Living in a forest, obtaining fuel for the wood-burning stove was no problem. The biggest problem was food. There was nothing to eat on the mountains, as only pine trees grew there. Food had to be obtained from the plateau and the valleys around it, all of which were occupied by the enemy. There were four different enemy elements: first, German Army units; second, SS field units including Cossacks; thirdly, Italian police; and fourthly, Italian Fascist troops who had remained loyal to Mussolini after the September 1943 armistice. With all these competing for food with the local civilians there was little to spare for partisans in the mountains.

Nevertheless, foraging parties were sent down to into the valleys, sometimes returning empty handed after a brush with the enemy, but occasionally bringing maize flour to make *polenta*, a sort of porridge. Once, and once only, our group acquired some black bread in the shape of hard, stale rolls. With it they brought some hard cheese – a refreshing change from the daily polenta.

Polenta was prepared in a large cooking pot, the only one that the partisans possessed. The cooking was always performed outside, over an open fire. When the water was boiling, a little salt was added, followed by handfuls of the maize meal. This was constantly stirred with a large stick about the size of a pick handle until thick. It was left to set for a minute or two, and then scooped out with a large spoon onto a special board. Attached to the board was a piece of string used to carve slices from the whole. It looked quite appetizing, like a large omelette, but to us it seemed to have no taste at all. The partisans called polenta 'poor man's bread', and it certainly held body and soul together, but served up daily, with nothing else, it left a lot to be desired. On peacetime visits to Italy I have never been able to touch the stuff again.

The Allies had divided German-occupied Italy into separate partisan zones. With the aid of SOE and OSS missions these zones could be kept in touch with each other via radio links with Allied No. 1 Special Forces HQ, with Fifteenth Army HQ in the south. These missions, usually two or three Italian-speaking officers and a wireless operator, were vital for the purpose of arranging arms drops to the partisans. Communications within a Partisan Divisional Zone was mainly by courier, usually by women, known as *staffetti* – dispatch riders. Women could usually roam about unmolested, whereas a male partisan would be shot, or sent to forced-labour camps in Germany.

Our partisan band, the twenty-strong 'Gruppo Dingo', was named after the *nome di battaglia* (battle, or code, name) of its OC, Giovanni Bonato. The *gruppo* was a sub-unit of *Brigata Fiamme Verdi* (Green Flames Brigade), the CO of which was Rodeghiero Domenico (*Falco* – Hawk), part of *Divisione Alpina Monte Ortigara*, named for a famous local Great War battle, and which operated throughout *Zona Ortigara*. Every partisan had a *nome di battaglia*; if captured they could not reveal the true names of others, thus protecting them and their families. *Falco*, an intelligent man in his mid-twenties who spoke a little English, was fair-skinned with a reddish-blonde beard; he spoke softly, and was well respected by all.

Attached to *Dingo* for liaison with the local SOE Mission, codename *Fluvius*, was a tall, slim, well-educated young Roman, battlename *Conte*, who spoke excellent English. He stood out from the bearded partisans as he was always clean shaven. I only once saw him scared. We had to move along a high snow-covered ridge with a sheer drop on either side. He didn't like heights but traversed it nevertheless.

My particular partisan friend, battlename *Bull*, was short, with black, curly hair worn long, with a beard to match. He had a great sense of humour, and as he spoke French we were able to talk freely. His real name was Giovanni Fabris.

The Yugoslav girl, battlename *Yola*, was a *staffetta*, and also sat in Asiago cafés listening to enemy conversation to glean information about their movements. It was rumoured she had been known to entice an enemy soldier to a secluded rendezvous, then shoot him. Whether that was true or not, I do not know. However, when my boots wore out she presented me with an almost new pair of German jack-boots. When asked her how she had obtained them, she smiled and drew her finger across her throat.

With the Italians' reputation for women chasing, I had expected to see some advances made by some of the group toward this attractive young woman. But such behaviour was strictly banned by the partisans to prevent any conflict between its members. As far as I could see, this ban was strictly adhered to, but even without the ban, I do not think any of them would risk upsetting this tough young woman, who reminded me of a tigress. Strange to relate, Yola was reputed to have fond feelings toward the group's cook. He was a tall, gangling, skinny lad with a pale complexion and he had not much to say about anything. He never had the opportunity to demonstrate his culinary skills, if he had any, as all he had to do was make polenta. Perhaps she had motherly feelings for him. Whatever the case, their relationship was obviously platonic.

Asiago had a German garrison based near the town centre in the hotel *Croce Bianca*, in the Corso IV Novembre, a long street named for the Great War Italian Armistice Day. There were small detachments at each of the five village railway stations on the plateau; a narrow-gauge railway linked Asiago with the plains. These detachments, and the garrison, supervised and protected *Organization Todt* teams building defences and timber-cutting, and, of course, the railway.

The majority of the partisans in the Asiago area had been living in the mountains since late 1943 and had become hardened to the life. They were the hard core, survivors of several enemy roundups or *rastrall-amenti* ('rakings'). The last big one had been in September 1944, when many partisans had been killed, or captured, then shot or hanged. I was shown a photograph of a tree-lined boulevard in Bassano del Grappa, and from every tree hung a partisan. Usually the Italian Fascists were responsible for these atrocities, but the Germans and Russians often resorted to terror tactics, particularly the burning of farms and houses. A mutual armistice existed in the depths of winter, largely due to the difficulty of movement, but another *rastrallamento* was expected when the snow melted. Most partisan groups were too poorly armed to afford substantial resistance and the usual tactic was to retreat to another area.

On our second day at the hut we duly contacted base by radio and were informed that a parachute drop of supplies and reinforcements would be made at map-reference X two nights hence. To pass the time until then we demonstrated to the partisans how to make up explosive charges, using PE and Cordtex from the supply drop. We also queried them as to the whereabouts of any worthwhile targets in the area. They were less than enthusiastic in this regard, maintaining that it would be much too dangerous for offensive actions until the snow was gone.

The following day some of us tried our hand at skiing on a nearby slope, which was clear of trees. None of us had skied before; one could hardly take into account the lesson we had received on the beach at Villa Sabine. Our antics provided some amusement for the partisans as we were pretty hopeless, and in my own case I fell and sprained a thumb. So the general consensus was that we would take our chances on our own two feet.

After this we went to the partisan OP, sited so that the sentry had a panoramic view of the valley below, and of Camporovere. Any movement of the enemy troops leaving the valley could be seen, so it was always manned during daylight, but not at night. If a sentry had been kept there at night he would probably have frozen to death, and even if not, he would not have been able to see anything. The partisans were complacent that they would not be attacked at night, but we British were not so sure. There was nothing to prevent the enemy from getting his troops in position under the cover of darkness then attacking at dawn. There was no doubt at all that they knew the partisans were on the mountains. Of course, we all slept fully clothed and kept our weapons very close at hand.

On the night of the proposed supply drop we set off at dusk to the DZ, which was a few miles away. We reached it by mountain paths without incident. We towed the sledge with us as it would be necessary for carrying the supplies we expected. We also carried dry wood for the line of small fires that would indicate to the aircraft the direction he should follow when dropping containers. The partisans were adept at preparing these fires. They stacked the dry wood in the shape of cones, very small twigs on the inside and thicker sticks on the outside. A small opening was left in front of the cone in which to insert the lighted match.

Morale was high as we waited in cheerful anticipation of the goodies that would soon be falling from the sky. After an hour or so a faint hum of an aircraft was heard. It got nearer and then it receded again. This occurred several times until we decided that it was near enough to see our fires. They were lit and soon blazed up. Simultaneously the pre-arranged Morse letter was flashed by torch. In addition our SF Signaller made repeated attempts to speak to the aircraft with his S-phone. This was the latest piece of electronic gadgetry that we had been issued with, but we had never trained with it and so were unaware of its effective range. It must have been quite limited as we never did get through to an aircraft with it. Sad to relate, the aircraft noise finally disappeared completely, and there was nothing to be done but to rebuild the fires and hope that the aircraft would return to us. This we did, and settled down to wait again. But our luck was out, and after waiting for a further two hours, we had to get back to the hut before daylight. So it was a disappointed little column that trudged back through the snow, dragging their sledge behind them.

Some hours later we contacted base by radio and were told that the aircraft had not been able to find us. They said to make contact the next day, when we should be given details of the next supply drop. Daily radio contact was maintained for several ensuing days, and the gist of the order from base was always that something was being arranged, and to keep in touch.

During this period we had a brief visit from two SOE officers, Major John Wilkinson, codename *Freccia* (Arrow), and his deputy/training officer, Captain Chris Woods, *Dardo* (Dart). Both wore civilian clothes and had been in the area since summer 1944. Major Wilkinson made a good impression on us, taking pains to shake hands and have a word with everyone, saying he hoped to be of assistance in the future. Unfortunately the next day he was killed by Fascist policemen, and is now buried in the CWGC Padua War Cemetery.

We were unaware that when the SAS mooted Operation COLD COMFORT *Freccia* and *Dardo* protested strongly against it taking place until the snowfields had melted. This had been ignored, which did not enhance relations between us. In fact, we never saw or heard from SOE again, although we heard that *Colombo*, Captain John Orr-Ewing, had replaced *Freccia*.

In the weeks that followed two more supply drops were arranged with base, but nothing materialized. Inevitably we began to get the feeling that base was losing interest in us. We pondered that perhaps they were devoting scarce resources to other 3 Squadron operations.

One morning a breathless partisan came to the hut on skis, saying that a supply drop had been made during the night at a point not far away.

Without further ado we asked him to show us the place and within less than an hour we were there. Unfortunately for us, we had arrived too late, for a different band of partisans had got there before us, communist *Garibaldini*. Although they sometimes took action against the enemy in order to capture weapons and ammunition, their purpose for doing so was to be strong enough to take over the Italian government when the war was over.

Relations between the *Garibaldini* and the Christian Democrat *Fiamma Verde* were sometimes strained, and this was one such occasion. We faced them in a line and told them that the supplies were ours and they could see that we were British soldiers. They outfaced us for a minute or two, but then gave us dirty looks and moved off. The bulk of the supplies had already been removed by them and the chances of recovering them were nil. We were left with several empty containers, and two full ones, which contained a Bren, ammunition, spare magazines and some PE.

Our partisans were delighted to have the Bren, as up to now they had been very poorly armed. Most carried a 9mm Beretta pistol, some had Stens and two had German Army rifles. These were referred to as 'ta-pooms', from the noise they made when fired. The expression is also the title of a song sung on the Asiago plateau about the dreadful slaughter of *Alpini* during the Ortigara battle. There was a shortage of ammunition for all these weapons.

Stens had to be handled with caution as they could fire if dropped. This happened one night when we were on patrol. A partisan accidentally dropped his Sten and it fired, sending a bullet up through his arm and out near his shoulder blade. He made such a noise moaning that I gave him a shot of morphine before we left him at a farmhouse for safe keeping. If I was wounded I should have to rely on one of my SAS colleagues to inject me with his morphine as we only had one ampoule each.

We had another partisan casualty shortly after this. A patrol had been down in the valley one night, searching for food. They had been fired on by Cossacks, hitting one partisan, Tommaso, in the stomach. His fellow partisans carried him clear of the valley then left him under cover temporarily, then made their way back to camp to get help. We made a stretcher with two saplings and a blanket and hurried down the mountain track to pick him up. He was quite heavy and it was hard going, with frequent stops for rest, before we got him back up the mountain. He was conscious and groaning the whole way and continued so for the rest of the day. During the day a doctor arrived from Camporovere, but there was little he could do. Tommaso died during the night and after a moving little ceremony he was buried there on the mountain top.

Word came that a *rastrallamento* was being prepared. According to the partisans, the usual method was for the enemy forces to encircle an area and then move inward, gradually decreasing the circumference of the search area. They had spies in the valley so their information was usually accurate. That night we moved out and headed for another partisan group some miles away. It took us most of the night to reach there, but we were well acclimatized by this time and were feeling fit, though hungry. This partisan group had a similar mountain hut, though larger than ours, and they seemed happy to see us. Both groups appeared to know each other and there was much laughter and hand-shaking all round. There were also three escaped British PoWs, who had been on the run since the Italian armistice in 1943, and all of them were quite fluent in the Italian language. They told us that they had not been long with this particular group and that they preferred to move from group to group so that they did not wear out their welcome. None of them were armed so they were not a lot of use to the partisans. We suggested that they could come with us and act as interpreters, but they were not keen on the idea and said that they would wait for the Allies to arrive.

We stayed only a few days at this new location and then returned to the old one as we wanted to keep in touch by radio with base. Our transmitter had been concealed in a camouflaged pit during our absence. We were still hopeful that some supplies might be parachuted to us. Our boots were beginning to deteriorate, caused by constant immersion in the snow, which rotted the stitching. The partisans all wore strong, well-made ski boots, which were much superior to ours. We got off a signal to base asking for a supply of new boots and were astonished to receive the reply 'Partisans can operate without boots – why can't you?' This was absolute rubbish, and did little for our morale. But, as previously stated, Yola solved the problem for me.

Easter came, with the church bells in the valley ringing to celebrate the occasion. One of our food foraging parties procured some bottles of *grappa*. This was powerful stuff and soon went to our heads, leading to a certain amount of drunken behaviour. One of the partisans started to fire up into the air until his weapon was taken away from him. Someone else put too much wood into the stove, causing sparks from the chimney, which ignited the nearest pine tree. Fortunately the tree still had snow on it and so the flames did not take hold.

Soon the heat of the sun got stronger and the thaw began. It was time to get out and earn our pay, even though we did not have a British officer to command us. It was decided to split up into two parties, one under Sergeant Rigden to go north to the Val Sugana and the other under Sergeant Lipscombe to go east to the Val Brenta. Both valleys had roads and railways running through them so were main arteries to and from the German front. Each party was accompanied by any partisans who wanted to tag along. Corporal Nobby Clarke and I were in Bill Rigden's party, heading for the Valle de Selva, then down its small river towards the railway station and sidings at Borgo.

In the afternoon of our first day's trek north towards the Val Sugana we encountered a different band of partisans. We had been attracted by the sound of a cow mooing, and when we reached it, we observed these partisans trying to stun the poor beast by hitting it on the head with a rock. It only succumbed after they cut its throat. They had probably stolen the cow from a local farmer. They were *Garibaldini* and made it plain that they did not want to share their ill-gotten gains with us, so we moved on. That night we slept out under the trees.

Breakfast next morning was a non-event, as we had no food, coffee or tea. Furthermore, it looked as if lunch and dinner would follow the same menu. Our Bergans were very light as the only thing in them was our sleeping bags and some PE. Spare ammunition was carried in our pockets. All of us were smokers, and we would have given our right arms for tobacco or cigarettes. A week before, one of the foraging party had brought some leaves, which he said were tobacco, stolen from some peasant's garden. We were advised by those in the know that the leaves should be soaked in water and then dried in the sun. This we did, and then chopped them as finely as possible. As we lacked cigarette papers we had to improvise with old bits of newspaper. I was in luck, being the only pipe smoker. Then came the magic moment of the first puff, quickly followed by a paroxysm of coughing and watering eyes. The stuff was so strong it made our heads spin. Obviously we still had a lot to learn about the art of curing tobacco. The partisans advised soaking the product again and we did this twice more, by which time it was tolerable, but still strong. But the small quantity of leaves had long since been consumed and prospects of obtaining any more were minimal.

That afternoon, as we were approaching the valley, we heard the sound of gunfire not far away. It was prolonged and intensive, and so we headed towards it. Within a few minutes we came upon the scene of an ambush being carried out by partisans. The target was a column of Cossacks, some on foot and some driving horse-drawn carts, their normal mode of transport. The partisans had chosen a good spot for their ambush. They were firing from the cover of trees on top of a slope, which gave them an excellent view of the narrow road below. The road was strewn with corpses and dead horses. Some of the horses were wounded and were screaming in their agony. One or two of the Cossacks were waving white handkerchiefs as a mark of surrender, but the partisans kept shooting – they had old scores to pay. We British joined in the shooting as some of the enemy were still returning fire, but my first priority was to shoot at the heads of the wounded horses to put them out of their misery. Of all animals, horses have always borne a disproportionate share of suffering in warfare. In the Great War hundreds of thousands of them lost their lives. The slaughter continued in the Second World War, as both the German and Russian armies employed horse-drawn transport for their non-mechanized divisions. These provided easy targets for strafing aircraft, and many froze to death in the Russian winters.

The firing diminished and finally stopped, probably because the partisans were running short of ammunition. The surviving Cossacks were ordered to come out with their hands up. After a little hesitation, for they suspected a trap, they came out in the open. There were very few of them. A partisan told me, some days later, that nearly 200 Cossacks had been killed. We left the partisans sorting out the spoils of war. After this action they would be well supplied with rifles and ammunition.

As darkness fell we found ourselves on a mountain slope with no flat ground within view anywhere. However, we kept moving for a couple of hours in the hope of finding somewhere more hospitable, but without success. So we laid ourselves down on the sloping ground, which is not a good way to sleep as one keeps sliding downhill. As the first glimmers of light came over the hilltop I was astonished to see that no more than 300 yards below us was a collection of wooden huts, laid out in lines. Quite certainly it was a permanent camp for the enemy. As I looked, a man in shirtsleeves came out of the nearest hut and threw a bucket of slops of some sort into a ditch. Then he gazed up the hill and must have seen us, as he stood transfixed for a full minute before going back inside the hut. I immediately woke the other chaps and told them to get moving up the hill as quickly and quietly as possible. They did not need any urging, as they could see for themselves the reason why. The man I had seen must have been slow to raise the alarm, because we were well clear when some random firing came from the camp. We headed back into the woods in case there was a pursuit from the camp.

Shortly after this we came upon another partisan band, about twenty strong. We questioned them about targets in the valley, in particular with regard to the railway. They advised against going into the valley, as it was swarming with German troops who were constructing a second defence in the hills north of the valley in case the Allies got up into the Asiago plateau from the Venetian plain. As for the railway, they claimed it was no longer in use owing to continuous strafing and bombing by the Allied air forces. They recommended that we should restrict our actions to ambushes on the minor roads, which was what they themselves did.

After some discussion, we decided that we should probably be more use if we returned to our original area where we knew the country and the partisans. Also that we should get something to eat there, even though it would only be polenta.

Our welcome by *Gruppo Dingo* was not ecstatic. Who could blame them when it meant more hungry mouths to feed? Consequently, Corporal Nobby Clarke and I persuaded Sergeant Rigden to allow the two of us to go off on a prolonged reconnaissance patrol. We took the Bren, some magazines and PE, and, as rations, a couple of slices of dried polenta.

Our two-man patrol was just right for observing enemy movement. We headed towards Camporovere as the partisans had told us that currently the place was devoid of enemy troops. Before entering it we kept it under observation for a while just to be sure there were no enemy present. Once we were satisfied, we entered, and had a chat with the locals, who informed us that though the village no longer had an enemy garrison, their troops frequently passed through there on the way to the Val Sugana, like the Cossacks ambushed previously. We managed to buy a few potatoes and half a loaf of bread, which we stowed away in our Bergans for future use.

For the next few days we covered a good deal of ground and were able to observe a lot of enemy activity. On one occasion we witnessed several batteries of German 88mm guns heading north through Asiago towards the Val Sugana. The partisans were also able to inform us of the location of fixed defence points on the plateau and which road and narrow-gauge railway bridges had not been demolished. This information was not of much use unless it could be passed on to the advancing Allied forces. Consequently, Nobby asked me if I would be willing to try and get the information through by passing through the German lines to the Allied ones. As the lines were somewhat fluid at this time, it was not as dangerous as it sounded, and so I agreed to give it a try.

The partisans had told us of a bridge far below in the Val Brenta and near a village called Campolongo, over the river Brenta, which had been blown by the Germans but which could probably be crossed by a man on foot because much of the wreckage was above water. They could also provide us with a guide to this bridge. With the aid of a map, Nobby briefed me on the main points of information I should pass on. Then we found the Italian guide and moved off at a fast pace.

It took nearly two days to reach the demolished bridge and it was late afternoon when we got there. We had to make several detours on the way to avoid groups of enemy troops and roadblocks. We also had to keep an eye peeled for Allied fighter aircraft, which had the habit of strafing anything that moved. When we started the steep descent down to the river we were actually looking down on fighter aircraft that were patrolling the valley.

I had a good look at the wreckage of the bridge and I could see that with some dexterity and a little care I should be able to get across it. But I decided to wait until nightfall before attempting it; at least then no one would be likely to take a pot-shot at me. So, soon after dark, I started to scramble over the girders that protruded out of the river at all angles. The partisans said that they thought there were American troops on the other bank. With this in mind, and not being anxious to be shot by an over-anxious trigger-happy sentry, I decided to sing a verse of a currently popular song, 'Lay that Pistol Down, Babe', which I thought was rather appropriate to the circumstances. This elicited no response, and so I called out very loudly, 'Don't shoot. I'm a British soldier and I'm coming across.' Still no response. So I pressed on a little further until a voice came out of the darkness saying 'Hold it right there. Don't move.'

A flashlight came on, momentarily dazzling me. After a few seconds the sentry seemed to be satisfied and led me into a nearby damaged building and told me to stay there until he fetched an officer, who checked my dog tags. After hearing the reason for my visit he ordered two men to take me in a Jeep to their Divisional Intelligence Officer. Div HQ was in Bassano del Grappa and we were there within the hour. The DIO, a Lieutenant Colonel, showed great interest in my information and I spent about an hour with him. Finally, he asked me where I should like to go now. I replied that if it wasn't too much trouble I should like to be taken back to the bridge. I said that as my group was still over there I would like to rejoin them. He then ordered the two GIs who had brought me to take me back again.

On the journey back the driver was constantly grousing about life in general and the Army in particular. He had a whining voice that did

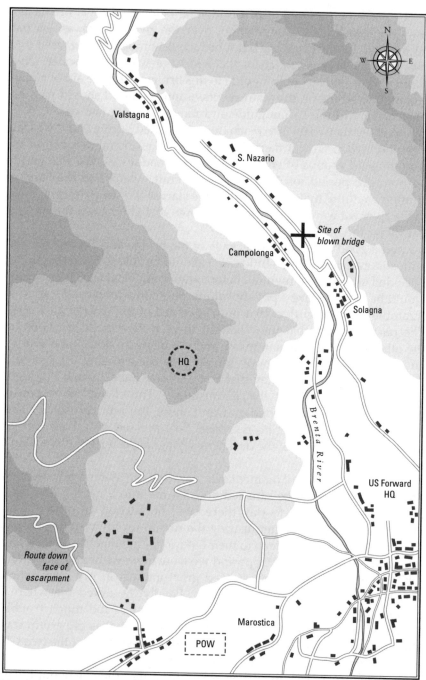

Map 8. Val Brenta: Charlie's recce and delivering PoWs to Marostica.

128

not endear him to me, so I started to converse with his colleague. I told them that we were not far from Venice and how unique it was with boats in its streets, to which the driver replied: 'Have those goddamn Krauts flooded the joint?' End of conversation!

When we got to the bridge again, dawn was breaking, and so I recrossed in daylight, which was easier and quicker. My guide had waited for me and we started at once to retrace our previous journey. The next day I rejoined Nobby in Camporovere and he seemed pleased with the outcome of my trip. The following day we were in the village barber's shop and Nobby was relaxed in the barber's chair, having his beard removed. I decided to keep mine, such as it was, until we got back to the regiment. The barber had removed half of Nobby's beard when, suddenly, a young partisan burst in the shop and yelled: 'A German convoy is coming and we are going to attack it!' I picked up the Bren and dashed out the door, closely followed by Nobby with half a beard, wiping the lather from his face with his fingers.

We ran down the road following the young partisan, and as we ran we heard an explosion, quite close by. This was followed by the clatter of small-arms fire. As we rounded a corner onto the main road we were confronted by a bus with one of its front wheels blown off. In line behind it were another three buses, all intact but empty. The site of the ambush was a good one. The partisans were deployed in the bushes above the road and there was a steep slope below the road ending in a deep ravine. The first bus had activated the mine placed by the partisans. The road was so narrow at this point that the other buses could not pass the front bus, nor could they turn round.

The occupants of the buses had made a hasty evacuation and run down the slope below to take cover behind whatever rocks and bushes they could find. They were returning fire, but very spasmodically, as they probably had very limited quantities of ammunition with them. The partisans, on the contrary, were blazing away in real Hollywood style. I noticed that some of them did not seem to fire at any particular target, but just blazed away at the general area of where the enemy might be. Since the enemy was well scattered and well concealed, it was probably as good a method as anything else.

After some minutes a German soldier popped up out of the bushes with his hands above his head. He was wearing a steel helmet and a Red Cross brassard, and he was unarmed. I told him in my best Italian to shout out to his comrades that if they surrendered it would be to British troops and not partisans. I said this because it had occurred to me that in view of the atrocities that the Germans had perpetrated against the partisans, they might well feel reluctant to become their prisoners. However, I did not seem to be getting through to this man – perhaps he did not understand Italian, and I knew no German. He just stood there looking stupid and very frightened and after a while I gave up on him.

The partisans had no machine-guns and neither had the Germans, at least not with them. So I thought it was time to bring my Bren into play. I walked until I was just past the fourth and last bus and then started to sweep the lower slope from left to right with short bursts of fire. Almost immediately groups of German soldiers came out of cover with their hands above their heads. I motioned to them to get up onto the road. There were about forty of them, and they were all paratroopers, well decorated with iron crosses and wound badges. Most of them were tall and all were of good physique. No sooner had they got onto the road when they were joined there by some two dozen young uniformed women soldiers. Presumably these girls were some sort of administrative staff, as they were not nurses. One of the Germans told me later that if they had not been escorting these girls they would not have surrendered so easily. I believed him, for these were men who had fought so stubbornly and bravely at Cassino and numerous other battles.

As the road was now blocked it became necessary to remove the obstacle. All the partisans got to one side of the bus, and the Germans were made to help too, and with much heaving and straining, the bus was pushed over and went clattering down to the bottom of the ravine and into the small river. The prisoners, after being searched for weapons, were put onto the remaining three buses together with partisan escorts and the convoy turned round and drove off in triumph to Asiago, which had been taken over by the partisans that day.

Asiago was only a small town, with a population of perhaps 5,000 to 6,000 inhabitants, but was the biggest town on the plateau known as the 'Altopiano di Asiago'. It had been on the front line for most of the Great War, when the Italians were fighting the Austro-Hungarians. In 1918 British troops had fought here, and there are no fewer than five CWGC cemeteries on the plateau with more on the plain below. Many of the trench systems of that time could still be seen as they had been blasted out of solid rock.

Our convoy drew up outside the Hotel *Croce Bianca* in the Corso Novembre IV, Asiago. The four wounded Germans were taken to the local hospital, which was run by nuns. Miraculously, considering the expenditure of ammunition, no one had been killed. The German girls were escorted Asiago's handsome town hall and placed under armed guard, while the German soldiers were taken to a partisan PoW camp in Marostica, on the Venetian Plain.

Nobby and I decided to join the joint SOE–Partisan HQ in the hotel. The hotel had been used by Organization Todt, then the Germans Army then an SS counter-terrorist team, and now by partisans and SOE as a HQ for the *Divisione Ortigara*'s operational area, and finally by us. The bedrooms were kept securely locked by the proprietor and his family – maybe they did not want scruffy, smelly partisans or paratroopers in them. But to give them their due, they served up platefuls of spaghetti to the chosen few, including us, free of charge.

Later that day, while tucking into spaghetti, we spotted a German NCO looking at us rather wistfully. Nobby asked him why he was not with the others. The NCO, who spoke near-perfect English, said he had been in the lavatory and when he came out the rest had gone. He seemed a decent chap, so we shared our spaghetti with him and got into a long conversation. He told us that he had been sick of the war for a long time and that even though he had long been aware that defeat for Germany was inevitable, he, and most others, had had no alternative but to keep on fighting. His name was Hans and he was from Berlin. He had been at university when the war began and had been mobilized immediately. Since then he had fought in France, Russia and finally Italy and had twice been wounded. For several weeks he had not received news from his fiancée and family in Berlin. We asked him what he would do if the Germans came back and re-took the town. He said that he did not think there was much chance of that happening, but if it should happen he would take to the mountains with us.

There was a piano in one corner of the large dining room and we asked Hans if he could play it. He replied that it was a long time since he had played but he was willing to give it a try. He played surprisingly well, and entertained us with excerpts from the works of Beethoven and Mozart. Then, feeling in the mood for singing, we asked him to play some popular songs of the time. Naturally, he did not know our British songs, but he had the musical ability to quickly pick up a tune if we first sang or whistled it. So we soon had him playing 'Roll out the Barrel', 'Run, Rabbit, Run' and other wartime ditties. Nobby, a pre-war medical student, got him to play 'Lily the Pink', which apparently was a special favourite of the students.

Suddenly, while we were happily singing away, I noticed through the large windows that an open-backed lorry had stopped outside. Men wearing German helmets were descending from it. It was quite a shock, and my first instinct was to get out via the back of the hotel. But then, on a closer look, I realized that they were partisans flaunting German souvenirs. They came into the hotel en masse, chattering and shouting like excited children, and their noise put an abrupt end to our musical soiree. In any event, we were bone-tired after the day's events, and it was time to find a quiet corner to sleep in. I found a small storeroom containing only a long table. This would suit me admirably as a bed. I climbed onto it, rolled up my jacket as a pillow and was soon asleep.

In the morning Nobby and I looked around for Hans and we were told that he had been taken to Marostica. We were also given the bad news that our friend Conte had been killed the previous day. He had been travelling in a truck with a group of partisans and they had been shot up by an Allied fighter aircraft. Unfortunately, this sort of occurrence was not a rare one.

During the weeks that we had been on this operation we had got used to seeing the US bombers passing very high in waves. Unless the weather was bad they flew over daily, and we watched the German flak bursting in little puffs around them. They always flew north, presumably to bomb targets in Austria and Germany. On their return the pattern of their formation was often ragged, as if broken up by German fighters. Once we saw parachutes emerge from a crippled bomber, but they landed far away from us, as did their plane when it crashed. Unlike the fighter aircraft, the bombers presented no danger to us.

That day there was a lot of activity at the hotel with the chiefs of the various partisan groups coming and going. One in particular was accorded a great deal of fawning attention. He was the chief of all the communist partisans in the whole area and stood on the hotel steps wearing a bright red hunting jacket, surrounded by sycophants, with the air of a Roman emperor. We were introduced to him, but apart from a brief handshake he showed no interest in us.

Nobby and I decided to get away from all the excitement for a while and soon found a quiet bar in a side street. As we stood there sipping grappa we wondered what we should do next. We came to the conclusion that it looked as if the war would soon be over and our best bet would be to take it easy for a while. With that momentous decision made, we called for another round of grappa. As we were drinking it a Jeep stopped outside and four tough-looking American soldiers came into the bar. They were members of the elite US Rangers, and were at first puzzled, and then amused, to find two Brits nonchalantly drinking at a bar, because as an advanced patrol they had been under the impression that they had just liberated the town. They joined us and we became good friends after a few drinks.

We compared the merits of our various weapons. Their Garand M1 rifle was undoubtedly superior to the British No. 4 bolt-action one in which the bolt had to be pulled back after every shot in order to eject the empty cartridge casing, and then forward again to push a new round into the breech. The Garand was semi-automatic and all one had to do to keep on firing was to keep on pulling the trigger. On the other hand, I thought our Bren was much superior to the Browning Automatic Rifle that the Rangers had with them.

Being typical Yanks, it was not long before they were asking where they could 'get a piece of ass', as they delicately phrased it. The proprietor directed them to the right place and they took off in a cloud of dust. They had with them several bags of sugar as payment: the Italians preferred scarce commodities to dubious Allied Forces paper money. Before the Rangers left we bummed a couple of packs of cigarettes from them as they had a good supply. What a joy it was to enjoy a decent smoke again.

Late that night they returned to the bar where Nobby and I had been sleeping on the wooden benches that were on two sides of the room. The proprietor had long since retired to his bed upstairs. One of them turned on the radio on the bar. As he twiddled the tuning knob a lot of excited voices in many languages could be heard, and then, suddenly, loud and clear, came the cultured voice of a BBC announcer saying that a ceasefire was in effect from midnight in the West, owing to the surrender of the German forces there. This was followed by a lot of patriotic music and songs. When they got to 'Land of Hope and Glory' Nobby and I could not restrain ourselves, and gave it all we had got in a boisterous rendering of the well-known words. This was an occasion that definitely called for a drink, but the proprietor-cum-barman was upstairs in bed. Loud calls were made demanding his presence, but after several minutes he still had not appeared. So we decided to help ourselves, but as soon as he heard the clink of glasses and bottles, he appeared as if by magic. He presented a bizarre appearance, in that although he was wearing a trilby hat, jacket and collar and tie, he had no trousers on. Instead, his lower regions were covered in white woollen longjohns ending in well-worn carpet slippers. He was not too pleased to be turned out in the middle of the night, even though we told him *'La guerra e finito!'*, but a bag of sugar and a packet of Lucky Strike cigarettes did much to console him. A lot of grappa was drunk that night, fortunately not on empty stomachs, as the Rangers had the foresight to bring a case of C-rations.

After a couple of hours' of sleep we shook hands and said goodbye to our Ranger friends. We had errands to perform in Vicenza, a big city down on the plain. While we waited in Asiago town square a company of about 200 young German soldiers came into view. They were unarmed but showed no sign of humiliation or defeat. On the contrary, they marched arrogantly and were singing some martial song loudly and in complete harmony. Shortly after this a large 10-ton Fiat lorry entered the piazza. Standing in the back of the lorry were the captured German Army girls. Nobby got into the cab with the driver and I joined the partisan escort, who was sat on the tailboard of the vehicle. They told me the object of the exercise was to lodge the girls in a convent in Vicenza until more permanent arrangements could be arranged for them. After that it was hoped to beg, borrow or steal some supplies for the partisans from the bounteous supplies of Uncle Sam – in effect, an early exposition of the famous Marshall Aid. The partisans had shared their meagre supplies with us: now it was payback time.

The journey down to Vicenza was hair-raising as we took the Pedescala route, which had hundreds of hairpin bends. Many required two separate attempts to get round, and to add to the tension the brakes were practically useless. The German girls were a pretty dour lot and endured the journey with stoic indifference, except, that is, for one little dark one who was as pretty as a button, and who kept giving me unmistakable enticing glances. But it was the wrong place and the wrong time, and she would be left at the convent with the rest of them. Our driver knew the location of the convent and so there was no delay in disposing of the *frauleins*. No doubt they would soon be transferred back to their battered Fatherland.

We drove around Vicenza until we came across a US fuel supply dump, piled high with jerrycans. We approached the sergeant in charge and told him we were collecting fuel for our unit. Nobby used his best upper-class voice for the purpose. Our request for fuel was quite a feasible one to make as we were in the Fifth Army sector, and although that army was mainly American it also had some British and French elements. So we quickly filled half the truck with cans of petrol before the sergeant found that there was no such regiment as the Rutland Fusiliers, the unit on whose behalf Nobby had requested the petrol.

We drove around again until we came upon a US ration depot under the care of a bespectacled and pedantic PFC. We used a differed modus operandi, telling him we needed rations for 500 newly surrendered German PoWs. This cock-and-bull story did not seem to faze him, but he said he could not issue anything without a requisition form signed by an officer. He gave us a blank form and we departed promising to return soon with the form duly signed. We found a café a short distance away, where we borrowed a pen from the barman. Nobby signed the form as Major McGowan, AMGOT (Allied Military Government) and after a couple of glasses of *rosso* we returned to the ration dump.

The PFC was quite happy with the bogus form and told us to take what we needed but he stipulated that PoWs were only entitled to K-rations. These were packed in waxed cardboard cartons, each holding enough supplies for one man for one day. They contained small tins of meat and cheese, together with crackers, coffee powder, lemonade powder, a candy bar, some sheets of toilet paper and, best of all, a book of matches and four cigarettes. These rations were intended for the use of troops when they had no access to normal cooking facilities, such as in battle or on a journey. Once we had completed loading about 3,000 packs we got out of town before the MPs saw us and started to ask embarrassing questions.

Apart from a few cartons, which we kept for our own consumption, the whole consignment was given to the partisans, free, gratis and for nothing, to do with as they wished. It was our way of saying thank you and goodbye to them.

We left Asiago again next morning on a truck that took us to Vicenza. From there we hitched a lift in a Jeep to Florence, where 3 Squadron had established a base in a house that they called the Joy Box. The first person we saw there was Squadron Sergeant Major John Alcock, who told us to get our hair cut! He was right, of course – we did look like a couple of tramps. He also told us while we were away several of our colleagues had been killed. They were Lieutenant James Arthur Riccomini RASC MBE MC, a popular young officer, signaller Sergeant Sid Guscott, a talented musician, and Corporal Stanley Bolden, who had hummed 'The Ride of the Valkyries' on the way to the airfield and in 1943 had won a Military Medal with Commandos. Also killed was Bruce (not his real name), brother of Ramos the Spaniard. They had all died in action. Added to these were Major Ross Littlejohn and Corporal Joseph Crowley, both killed, plus one officer and six other ranks missing, although they eventually returned from PoW camps, very lucky not to have been executed. In addition, four men had been wounded, but not seriously.

We only stayed one day in Florence, so unfortunately were not able to explore the beautiful city. We went by truck back to the Villa Sabine, near Cecina. No sooner had we arrived than I developed a severe burning sensation in my esophagus when trying to eat or drink anything. There was a US hospital about two miles along the beach from us, so I rode there on mule back. The Royal Army Veterinary Corps had lent the squadron some mules for training purposes and they were used to carrying loads. However, they were not happy with whooping men on their backs. They demonstrated their distaste for this by breaking into a fast gallop, and then suddenly stopping dead, which had the effect of sending the rider flying over its head before hitting the ground. Since there were not any reins or saddles, just a rope halter, even experienced riders could be unseated by this tactic. These mules, though, had been invaluable during the Italian campaign. They had been used to take food and ammunition to front-line positions in the mountains and even to bring out the wounded.

On arrival at the US hospital I was told that my condition was due to lack of proper food and from drinking spirits on an empty stomach. I was given a dose of medicine on the spot and a bottle of it to take away with me. Within a couple of days I was fit as a flea again. The recuperative qualities of youth are wonderful. There were only a few of us at the Villa Sabine at this time, as most of the squadron had been given leave to Rome. Nobby and I had returned too late to take advantage of this. We did not mind too much as it was very pleasant just to loaf around on the beach.

A few days later we left the Villa Sabine and were flown by a Dakota aircraft to Naples. In the transit camp outside Naples we met up again with the rest of the squadron. There we would wait for a troopship to take us back to the UK, but in the meantime we had our photograph taken with a 75mm gun used by Major Farran on Operation TOMBOLA in front.

In typical SAS fashion, when not in training or on operations, we were left pretty much to our own devices. In consequence, we made many trips to Naples. Transport was no problem as there were many trucks going to and from the city. British drivers would usually stop for us, but quite often US drivers would not.

Naples was a sprawling, bustling city with not much to recommend it architecturally. The view across the bay was spectacular but one had to be on high ground to really see and appreciate it. The city centre was flocked with a multitude of soldiers of many nations, though the majority were British and American. There was a massive NAAFI canteen with games and rest rooms, and, of course a bar, which unfortunately had no beer. The canteen was housed in a huge rococo building, which must have at one time been a palace.

Most of us went in search of feminine company but, as ever, the best had already been snapped up by the people working at the base, known as base wallahs. These soldiers really had their feet under the table and led a practically normal married life. Sometimes they would set their girlfriend up in a cheap apartment and provide rations for them both. Some even lived with the girl's family, with their approval, providing they supplied food and a little money. So what females remained were either the dross, with a high percentage of them infected with VD, or respectable girls who would not have any relations with soldiers at any price.

There were other diversions of course, such as a visit to the San Carlo Opera House to see Bizet's *Carmen*, which started me on what became an abiding interest in opera. Entrance was free to Allied troops, but not many seemed to take advantage of it – I suppose they preferred the Forces entertainment shows put on by ENSA. I forget the meaning of the letters of this acronym, but as usual the troops had their own version: 'Every Night Something Awful'.

On entering the Opera House I was most impressed that we were directed to seats in a box, to the right of the stage, which gave us a superb and close-up view of the cast. The only other occupant of the box was an old lady dressed in a long black dress that was turning green with age. She regarded us disdainfully and muttered something we did not understand, but the tone of it was disparaging. We tried to keep well upwind of the old crone, as it soon became obvious to our noses that water was an alien substance to her, except possibly as a beverage. Nevertheless, we enjoyed the show.

Another diversion of interest was a visit to Pompeii, which had been buried under a mass of volcanic lava and ash centuries ago. It had recently been disinterred from this condition and much of it was remarkably well preserved. The Italian guide pointed out various items of interest and for a little extra payment unlocked the door of the ancient brothel. Above each stone bed in this room was a picture done in mosaic; each one illustrated a different position of the sex act. Outside on the walls of different streets our guide pointed out engravings of a penis and scrotum with wings attached, which we thought it would make a good squadron badge! He explained that these symbols served as signposts pointing in the direction of the brothel. Much to our amazement we were later accosted by a pretty young girl who was selling these flying penises. They were miniatures made of bronze and she had a whole tray load suspended from her neck. As they had a little ring on them, presumably they could be worn on a watch chain or on a lady's bracelet. There's no doubt they would make a good talking point if worn at a village vicarage tea party. I regret not having bought one. There must have been a lot of lechery going on in ancient Pompeii – but then, they did not have radio and TV. Lucky devils.

Not long after our arrival at Naples I was told that Major Bob Walker-Brown, commanding 3 Squadron, wanted to see me. I found him outside his office talking to two other men, one of whom was Ramos the Spaniard, and the other a young chap called Fitzpatrick. He informed us that we had all been awarded the Military Medal and that we should go to the QM Stores, draw the ribbon and sew it on as soon as possible. Naturally, I was delighted, though I could not think of any reason why I had been chosen for the award.

After some ten days in the transit camp we boarded a troopship to take us to England. We realized that we were fortunate to be going back so early since some troops had been overseas for up to three years and were still waiting their turn. We could only assume that the powers that be had other plans for us in the Far East or who knows where.

The voyage home was run of the mill, except that we sailed alone, not in convoy, which meant a shorter journey in time as our ship had a good turn of speed. But we lost the best part of a day hove-to off Gibraltar. We were told that General Hawkesworth, who had been a passenger on board, had died, and had been landed at Gibraltar for burial. The only incident that concerned me personally was when I was put on guard one morning in one of the ship's alleyways. I was stationed by a hatch that led to the engine room to prevent unauthorized persons from entering. Standing and looking at an iron door for a spell of two hours is the epitome of boredom and I soon tired of it. I decided that a surreptitious smoke would help pass the time. So I made my way along the deserted alleyway for about fifty feet until I came to a porthole, which I opened. I then lit my cigarette and gazed out at the white-capped waves. I was lost in my thoughts when suddenly I heard voices very near and coming my way. I just had time to throw my cigarette out the porthole before they were upon me. It was the procession that made up the daily morning inspection, and led by the ship's Captain, the Army OC Troopship, accompanied by the ship's RSM, RQMS and various hangers-on.

The ship's OC, a lieutenant colonel, thundered, 'Sentry, why have you left your post?' and they all glared at me as if I was the basest criminal. But when I told them that I had had a bout of sea sickness and had come to the porthole for some fresh air rather than vomit on the clean deck, they became quite sympathetic, and even smiled. The Colonel asked me if I felt fit enough to finish my spell of duty and I bravely replied that I could. And they went on their way, probably feeling quite virtuous.

To sum up the squadron's brief stay in Italy, it is fair to say that it had been largely successful. COLD COMFORT had been a disaster, but Operations GALIA, TOMBOLA and CANUCK had caused mayhem behind the enemy's lines. This had had the effect of forcing the enemy to use extra troops to guard his lines of communication and thus keeping them away from the front where they were needed.

Operation TOMBOLA, commanded by Major Roy Farran, had been very effective. His group had attacked a German Corps HQ and caused a number of casualties to the enemy there. In defence of our efforts on Operation COLD COMFORT it should be realized that we received no resupply drops, and that, unlike the other operations, we lacked heavy weapons. They had the use of heavy machine-guns, 3-inch mortars and even a 75mm pack howitzer. Probably the biggest drawback was that after the capture and death of Major Littlejohn we lacked any effective leadership. An officer or sergeant with a strong will to get things done, whatever the odds, could have made a considerable difference. On the other hand, such a person would have probably got half of us killed, so on reflection perhaps everything worked out for the best in the end. As they say, there are old soldiers and bold soldiers, but there are very few old and bold soldiers.

Chapter 12

Moussey

On arrival in Britain we were given fourteen days' disembarkation leave and I headed directly for Yeovil. My submariner pal Phil Hughes was also on leave, as were several more of my friends. The forces were very generous with leave now that the war in Europe was over. Although it had now been over for a month or more, the population in general, and servicemen in particular, were still in celebratory mood. The pubs were doing a roaring trade and there was a palpable feeling of relief in the air.

One night, after a few drinks in a pub, a group of us servicemen, about twenty strong, linked arms and made a line from one side of the main street to the other and proceeded along it to the next pub. Any female, irrespective of age, encountered en route received a hearty kiss. None raised any objection; indeed, many of the older ones looked delighted.

During this leave my boyhood sweetheart came over from Taunton to see me. At that time only my mother was living in our house and so she was given a bedroom to herself. Of course, that did not prevent me from creeping into her room, once I considered my mother was asleep. We were both stark naked, yet she would not go all the way, much to my disappointment, as she was engaged to an officer serving with Fourteenth Army in Burma, and wanted to preserve her virginity. So what the hell was she doing chasing me? Even so, it was good to see her again, and she was pleased with the present I had brought from Italy for her.

My leave flew by, as it always does when one is having a good time. Soon I was back in Wivenhoe with the regiment. In the evenings we renewed our acquaintance with the local. It was now high summer and the walk to and from the pub was pleasant along the leafy lanes. We got down to serious training again, mostly with heavily armed Jeeps. There was a rumour that we were going to the Gobi Desert in north-west China and southern Mongolia, where there was a puppet Japanese state, Manchukuo. We would operate behind enemy lines, like the original SAS unit in North Africa. While we had been in Italy the SAS Brigade had been given a new commander, Brigadier 'Mad Mike' Calvert, like me a former sapper. He had twice commanded a Chindit column in Burma, where he was second only in fame to General Orde Wingate. He was a very suitable SAS commander and we expected to do great things under his direction.

In early August I was one of six men selected to form a guard of honour at a burial service for ten SAS and Phantom men executed near a small village in the Vosges called Moussey. Our little detachment was under the command of SSM John Alcock, from the Coldstream Guards. We practised the slow march and firing volleys. It is a British Army tradition to fire a volley of three rounds of blank ammunition after the coffins have been lowered into the ground. The volley must be fired in unison, the six shots sounding as one, and this requires some practice to achieve perfection.

We left Wivenhoe one afternoon and drove to London where we were put up for the night in a small hotel that had been requisitioned for the Army. Next morning we crossed the Channel by ferry and drove across France to Moussey. Moussey had paid a heavy penalty for helping SAS parties operating in that area between August and October 1944. As a reprisal the Germans rounded up 187 men of the village and transported them to concentration camps in Germany. Only thirty-three returned to their village when the war ended. They are commemorated on a monument, while the place where the SAS men were killed is marked by a plaque on a rock, placed by the local section of the Maquis Association.

The bodies of our ten colleagues, originally buried in different parts of the area, had been exhumed and were now in the village churchyard awaiting reburial. Three had been killed in action, but the others had been captured by the SS, interrogated under torture, then executed. That evening our group was billeted in pairs to different houses in the village. In my house there was only a mother and a daughter in her early twenties. The daughter, a very attractive woman, had come over from Paris, where she worked, especially for the occasion. After dinner that evening I asked her to teach me the words of the French national anthem, 'La Marsellaise'. We then went on to the words of 'J'attendrai', a popular French song of the time. Finally, she taught me the words of 'Madelon', the famous song of the French Army during the Great War. I must have tried her patience, as it took many repetitions before I got them off by heart, but she did not show any signs of it. She was a very charming lady.

Next morning, at an early hour, we paraded at one end of the long, straggling village street. Also present were the survivors from the German camps and ex-Resistance men from surrounding villages, and some of their womenfolk. Leading the procession was a local brass band and we SAS were situated immediately behind it. Fittingly, for such a sombre occasion, the sky was grey and a slight drizzle was in the air. Soon we were given the order 'Slope Arms' followed by 'Slow March' at the same time as the band struck up a funeral march. The British slow march looks very dignified but tends to become tiring over long distances. As the church was at the other end of the village the twenty or so minutes it took to get there seemed more like an hour.

At the churchyard a short religious service was held. The congregation of several hundred then watched as we, the guard of honour, laid down our rifles and went to the line of plain coffins, hoisted them onto our shoulders one by one, marched slowly to the burial plot and placed each next to an open grave. One of the coffins had not been properly sealed and an evil-smelling fluid oozed out from it onto our shoulders. Like good soldiers we pretended not to notice it, but it was a sobering thought that our erstwhile healthy and happy young comrades should have come to this.

We then retrieved our rifles and formed a line just to the rear of the coffins. The three volleys were fired with perfect precision, followed by a French bugler who played 'Tattoo', their equivalent of the Last Post. After that we marched smartly away, leaving the task of lowering the coffins into the graves to the professional gravediggers.

We halted outside a village bar and were dismissed there, as that was the end of our official duties. Needless to say we were into that bar like a flash – a glass of wine had never tasted so good. We were soon joined by crowds of Frenchmen who insisted that we did not pay for our drinks. The bar was soon bursting at the seams and the air was full of Gauloise smoke. There was a great deal of noisy chatter but no laughter and we soon tired of the sombre atmosphere and were glad to get into the fresh air outside.

This was a village still in a state of shock and mourning, and we realized that if it had not been for the presence of SAS troops and the assistance given to them in 1944, then the tragedy that had befallen them would not have happened. Since then, Moussey has become a place of pilgrimage for the SAS, especially wartime veterans. Near the font in the church an SAS flag may be seen. On the wall of the churchyard, beneath which our ten comrades are buried in a line, there is a marble plaque inscribed with their names and citing the manner of their deaths. Long after the war I visited the churchyard several times,

142

once, in 2004, with other wartime members of the SAS, SBS and Phantom on a Regimental Pilgrimage, and was honoured to lay the wreath, being the only person present who had attended the earlier ceremony.

Next day we went into the woods, some three miles from Moussey, to the spot where eight of our comrades had been captured and then executed by the Gestapo. The place is marked by a large natural rock, inset with a small marble plaque bearing the names of the eight men and telling how they died. This monument was erected by the local people. For some reason the bodies were taken to Durnbach, near Bad Tolz, Bavaria, for burial, and are now in the CWGC cemetery there.

Anyone reading this narrative may wonder why so many SAS soldiers were taken prisoner. There are many answers to this question. First and foremost was the lack of any Escape and Evasion training, and, sad to relate, there were some Frenchmen who were pro-German and who would betray our soldiers when they could. This applied particularly to the Alsace region, which had been under German control from 1870 to 1918.

Other reasons, previously mentioned, were the giveaway rubber soles, and that of being over confident and relaxing one's vigilance when operating in enemy territory. When a party consisted of only two or three men it was difficult for them to maintain an all-night guard system, particularly if they were exhausted and short of food. Furthermore, the enemy always had the advantage of superior numbers and was in a position to be able to completely surround a small SAS party if he knew where they were located.

Finally, and most importantly, SAS troops who operated behind enemy lines in France in 1944 were not aware of the infamous *Fuerherbefehl* mentioned earlier, that all SAS- and Commando-type troops who were captured should be handed over to the Gestapo or SS for execution. Had they been told of this, I am sure that rather than be captured they would have chosen to die fighting.

We left Moussey the following morning and headed for Paris, where we were given three days' leave. We arrived there to find that the war with Japan had just been officially declared over. The Americans had dropped atomic bombs on Hiroshima and Nagasaki, causing complete devastation and much loss of life, and so the Japanese had surrendered. The city was full of US troops and they were in celebratory mood as they thought that they would soon be going home.

143

We were given rooms in a small hotel that had been taken over as a leave centre and told that we were free to do as we liked for the next three days. I decided that I would spend the rest of our short stay in Paris by visiting some of the sights of the city. I found this quite easy to do by using the underground trains of the Metro. There was a lot to see and I became engrossed in the beauty of it all.

The sea crossing back to England was a really rough one, with gale-force winds. We drove back to Wivenhoe to find the regiment awash with rumours about its future, the main one being that we were to be disbanded. This filled me with foreboding as I had enjoyed the free and easy life of the SAS immensely. One thing was obvious – the intense training that we had been undergoing had now been discontinued and leave was easily available.

Just before its disbandment the regiment held a sports day, an event that very few took seriously, though the beer tent did a roaring trade. For early October in England it was uncharacteristically warm and sunny, and after the racing events were over it was a pleasure to walk to Wivenhoe village. In the garden of our favourite pub I encountered our QM, Major Tom Burt. He had a round, rosy red face and a rather rotund body to complement it. He would have made a perfect Santa Claus. Tom Burt was a legend in the regiment. He enlisted in 1911 as a bugler in the infantry, served in India, then in France during the Great War. Between the wars he served in many parts of what was then the British Empire. In the Second World War he served with the Infantry in North Africa until transferring to the SAS as a Major QM. He was easygoing with those who showed him respect, but woe-betide anyone who tried to be funny with him. When I saw him on this occasion he must have taken a shine to me because he bought me a drink. He was drinking pints of draught Bass, so I had the same. He would not let me pay for a round and bought me a couple more pints. This could only happen in the camaraderie of the SAS – a major buying drinks for a private. All went well until Tom bought a jar of cockles, which he invited me to share with him. I did so, but within two minutes I felt violently ill and was forced to make a hasty departure. I found a convenient tree in a nearby field, and there I lay for three or four hours until I had recovered from the bouts of vomiting. I imagine that I must have an allergy to shellfish – I have never eaten them since.

Chapter 13

A Sapper Again

A few days before the regiment disbanded 3 Squadron was told to assemble for a talk by the Major Bob Walker-Brown. He told us that he was going to a battalion of the Parachute Regiment that was being formed for service in Palestine. Because of the influx of Jewish immigrants from Europe the indigenous Arabs were taking up arms against them, and more troops were required there to keep them apart. He emphasized that life there would not be boring and asked for volunteers to go with him. He also promised that if any of us should later decide that we did not like being in the Parachute Regiment we would be allowed to return to our parent regiments or corps. About ninety men, including me, volunteered to go.

We were sent to Bulford Camp and on arrival there were split up and posted to different companies in the battalion. That did not please any of us as we would have preferred to stay with our friends, all in the same company. We found that the battalion was mostly made up of young, inexperienced soldiers who had never been in action. The Parachute Regiment of those days had earned a reputation in the war of an elite fighting force and was justly proud of it, but it did not have the ethos and character of the equally young SAS. In the SAS one had a friendly relationship with the officers and we trained with them and went on operations in small parties with them.

I soon realized that I had made a mistake in joining the Paras because I felt like a very small cog in a very large machine. In the SAS I had felt like an individual and someone who was valued. In any case, what was I, a trained sapper, doing in the infantry? So after two weeks I asked for an interview with my Company Commander and requested a transfer back to the Royal Engineers, which he granted, albeit reluctantly.

Next day I was on a train going north to Halifax in Yorkshire where the RE Depot was situated. Accommodation for the troops was in the usual familiar cotton mill. The beds were wooden framed, one up and one down, with straw palliasses supported on wire frames. There were about 200 beds on each floor. I was interviewed by a friendly captain who asked me what I would like to do next. I told him I would like an overseas posting and he said he would put me down for East Africa, but that I would have to wait a few weeks for a troopship.

There were several hundred sappers of all ranks at the depot, mostly waiting for postings. We all paraded each morning after breakfast on the large square in front of the mill. A few people were then selected for various jobs but the vast majority were dismissed to spend the day as they wished. The sergeant major who took the parade had a sense of humour and on Sunday mornings always addressed the parade as follows: 'Fall out the CofEs, RCs, Burmese, Sudanese, Japanese and Stand at Ease.'

Occupying the bunk bed above mine was an ex-Royal Marine Commando who like me was returning to the RE. As we were the only two ex-Special Forces on our floor we became friends. One morning after a heavy night out he did not want to get up to go on morning parade. I shook him several times before I left and he said each time that he was OK and would get up in a minute. In the event he did not get up, and at 1000 hrs when the CQMS was checking barrack stores he was discovered still lying there. When he was shaken awake by the indignant NCO he had the presence of mind to groan and say that he was suffering from a relapse of Sandfly Fever, which was cheeky because he had never been further east than Germany. The CQMS became very concerned and told him to stay where he was until a stretcher party was organized for him. They duly appeared and carted him off to see the MO. When he got there he made a remarkable recovery, telling the MO that such was the nature of his relapses that they came and went with alarming rapidity. Fortunately for my friend, the young MO did not know anything about Sandfly Fever either. One can get away with a lot in the Army with a bit of cheek. As we used to say, 'bullshit baffles brains'.

One night some of us went to a dance in the town. I was not keen on dancing as I do not have much sense of rhythm, but dances were the best place to meet unattached females. Order was maintained in the dance hall by the simple expedient of only selling soft drinks. At this dance I met a girl called Bobbie. She was a jolly girl from a good family and had a very healthy sexual appetite – just what I needed to dispel the gloomy thoughts I had at the prospect of another four years to serve in a peacetime army. I walked Bobbie home that night and we arranged to meet again the following night. After that we met every night. On the third night she had a surprise for me – we took a bus to the outskirts of the town to a cottage that belonged to her family. As it was un-occupied, her mother thought it would be sensible if Bobbie visited it occasionally, to light a fire in order to keep away the damp. After that if became our nightly love nest. It was well furnished and had a plentiful supply of coal so we usually made love in front of a roaring fire. I do not know if Bobbie's mother knew of our affair – perhaps not, Bobbie never invited me to her home to meet her.

She told me that prior to meeting me she had been going out with a sergeant on the permanent staff of the RE Depot. I had seen this man and he had given me the impression that he was a real sour-looking character. From the black looks he had given me I surmised that he was aware of my affair with Bobbie. It was a mystery to me how a happy-go-lucky girl like her could go out with such a dismal man as he was. Attraction of opposites, maybe. All things come to an end, and I was notified that I would be leaving for Southampton in two weeks' time to board a troopship for Mombasa. Before that I had fourteen days' embarkation leave at home.

I noticed a lot of changes on this leave. The euphoria that had been engendered by the ending of the war had gone. The people in general looked weary and drably dressed. There was still rationing for clothes and petrol and many other things, including certain items of food such as meat and sugar. At the July 1945 election the populace turned its back on Winston Churchill and his Conservative Party and voted over-whelmingly for Labour. The votes of servicemen may have seen partly instrumental in bringing about this swing. The vast majority of them were heartily sick of being treated as inferior beings by the so-called 'officer class' and demonstrated with their votes.

But no matter which party was in power, the war had cost Britain dear – it was tired and it was broke. It was going to be a long, uphill struggle to bring it back to prosperity. I found that many of my friends had been demobilized and were back at their old humdrum ways. The Americans, with their big spending habits, had gone. The local pubs were empty and I was not sorry to be leaving England for Africa.

I returned to Halifax for a few days and then, after a tearful farewell with Bobbie, went by train to Southampton and, yet again, boarded a troopship.

147

Chapter 14

Around Africa

On the troopship *Franconia* I met up with an old friend from 3 Squadron in France and Italy, Jack Paley. He had recently been at a school for experimental parachuting and was off to join the Parachute Regiment in Palestine, so we had plenty to talk about. Most of the troops on board were young National Servicemen and the majority of them would leave the ship at Port Said for service in the Middle East.

The voyage to Port Said was uneventful and, apart from the usual cramped accommodation and uninspiring food, was quite enjoyable. I said goodbye to Jack and we promised to keep in touch. In the event, we did not do so, at least not until fifty years later, when we got in contact through the SAS Regimental magazine. By then he was living in Canada and I in Cyprus, but even so we managed to meet up in London, France, Italy and Cyprus and to keep up a regular correspondence.

As we sailed through the Suez Canal I was able to identity the place where we had been camped in early 1944. The tents were gone and it looked even more desolate. The Red Sea was hot as usual, but bearable, as it was still February. In the middle of the night we passed a naval frigate lying hove-to and with not a glimmer of light showing – quite mysterious. Perhaps she was looking for slavers. It still continued in that part of the world. We had stopped briefly about half a mile off the port of Berbera. No one had disembarked there, but a lighter had come out and taken some cargo from us. The town was shimmering in the fierce heat and its cluster of low white buildings looked lost in the treeless desert that surrounded them. After two days we left the Red Sea and eased through the straits of Bab-el-Mandeb, and my tour of East Africa started in earnest. Next day we passed the isolated Socotra islands off the Horn of Africa. No ships ever seemed to stop, but I suppose an occasional Arab dhow put in there now and then. It seems to have changed now. We then stopped briefly at Aden, another godforsaken place: I was glad not to have been posted there. It was dry, hot and with not a piece of greenery in sight.

When we sailed into Kilindini Harbour at Mombasa there was an abundance of green vegetation, including banana plants and palm trees. Here on the coast the climate was hot and humid and our khaki drill uniforms were soon sodden with sweat as we carried our kit-bags down the gangplank. On the dockside a train was waiting, and members of the RE Movement Control Staff quickly directed us to our compartments, six men to each. There were no cattle trucks this time, but proper carriages with padded seats. Our destination was Nairobi, the capital of Kenya, in the Kenya Highlands, at an altitude of 6,000 feet.

It was dark when we left Mombasa and we were told we would be travelling all night and part of the next day. The train went at a leisurely pace and made many stops. No matter what the hour was there were always crowds of Africans at each station. Some tried to sell us bananas, but mainly they just stood and stared, and some just lay sleeping on the ground, wrapped in a thin blanket and oblivious to the clamour.

For most of us this was our first sight of bare-breasted women, but we soon became accustomed to it as the sight was so common. Many of the women practised self-mutilation by boring their earlobes and inserting wooden plugs into the holes. Progressively larger plugs were used until the lobe made a loop two or three inches in length. Then, in place of the plug, metal ornaments were hung on the loop to dangle there. Later, I was to find that some of our black soldiers (known as Askaris) had these ear loops. However, as they were not allowed to wear adornments on them, they devised a method of rolling the loop back over the ear to make a neat little bundle.

We arrived at Nairobi about noon and were taken by truck to the East Africa Command Reinforcement Depot, from where we would be appointed to our respective units. I met an RE Corporal who, like me, had also just arrived in the colony. He was a little older than me and had been a coal miner before joining the Army. With his broken nose and work-scarred hands he looked a pretty tough character. During the war he had served in a Field Company in France and Germany. That afternoon we were informed that we had both been posted to 109 Road Construction Company RE, based at Arusha in Tanganyika, so we decided to have a look at Nairobi that evening, as we should be leaving for Arusha the next morning. Nairobi was not very big in those days and all the bars seemed to be in the hotels. As we had not yet had the time or the opportunity to buy civilian clothes, we were rather reluctant to enter hotels in uniform. So we thought it might be fun, and cheaper, to go into the native quarter, which was known as the Majengo. We very soon came across an 'Out of Bounds' sign but chose to ignore it.

The native quarter of Nairobi was a rather depressing place. Most of its houses, if one can call them such, had roofs and walls made of flattened-out petrol cans, the type we called 'flimsies' before we had the jerrycan. There were no pavements and the roads had dirt surfaces, and as for sanitation . . . there wasn't any. Not a good example of the benefits of colonialism.

We had not been there more than fifteen minutes, and were on the point of leaving, when an RMP paddy-wagon drew up alongside us. Out jumped a sergeant, backed up by two corporals. The usual questions were asked as to why were we there, and did we not see the 'Out of Bounds' notices? We pleaded ignorance and that we had only just arrived in Kenya. Then one of the corporals made some disparaging remark about the medal ribbons on my bush jacket. I responded with words that cast doubts about his parents being married. I was immediately arrested and bundled into the van. My friend the Corporal was released with a warning.

When they got me to their office they prepared a charge against me and then proceeded to have fun with me by making me stand rigidly to attention to a mere lance corporal while making insulting remarks about my appearance. Their object was to humiliate me and perhaps provoke me into retaliating, so that they would have something further with which to charge me. But I held my peace, even though I was seething inside, and after half an hour or so they released me. The RMP had gone down even lower in my estimation.

Next morning, just before we left for Arusha, my corporal friend, Joe Armstrong, was called before the Depot CO. He told Joe a charge had been made against me and asked him what sort of chap I was. Joe pulled out all the stops and praised me to the skies, saying what a good war record I had and so on. I do not know what the major did with the charge sheet, but I never heard another word about it, and it was never recorded on my personal records.

A little later we joined the convoy that was taking demobilized African soldiers to their home towns in Tanganyika and Nyasaland. There were about a dozen 3-tonners, driven by Asian civilians. Joe and I were the only white soldiers, known in East Africa as BNCOs (British NCOs). Joe sat next to the driver in the leading vehicle and I sat next to the driver of the rear vehicle.

The Askari were in good spirits. They had served with Fourteenth Army in Burma, and had not seen their homes for two years or more. The trucks they were in were open at the back and many of them were perched on the sides. There was a good deal of singing and shouting and good-humoured banter. After we had cleared Nairobi and the asphalt road surface had abruptly finished, I got my first taste of East African roads. They were, of course, very dusty, and most of the time deeply rutted, which caused vehicles to shake alarmingly. It was said that the best way to alleviate the discomfort caused by the corrugations was to drive at a steady 50mph. About ninety miles south of Nairobi we left Kenya and crossed into Tanganyika at a place called Namanga. Here I had my first glimpse of elephants in the wild, a family group of about a dozen, some 300 yards from the road. They seemed to ignore us completely.

We were making good progress, albeit very dusty, when the truck in front of us started to try and overtake the truck in front of it. It was tooting its horn incessantly and the Africans in the back were cheering wildly in encouragement, but the truck being overtaken did not pull over, and suddenly there was a screeching of metal as the sides of the two vehicles met and the rear truck went over on its side. Bodies were spilled all over the place and we were fortunate not to run over any as we made an emergency stop.

The Asian driver crawled from the cab of the crashed vehicle, and immediately the Askari started to berate him and then to beat him with their sticks. The poor man took to his heels, closely pursued by the stick-wielding Africans. I did not know any Swahili at that time, but I ran after them shouting in English, and they soon gave up the chase.

By sheer good luck no one had been killed and the African medical orderly was able to put rough splints on two Askari who had broken arms. Other cuts and bruises would have to wait until we got to Arusha. The overturned truck and its driver were left behind until a breakdown truck could be sent to their aid. The passengers from it were re-distributed among the other vehicles, and the convoy set off again.

We arrived in Arusha during the afternoon. In those days it had one street lined on each side with corrugated iron-roofed buildings, some little more than shacks. They were mainly Asian shops, 'dirkas', selling a variety of objects. At one end of the street was a garage and workshop, the only business being run by a European. The Asians, mainly from India, were the shopkeepers of East Africa. They had originally come to Kenya in the 1920s to build a railway from Mombasa to Lake Victoria via Nairobi. After the railway was finished many remained in the colony to run small family businesses. Through hard work and frugal living they had been successful and provided an important part of the colony's infrastructure.

109 Company had sent a Tilly to take Joe and me to its camp, which was about 10 miles from Arusha. It was a temporary camp, everything and everybody in tents, so there was not much in the way of comforts or amenities. It was moved to whichever section of road required its attention. Although the unit was called a Road Construction Company, this was something of a misnomer in that it was employed in road maintenance rather than in building new roads. The company was shortly to become 54 Field Squadron, East African Engineers, and would be equipped with bulldozers and well-boring machines. It would be the only RE unit in East Africa Command, to provide services to Kenya, Tanganyika, Uganda, Somaliland and Ethiopia.

The unit was commanded a Major Cumberlage, with a captain as second in command, and two, sometimes three, lieutenants or second lieutenants, who were usually National Service, not Regular, officers. The BNCOs were the CSM, the CQMS, a staff sergeant, two sergeants, two full corporals and me, newly promoted to lance corporal. There were about 200 Askari sappers who also had their own NCOs, from a sergeant major down to lance corporals.

There were two messes for the Europeans ('*Wazungu*' in Swahili), an officers' mess and a sergeants' mess, the latter used by all BNCOs irrespective of rank. I sensed straight away that this was a happy unit and that the atmosphere was relaxed though workmanlike. This usually was the case with small working units, especially if they were roughing it.

After a rather plain meal in the sergeants' mess marquee I was shown to my tent. There was a bed in it complete with mosquito net, a canvas washbasin on wooden legs and a folding camp-chair – and nothing else apart from wire coat-hangers strung around the walls. As it was a malarial area I was given some anti-mosquito sprays. These were in the form of small bomb-shaped metal containers. The drill was to get into bed, making sure that the net was tucked in all round, then break off the top of a bomb, which released a chemical spray. In addition to the ubiquitous mosquitoes there was a variety of other insects to make life interesting. In this particular area there were large flying insects known as 'sausage flies' as their bodies, one and a half inches long, bore a marked resemblance to chipolatas. Like most flying insects they were attracted to light at night. When I got up in the morning I found the floor of my tent literally covered with dead insects.

Further south tsetse flies were endemic. Their bite could cause sleeping sickness in humans, which can be fatal, so strict precautions were necessary against it. Other minor hazards were snakes and scorpions. Regarding the former, they would usually get out of one's way unless one had the misfortune to accidentally step on a sleeping one. As for scorpions, they often liked to crawl into dark corners, so it was a wise precaution to examine one's boots before putting them on in the morning.

Our Askari sappers came from a variety of tribes, such as the Jaluo from around Lake Victoria, Wakamba from the Machakos area, the Nandi, who were reputed to be a great warrior tribe in the past and who made good NCOs, and the Kikuyu, Kenya's largest tribe. In spite of them being the majority tribe there were only a few Kikuyu in the unit and they tended to be mess waiters, cooks and clerks.

The OC placed me with the MT Sergeant, Bob Hardy. I knew nothing about the mysteries of the internal combustion engine, so here was my chance to learn. Our vehicles, many of which were clapped out owing to the shortage of spares, were Tillys, 3-tonners, a Jeep and one 10-ton Mack truck. I had never driven anything bigger than a Jeep so was given driving lessons on these larger vehicles.

In my spare time I learned Swahili, essential, as very few of the Africans knew English. All the tribes had their own languages, but Swahili was the *lingua franca* throughout East Africa. I picked up the language quite easily and by using it all the time soon became fluent.

Like everyone else in East Africa we worked 'tropical hours'. That meant morning muster at 0600 hrs, finish for the day at 1300 hrs, with a post-lunch siesta. Being so close to the equator there was no twilight and darkness came suddenly around 1800 hours. Not long after I arrived the rainy season began and work on the roads became impossible. The rain during this period of several weeks is so heavy and prolonged that the earth roads become rivers of mud. Any essential traffic could only move slowly and with the use of wheel chains. Before it became too wet it was decided that the squadron, as it now was, would return to its permanent camp at Nanyuki in Kenya.

Nanyuki is situated in the Kenya Highlands about 120 miles north of Nairobi. At that time, 1946, it consisted of one street lined on both sides with Indian-run shops and a couple of bars. Outside this area was a sprawl of shacks, which formed the African quarter, the Majengo. Our camp was situated on the plain at the approaches to Mount Kenya, at a height of 6,000 feet above sea level. It was a healthy area, too high for mosquitoes and pleasantly cool in the evenings. We wore khaki drill uniforms, that is, shorts, bush jackets and slouch hats, all the year round. Long trousers and long-sleeved shirts were worn at night, especially during the rains.

153

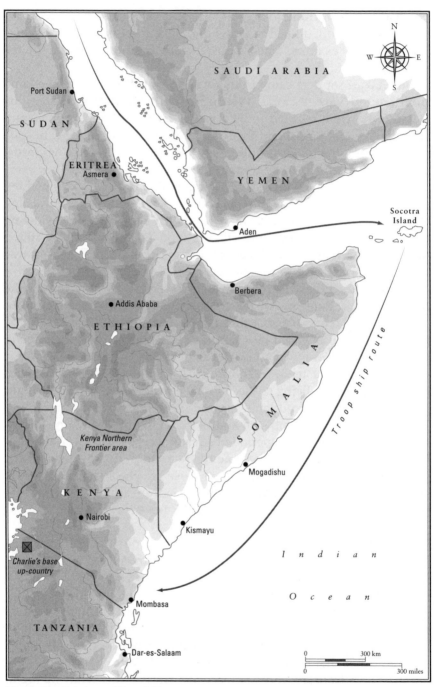

Map 9. Charlie's tour of East Africa.

154

The 17,000-feet high Mount Kenya, the second-highest mountain in Africa, was plainly visible from our camp and its snow-covered summit could be observed every morning until the daily clouds covered it up. The lower slopes of the mountain were heavily forested and provided the habitat for elephants, buffalo and other wild animals. A few years later it also provided a hideout for Mau Mau fighters.

The buildings in our camp were mainly wooden framed, with walls and roofs covered by bitumenized material. The interiors were lined with elephant grass, which looked quite attractive, but was often infested with white ants. At night when it was quiet one could actually hear them chewing. The cookhouses, ablutions and various stores had corrugated iron walls and roofs. The only brick building was the guard room, which was also the armoury, housing weapons, ammunition and explosives.

The camp covered quite a large area as, apart from accommodation, there was a compound containing road-making and well-boring equipment, officers' and BNCOs messes, QM Stores, ablutions and offices. In the middle was the drill square with a flag post. Every evening the Union Jack was lowered as the bugler sounded 'retreat', and every morning at 'reveille' it was raised again. Our square, made of beaten earth, was not sacred, as it was with some units. We used it for sports and the occasional African *ngomie* (dance).

Every BNCO had his own room with a bed, a table and a cupboard, and it was up to the individual to make it as comfortable as he wished. Also every BNCO, irrespective of rank, was allocated a batman, known as a 'personal boy', whatever his age. In retrospect, I find this term demeaning to the Askari, but in those days did not give it a second thought. My 'boy', Tarafa, was the only Ethiopian in the squadron, and he was very black.

The duties of a personal boy were not arduous, which was why they volunteered for the job. They had to keep their *bwana*'s uniforms clean, starched and ironed, and bring him hot water and a cup of tea at 'reveille' each morning. Apart from that their time was pretty much their own. *'bwana'* ('Father') was the word used when the Askari addressed an officer or BNCO, but was occasionally replaced by *'effendi'* ('Lord').

Nanyuki did not offer much in the way of entertainment. There was no cinema – the nearest one was in Nairobi, 120 miles away. It was rumoured that some of the older and more conventional white people still wore dinner jackets when they went to it. The two bars in the town were run by Indians and they lacked British pub ambience. There was a

NAAFI canteen, but without NAAFI girls. We went there once in a while to see different faces and enjoy a bit of singing.

However, most of our leisure time was spent in the BNCOs mess, sitting at the bar and talking about every subject on earth. Of course, there was no TV, videos or DVDs. We did have two radios, but neither worked. Apparently we were too far from the transmitter station. The only newspaper was the odd copy of the *East African Standard*. Sometimes paperback books could be bought from one of the small Indian dirkas, but the choice was rather limited. There were no touring entertainment shows in East Africa as were common for troops in Europe, the Middle East and the Far East. We also lacked any female companionship as none of us were married except CSM George Hopkins. His wife came out from England but after a few months returned home. Who could blame her? She was the only European wife in the camp.

Despite our social deprivations, we were a happy bunch and got on well together in the mess. We were fairly hard drinkers and always got through the mess's monthly whisky ration long before the month was out. We would then start on the gin ration, which no one really liked. But in spite of our drinking habits, in the three and half years I spent in that unit, only one of our members became an alcoholic, and even he never failed to carry out his duties. There was no rank in the mess and everyone was called by his forename or nickname if he had one. We had a sign over the entrance to the mess on which was written *Abandon Rank All Ye Who Enter Here*, and this applied to officer guests also, although they were always accorded proper respect. In effect, the mess was run in the spirit of 'on parade, on parade; off parade, off parade'. I remember a kindly old sergeant in boys' service who used to tell us, 'Work hard, play hard, drink hard', adding that we would come to the last part later. How right he was!

In our mess he could have added 'sing hard', because we indulged in a great deal of singing. In my time in the Army I learnt literally dozens of songs, and I do not mean the popular songs of the day because we had no means of hearing them. What we mainly sang were songs peculiar to the different areas that our Mess members came from. For example, someone from Liverpool would sing 'Maggie May' or 'On Mother Kelly's Doorstep'. Sentimental songs from Ireland were always popular, such as 'The Rose of Tralee' and 'I'll Take You Home Again, Kathleen'. Ribald and obscene songs were also delivered with great gusto, 'Frigging in the Rigging', 'This Old Coat of Mine', 'I Don't Want to Join the Army', 'Oh, Gethusalem' and so on being high on the repertoire. Some of these songs dated back to our grandfathers' days or even beyond and we really enjoyed singing them – we were a singing army.

Sadly, the soldiers of today do not seem to sing much, and the modem music that they listen to does not give them any encouragement to do so.

I was delighted when Major Cumberlage lent me his portable gramophone and collection of operatic records. They were all 78 rpm records of popular arias from *Tosca* and *La Boheme* and some Neapolitan songs. Most of the arias were by Beniamino Gigli, and even one or two by Caruso.

We had working in the camp three Italian PoWs, captured in Abyssinia during 1941. They were not confined in any way and lived in their own hut in the camp. I became friendly with them, particularly with Dante, who was well educated and came from Rome. He kept a pet dog called Sofia, who he left with me when he went back to Italy. The other two were Enrico and Giovanni, and all three of them were odd-job men for camp maintenance. It was the middle of 1947 before they were repatriated to Italy, which must have been very hard for them. So when I was lent the gramophone and records, I took them over to their hut several times to give them a concert. They really appreciated it and it brought tears to their eyes. Needles for the gramophone were hard to obtain and we experimented with some of the hard, vicious needles one can find in the bush, but they were not a success, so very reluctantly I had to return the records and gramophone to the OC.

The rainy season, which limited our activities on road work, gave me a good opportunity to improve my knowledge of Swahili. Our tutor was a young Kikuyu Askari who had been educated in a school run by missionaries and so had a good command of English.

When the weather became dry and sunny again, HQ East Africa Command in Nairobi decided that it would put on a military tattoo, and our squadron was asked to provide a small detachment to participate. Our party consisted of the OC, a Sergeant Forse and me, plus our personal boys. Our job would be to provide the explosive effects for the various battle scenes.

This detached duty gave us the chance to meet other units in 70 Brigade, the 'teeth' of the command. We used the mess of the 156 Battery, East African Artillery; they had brought a whole battery of 25-pounder field guns with them. Also present were two battalions of the King's African Rifles (KAR) together with their very good military band. The tattoo was to last three days with a performance each evening and it would take place at the Nairobi racecourse. We arrived three days earlier to make our preparations. A dugout was excavated to hide us from public view and this was to be our control centre. Across the battle area many shallow holes were dug and each hole would contain a small explosive charge complete with an electric detonator. From the detonator wires were laid to end on a board in the dugout. The board had two contact points for each hole in the battle area. To activate the explosives one had to take up the two wires leading to a 12-volt battery and touch them on the two relevant contact points on the board. The idea was that every time one of the field guns fired a blank round we would activate an explosion to simulate the fall of the shell.

The other explosive device was the Cordtex net. This was a net with a mesh of about a foot square made of Cordtex instantaneous explosive fuse. These nets were intended to be laid over a minefield and when it was detonated it would also detonate any mines beneath it, so clearing a path through the minefield.

The simulated attack by the KAR was supposed to illustrate the role that they had played against the Japanese in Burma. In defence the Japanese Army had seldom used mines, but used sharpened bamboo stakes dug into the ground in great quantity in front of their positions. These stakes were known as *punjis* and during the performance we would detonate a Cordtex net as if we were destroying a belt of them.

The first performance of the tattoo went off very well. There was a very impressive war dance put on by warriors of the Wakamba tribe in their national costume, or perhaps it should be said lack of costume – it seemed to consist, very economically, of bits of fur and feathers. Their spears were well polished and lethal looking, as were their facial expressions.

The band put on an excellent show with their marching and counter-marching. This was followed by one of the KAR battalions performing a long exhibition of 'continuity drill', arms- and foot-drill carried out in complete silence, without any word of command. Their precision and smartness would have done credit to the Brigade of Guards.

Next came a pageant of the history of the KAR, mainly of their vital part in the campaigns in the Great War against the very able German General, Paul Emil von Lettow-Vorbeck. Finally, as darkness descended there came the mock attack on the Japanese position. With the commentator explaining the action over the PA system, the guns fired their blanks followed by the appropriate explosions from us; then came the explosion of the Cordtex net to make a path through the punjis, swiftly followed by an infantry assault firing blanks from their rifles. The show ended with the KAR band playing the National Anthem and everyone feeling satisfied that everything had gone so well.

158

The second night the show again went off without a hitch but with one addition to our part in the proceedings. To add authenticity to the infantry assault it was felt that some machine-gun fire would add realism. At that time one could not use blank firing attachments on automatic weapons so I fired live ammunition into the side of a pit at the appropriate time.

Came the third and last show, and again all went well until just before the final assault. The artillery barrage ended and in the darkness the commentator announced in hushed tones that the sappers were now creeping forward to lay their Cordtex net and that any second now it would explode. The seconds dragged on and on, and nothing happened. In the dugout there was a sense of panic as the OC kept applying the battery leads to the contact points. Still nothing. The commentator, who must have been a pro, saved the situation by saying that the sappers must have run into trouble and were probably casualties, but that the assault would go ahead in spite of that. I fired my Bren into the pit and off went the infantry attack, screaming like mad.

We never did ascertain for sure what had gone wrong, possibly the battery should have been recharged, but we took an awful lot of ribbing from other units, particularly from the gunners. We took this in good part, but decided between ourselves that we would have our revenge. It would have to be taken that night as on the morrow all units would return to their various locations. The Gunners were commanded by a major, a dapper man and a bit of a martinet. He had led the joking about Cordtex net failure and he was going to be our principal target.

There was a good deal of partying and drinking that night to celebrate the end of a successful tattoo. This aided our plan, in that the victims would be later sleeping soundly. At about 0200 hours the three of us got into our Jeep driven by the OC and armed with a good supply of thunderflashes. These were an outsize firework, about ten inches long, used on exercises to simulate gunfire. They were not dangerous, but exploded with a very loud bang.

We headed at speed for the Gunners' tents, stopped at the tent of the major, and after undoing his tent flap treated him to a salvo of three thunder-flashes. Then we drove along the line of tents throwing thunder-flashes into the open tent flaps – it was a hot night. At those that were not open we drove over their guy-ropes, causing them to collapse. The whole raid lasted about two minutes, but it left behind a scene of devastation.

The major told our OC some days later that one of the thunder-flashes had landed in his urinal bucket and that he had been liberally splashed with the contents. That would have taught him not to take the piss out of sappers!

When we got back to Nanyuki the OC decided to give our Askaris an *ngoma*, an evening of drinking, feasting and native dances. Preparation for this involved brewing beer from fermented millet seed. The containers for this were several empty 44-gallon petrol drums and the brewing was carried out by Corporal Samuels, a Jaluo and a giant of a man. He was acknowledged by the Askaris as an expert at the process. Also required was a large bonfire, which meant scouring the area for firewood for several days until a huge pyre was erected on the camp square. Lastly, a day's hunting was organized by us BNCOs and we returned with several assorted gazelles to provide meat for the party. The ngoma was held on a Saturday night so that Sunday could be given over to nursing hangovers. The native beer, in Swahili called *pombe*, did not look very appetizing, resembling a rather watery porridge, but the Askaris seemed to enjoy it. We officers and BNCOs took no part in the proceeding other than as spectators. The bonfire made a splendid blaze and apart from providing illumination was also utilized as a cooking fire. The Askaris put chunks of meat on pointed sticks and held them over the hot ashes, then consumed the result, which was part burnt, part raw. The dancing soon started with much chanting and stamping of feet and as our men were a mixture of tribes there were soon several different tribal dances in progress simultaneously.

Once the *ngoma* was in full swing we whites slipped away to our messes so that our presence would not inhibit the Askaris' enjoyment. We would only return if the tribal rivalry got out of hand. It never did in my three and a half years with them, though inevitably there were minor quarrels, but on the whole their discipline was good, both on and off duty. The majority of them were cheerful and willing and were a pleasure to work with. As in all armies, we had the odd lead-swinger, or barrack-room lawyer or other malcontent in the ranks of our Askaris, but the majority of them appreciated that they had a better life with us than they would have back in their villages.

To help them with any problem they might have, every Saturday morning a period was given over to a *shauri* session. In this period any African soldier could come to his section BNCO and tell him about his request or complaint, or anything else that bothered him. If possible the BNCO would deal with the affair and if not he would take the soldier before the OC and explain the matter to him and ask for his judgement. The usual request was for leave to his home, perhaps because the man's wife was ill, or one of his children. This would normally be granted at once, but if there was any doubt of the veracity of the man's story then a telegram would be sent to the his District Officer asking him to verify the claim.

One quite frequent request was for leave to attend a son's circumcision ceremony. This was an important tribal ceremony carried out on groups of boys as part of their rite of passage into manhood. It was carried out by their own tribal doctor, known as a *maganga*, irrespective of whether they were Christian or pagan. Probably this ritual has died out, but at that time a man's seniority in his tribe was based on the date of his circumcision. So it was not uncommon in the Army that a private soldier's date of circumcision could be earlier than that of his sergeant, and thus when off duty the sergeant would have to show respect to his tribal senior. This, of course, would only apply to members of the same tribe.

Another common cause for leave application was to attend disputes over bride price. When an African wanted to marry it was incumbent on him to pay the father of the bride for the privilege. In 1946 the price could vary from four to eight cows and was subject to hard bargaining before the final figure was arrived at. Back then a man's wealth was measured by the number of cattle he owned, so a young soldier needed to be there in person for the bargaining session. The Askaris were allowed to have their wives and children in quarters within the camp but few of them chose to do so. One reason for this was that the majority of them had a piece of land back in their villages and they preferred that their wives should remain there to tend their '*shambas*', as they were known. Those that did choose to have their families in camp probably left the care of their shambas to their parents.

No attempt was ever made by the Army to interfere with the Askaris' religion or beliefs – there was no proselytizing or church parades. As far as I could see their lives were dominated and controlled by tribal custom and they did not hold any religious or political beliefs (to my Western eyes, anyway). They seemed happy enough without them. However, this was to change a few years later when the Mau Mau insurrection started, particularly among the Kikuyu.

There were very few Muslims among the Askaris, and those that were came from the coast where the Arab influence is strong. I can remember only one in the squadron – Mohammad. He had a dour and silent disposition and keep pretty much to himself. When we went shooting game for the pot we always took him with us as he would not eat the meat unless it had been killed in the Islamic way. When we shot a gazelle he would dash up to it and cut its throat before it had died. If it were already dead when he got to it he would not eat the meat.

Because of our lack of social amenities our OC had no objection to our use of official transport for hunting or sightseeing trips. One of our favourite jaunts was to drive to Archer's Post, near the small town of Isiolo in the Northern Frontier District. At Archer's Post was what might be described as an oasis in an otherwise barren landscape. It had a few palm trees, a rarity for that part of the country, and three fresh-water pools. One was for the use of Africans, one for Europeans and the other for cooking and drinking water. The water was crystal clear and had little terrapins in it. In spite of the heat in that area the water was delightfully cool and deep enough to swim in.

Further north the road led to the Ethiopian border, but before it was the town of Marsabit, around which one could usually see roaming elephants. Packs of wild dogs also roamed in the area, as did many other types of game. One felt an overwhelming sense of freedom in such wild places as this, especially as they were so sparsely inhabited.

At the beginning of 1947 I was sent to a place called Gilgil on a Motor Transport Officer's course where the mysteries of the internal combustion engine were made known to me. After passing it successfully I was promoted to full corporal.

Not long after this I nearly lost my newly acquired second stripe. The OC, in its wisdom, decided that early morning runs would benefit all of us, as we were getting fat and lazy. A different BNCO would accompany the Askaris each morning. When it came to my turn I devised a cunning plan whereby the unit bicycle would be left in the Guardroom by the main gate. I would lead my merry men on foot as far as the Guardroom, then mount the bicycle and lead them in that fashion.

All went according to plan except for one thing. I had not seen the major while riding the bike, but he had seen me, and had taken a dim view of my behaviour. Later that morning I was marched into his presence by the Squadron Sergeant Major. I pleaded guilty, of course, and did not try to offer any mitigating excuses. I was given a monu-mental telling off, what was known in army jargon as 'a right bol-locking', and told that only my previous clean sheet saved me from being demoted. He was absolutely right of course, as my behaviour was unacceptable and not a good example to the Askaris. Though I have to say that when some years later I saw some archive films of British troops on the march during the Great War, I couldn't help noticing that the troops were on their feet, but their officers were on horseback.

I had now been in East Africa for a year and a half and was halfway through my three-year tour. I now took my entitlement of one month's leave in the UK. This meant another voyage on a troopship. The only incident worthy of note was the 'crossing the line' ceremony, which took place the day after we left Mombasa. We had on board about 200 young Mauritian soldiers who would be disembarking at Port Said for service in Egypt and Palestine. No one had bothered to explain to them the purpose of the ceremony and so when the ship slowed down and King Neptune and his retainers, clad in their weird costumes, came aboard, there was consternation among the Mauritians. This turned to panic when the Neptune party started to grab some of them as potential victims. They responded by yelling with fear and tried to climb up the rigging and even the masts in an attempt to get away. It was quite a while before order was restored and they were reassured.

The month at home was pleasant enough but the country was still enduring rationing of food and petrol and people still looked drab and tired. My brother Arthur had just been demobbed and was back at his solicitor's office and Kathleen had married and gone to India with her husband. My father was no longer needed by the NAAFI and had a job as barman at Yeovil Cricket Club. Most of my friends were back at work and only went out on Saturday nights, so my leave was rather dull and I was not really sorry when it was time to go back.

The troopship sailed from Southampton and arrived at Port Said ten days later. Everyone had to disembark there as the ship was returning to the UK. That evening we were put on a troop train to take us all to the Base Transit Depot at Suez. As we waited at Port Said railway station for the train to depart some lads were looking out of the windows with their arms resting on the window frames. As soon as the train started to move young Egyptians stepped forward and in a flash pulled the wristwatches off the soldiers' wrists. This was not as difficult as it may sound, since most of the watches had metal expanding straps. I had heard that if confronted with leather or plastic straps the thieves were not averse to making a quick slash with a sharp knife, even if it meant leaving the victim with a cut wrist.

As the train cleared the town and started to get up speed gangs of youths hurled rocks at it and broke several of its windows. Obviously the British Army was not popular in this country and I was told that this sort of thing was an almost daily occurrence.

The Base Transit Depot was a dreary place with hundreds of tents and not a tree or bush in sight anywhere, just the all-pervading sand. The worst annoyance of the camp was the blaring of the loudspeakers of the

PA system, which went on day and night, reading out lists of names of people who were posted to various parts of the Middle East. I was dismayed to be told that it would be three weeks before a troopship left for Mombasa. But all things pass, and apart from a few guard duties I was left pretty much alone. I was able to get to the beach occasionally and the local Stella beer was quite palatable. Suez town was out of bounds, but that was no hardship – I had seen it before.

So it was with a feeling of relief that I was called forward to board HMT *Ascanius* for Mombasa, and what a ship it was. It looked like something left over from the Boer War, and had certainly seen service at Gallipoli in 1915. It was quite small as troopships go, rather scruffy looking, and graced with a tall, thin blue funnel. It was a coal-burner, which accounted for its dirty appearance. Its itinerary was Mombasa–Suez–Mombasa. It was crewed by Lascars (Indian seamen) – the authorities probably could not persuade white crews to sail in this old tub. To add to all its other non-virtues it was slow and its old engines were unreliable, which would be demonstrated to us later in the voyage.

Troop accommodation was of the usual tinned sardine variety. There was no canteen selling beer, nor were any duty-free cigarettes or tobacco available. Deck space for exercise was very limited, except for officers, who had the whole of the boat deck for that purpose. On the forward well-deck, just aft of the forecastle, there were two wooden lean-to constructions. The one on the port side was the troop latrine. Inside it, and running the length, was a long box with holes cut into it as equal intervals. Under the box was an open metal trough through which sea water kept running. Opposite this primitive convenience, and situated on the starboard side, was a smaller hut that served as the troop's galley. The two Lascar cooks and their assistants were clad in grubby, off-white cotton trousers and singlets. I well remember an occasion when the ship was in the Red Sea and it was extremely hot. I stood outside the open kitchen door and watched the cooks preparing meatballs for the troops' dinner. As they moulded them in their bare hands the perspiration streamed down their bodies and arms and some of it, perforce, was minced into the meatballs. The moral of that was that if you wish to enjoy your dinner, keep out of the kitchen.

After clearing the Red Sea the ship turned east to head for Aden where she was to take on coal before continuing to Mombasa. That night the throbbing of the ship's engines ceased and she was left without forward movement; instead she began to roll in the swell of the Indian Ocean and it began to get unpleasantly warm. This situation continued for nearly thirty-six hours, during which time there occurred a lot of banging and clanging from the engine room. Finally we got underway again and next day sailed into the harbour at Aden.

Everyone was allowed to go ashore and everyone did because bunkering a ship with coal is something to keep away from. But before leaving the ship I was able to watch the process for a while. Two large barges full of bagged coal drew alongside and a gangway was rigged down to them. Then literally hundreds of labourers formed a long chain, each man with a sack of coal on his back, and one by one they came on board, dropped the coal from the opened bag into the open bunker hatch, then went back to the barge with the empty sack and collected another full one. It was hard, unremitting work and the overseers would occasionally strike a man with a cane to encourage him to increase his speed. It was little better than slavery but I imagine the poor devils needed the pittance that was paid to them.

Aden itself seemed to be asleep as we walked through its streets and apart from taking a few photographs there was little else to do. Later in the day we found a small cove where one could bathe in the sea safely as it had a shark net across it, but we were unable to take advantage of this as we had no swimming trunks with us. So it was back to the ship, even though coaling was still in progress and everything one touched on the open deck was covered in coal dust. To pass the time we crossed to the other side of the ship and threw coins into the sea for the Arab kids who were swimming there. They were very adept at diving deeply to retrieve the coins, even though there was a real risk of being attacked by sharks. In fact one of the kids had one of his legs missing from just above the knee, most probably from a shark bite, but he was still taking the risk.

Three days later we docked at Mombasa and never have I been so glad to leave a ship. The train journey to Nanyuki was sheer luxury. There were few passengers on the train and four of us BNCOs practically had the dining car to ourselves.

Chapter 15

Mount Elgon – Uganda

It was good to be back with the squadron again and to see the familiar and welcome faces of old friends. Major Cumberlege had been demobilized and replaced by Major D.G. Waller, a likeable, easy-going type. Shortly after my return he promoted me to Sergeant, so I must have been doing something right. This meant that I would now have my own section of Askaris. There would, of course, be a troop commander, a lieutenant, over me, but he was a National Service officer and only had a few more months to serve before he would be replaced by another National Service officer. By the time these officers had some grasp of Swahili and other local customs, their time was up, and so they tended to let the BNCOs run the show for them.

After I had been back for a month my section, consisting of my lieutenant, me and forty Askaris and native NCOs, was detailed to proceed to the Mount Elgon area on the border between Kenya and Uganda to take part in a brigade exercise. Our transport was one Jeep and four 3-tonners. Our equipment was rather basic, made up of various hand tools such as picks and shovels, crowbars, sledgehammers and carpenters' tools.

Other units taking part in the exercise were the 2nd (Nyasa) Battalion of the King's African Rifles, a squadron of armoured cars and our old friends from the Nairobi Tattoo, 156 Battery, East African Artillery, with 25-pounder field guns. In addition there were various odds and sods from the Nairobi garrison: RASC, REME, Royal Signals and so on.

Our journey westwards took us from the open savannah country of the Kenya Highlands into the moist heat and thicker vegetation of Uganda. We passed through Kitule, Mbale, Eldoret and Tororo, all small one-horse towns with the usual collection of Indian dirkas. I noticed that it was common in Uganda for women to smoke their tobacco in pipes, something I had not seen in Kenya or Tanganyika.

We arrive at the lower slopes of Mount Elgon, known to local tribes as 'Breast Mountain' for its perfectly conical shape, an area of dense rain forest, just before nightfall. Prior to our departure from Nanyuki an order had been given that no camp beds were to be taken on this exercise and that all ranks would sleep on the bare ground. I decided to ignore this order as my fear of snakes and other reptiles was greater than my fear of higher authority. So, just after darkness came, I was lying contentedly on my camp bed enjoying a cigarette when, to my dismay, a figure carrying a hurricane lamp emerged from the surrounding bushes. It was the Brigadier. I got off the bed in a flash and stood to attention in my stockinged feet. 'I see you have brought your camp bed, Sergeant!' he said. My heart dropped into my boots (or would have done had I been wearing them). Then, amazingly, he continued, 'Quite right. I've brought mine too. Any bloody fool can be uncomfortable. I expect you had enough of sleeping rough during the war, I know I did. Good night, Sergeant.'

From that moment my estimation of senior officers improved a thousand per cent. Not so that of my National Service Lieutenant, lying uncomfortably on the bare ground behind the next bush. I thought it politic to maintain a discreet silence in answer to his disgruntled comments about sergeants who did not obey orders.

Next morning early, the exercise started. The object of it was to evaluate the rate of progress of an all-arms advance through dense bush country. After an hour or so a halt was called, and my friend the Brigadier, who was in command of the whole show, approached me and asked if I could make some explosive effects in order to simulate an enemy response to our advance. I was only too happy to oblige. I made up a supply of small bangers by inserting short lengths of safety fuse into No. 27 detonators and then inserting the detonators into guncotton primers. I filled the pockets of my bush jacket with these prepared charges, lit a cigarette, which could be used to ignite the safety fuse, and rejoined the Brigadier.

For the rest of the morning we walked together among the leading platoons of infantry and occasionally the Brigadier would say something like: 'That chap over there looks half asleep. Drop one behind him to wake him up.' I would then touch the lighted end of my cigarette to the safety fuse and toss the charge a couple of paces behind the Askari who had been indicated. It was not dangerous, but it did make a significant bang, and served to accelerate the speed of the advance, which made the Brigadier happy.

That night, instead of sleeping after the exertions of the day, it was ordered that all units would go by motor transport and attempt to reach the summit of Mount Elgon, but without the use of vehicle lights. This was not easy because there were no roads on the higher slopes, only animal trails. The summit was about 14,000 feet above sea level. There had been no rain for some months so the vehicles stirred up thick clouds of dust, making it extremely difficult to see the vehicle ahead of oneself. The progress was no faster than a slow walking pace, but in spite of one or two collisions and breakdowns, the bulk of the transport reached the top.

After a few hours' rest and a makeshift cold breakfast, and most importantly a brew of hot tea, the Brigade moved off again. The convoy descended the mountain, a lot faster in daylight, and headed westward on the plains below. The vegetation was mostly scrubby bushes and small, twisted trees. It was very hot and dusty, much more so than the Kenya Highlands to which we were accustomed.

About midday we crossed a rickety wooden bridge that seemed to shudder as we passed over it. I turned round to look behind and was amazed to see a gap where the bridge had been and a huge cloud of dust arising. This brought the convoy to a halt as most of the transport was still on the opposite side of the erstwhile bridge.

Within seconds, up strode the bold Brigadier, looking very cross indeed. Glaring at my officer, he barked, 'How long will it take you to put another bridge across here?' to which my inexperienced officer replied, 'About two weeks, Sir.' As I watched, the Brigadier's normal rosy complexion started to become purple and I feared he might have a stroke. But he recovered his composure and barked out: 'I want the last vehicle across before dawn.' With that he strode off to his Jeep, leaving us to ponder how we were going to comply with his order when there was not a straight piece of timber for miles around. If we had possessed any proper bridging equipment such as the Bailey bridge there would not have been a problem, but we only had hand tools.

We made a quick inspection under what remained of the bridge and found that it had been a real Heath Robinson contraption. The supports had consisted of literally hundreds of intertwined branches, none of them thicker than a man's wrist and none of them straight. Fortunately the gap was no more than twenty feet across so with a little ingenuity and a lot of hard work we might be able to close it. Since there was no straight timber available we should have to make do with the twisted stuff. Work parties were sent out to cut down whatever trees they could find and told to return as quickly as possible.

The remainder of the men were employed with picks and shovels to make a ford adjacent to the bridge. This was done by cutting into the banks of the dry wadi and making a road across it. We worked all night and with some difficulty managed to close the gap in the bridge, but just before it was completed one of the Askari dropped a sledge-hammer into the gully below. I told him to get down there and bring it back but he said he was scared because they had seen snakes under the bridge. I asked for a volunteer but no one was prepared to oblige, so I had no alternative but to retrieve the hammer myself. It was pitch black down there but I had a hurricane lamp and soon found it. I did not see any snakes – probably the noise had frightened them off.

The repairs on the bridge were only just good enough for it to take light vehicles and my Jeep was the first across to the cheers of the Askaris. The heavier vehicles had to use the ford and some of them got stuck in the soft ground. Luckily the armoured cars were equipped with winches and these were employed to pull across any stuck vehicle.

After the last vehicle had crossed over I lit up a well-deserved cigarette and was piffling away contentedly when I heard a voice exclaim, 'Get your finger out Sergeant, the exercise is not over yet.' It was the Brigadier, of course. *Poor chap*, I thought sympathetically, *he probably didn't sleep very well*. But mere sergeants don't argue with irate brigadiers, so I jumped into the Jeep and took off in a cloud of dust to catch up with the convoy.

Later that day we came up to a river about fifty metres in width and about one metre deep in the middle. There was a good, sound bridge a few miles upstream, but for the purpose of the exercise a crossing had to be made at this point. We solved this problem by putting two parallel tapes across the river the width of a road apart. We then borrowed a company of the KAR to work with our own men and divided them into two parties; one party on the outside of each tape. Their task was to pick up stones that covered the riverbed and toss them into the area between the tapes. In less than two hours it was possible for vehicles to cross. Had the river been deeper and less sluggish in its flow, then this method would not have worked, but luckily the conditions were perfect and the Brigadier was pleased.

We watched the vehicles splashing across a Jeep came to a halt near us. It was in immaculate condition, as were the men in it. There were four of them, an Askari driver, two Askaris in the back and next to the driver a Royal Artillery Major, who was none other than our friend from the Nairobi Tattoo. The gallant Major descended from the Jeep, marched to the side of the track, did a smart salute turn and barked 'Prepare to dismount!' The already stiff Askaris stiffened a little more. A pause. Then he marched to the opposite side of the track, about turned smartly and stood at attention facing the Jeep. He then gave the orders 'Stand at ease – stand easy.' Our scruffy sappers were vastly amused by this demonstration of military correctness, and when I shouted at them 'Now you can see what real soldiers look like,' their smiles were even bigger than mine.

The exercise ended that day and all ranks were told to relax for the next thirty-six hours and to make themselves comfortable. I was immensely impressed by the way the Nyasa Askaris did this. Within a matter of three hours, and using only dried grass and sticks collected locally, they made a line of beautifully constructed grass huts. Inside these they made comfortable beds using the same materials.

I had an alfresco bath in a nearby crystal-clear stream and then made my way to the big tent, which was the exercise mess for the KAR BNCOs. Dinner was the first cooked meal we had eaten for three days and there was a plentiful supply of Tusker beer, which was kept cool by laying the bottles in the stream. Later in the evening I went outside in the dark night to urinate, and while doing so I felt a searing, burning pain which seemed to be affecting my legs, stomach and groin. I quickly realized that I was standing in the path of a column of vicious soldier ants. Without hesitation I pulled off bush shirt, shorts and underpants and clad only in my boots and stockings dashed back the Mess tent yelling blue murder.

There is an old army expression which says that Sappers are either mad, married or Methodist. The other members of the mess must have thought I was certainly qualified for the first category, or perhaps they thought it was some bizarre sapper ritual war dance. However, when they saw the ants swarming all over me, they set about slapping them off with quite unnecessary enthusiasm. One kindly soul even threw a bucket of water over me.

The RSM, a strait-laced Scot, took a dim view of the whole incident and ordered me to get dressed at once. He then ruled that the penalty for entering the mess improperly dressed was that I should buy drinks for everyone in the mess. This was greeted by loud cheers from all present and a groan from me.

After a day spent packing up, all units dispersed to their various camps around what was then called British East Africa and consisted of Kenya, Tanganyika, Uganda and British Somaliland. There were also British troops stationed in the former Italian Somaliland and Abyssinia. No. 54 Squadron was the only Royal Engineer unit remaining in British East Africa after the post-war demobilization and with all that territory to cover we were never idle. But the exercise had made a nice break and we had enjoyed playing soldiers.

On returning to Nanyuki my section officer left the squadron for onward travel to the UK where he would be demobilized, or, as it was usually called, 'demobbed'. His replacement was Lieutenant Gerry Ibbottson, a much more colourful character and someone who would make a reputation for himself. Seeing him on parade for the first time he did not present a very soldierly figure; but as a hard-working engineer squadron that was not so important.

He was quite short, about five feet four inches, and wore large horn-rimmed spectacles that gave him a rather owlish appearance. Having just arrived by troopship from England his bare arms and knees were still very white, but he looked fit enough with his rosy red cheeks. On his waist-belt he wore a holster containing a German Luger automatic pistol, which he had acquired from a fellow officer in the UK and of which he was inordinately proud.

I was to be not only his section sergeant, but also his guide and mentor. This was because I spoke Swahili and he did not, so he could not communicate with our Askaris except through me. Furthermore, I had several years' army experience, including active service behind enemy lines, behind me, a fact that he appreciated, and so we were on good terms from the start to the end of our relationship.

He was only nineteen years old and told me that he had been born in India, where his father had been a District Commissioner and a great hunter of tigers in his leisure hours. His father had invented a system in which dogs were carried in a howdah on an elephant's back. When they reached the vicinity of the tiger the dogs were sent to the ground through canvas chutes, much like those used for evacuating passengers from an airliner when on the ground during an emergency. The dogs then surrounded the tiger and kept it in position while the DC shot at it from the howdah above. Gerry had been encouraged by his father to carry on the family traditions of hunting, shooting and fishing. To this end, at the age of ten, he had presented him with a .22 rifle, a .410-inch shotgun and a large game book in which to record all his kills. He showed me this book and it contained hundreds of entries. When he was sent to boarding school in England he took his guns with him and considerably reduced the wildlife population in his area.

Later he went on to Cambridge where he got a Running Blue. Running was his second love, after shooting, and he indulged in it at every opportunity. Many times in the hot afternoons when the rest of us would be lying on our beds in an alcohol-induced torpor, Gerry would be charging through the bush with the sun flashing from his spectacles.

171

The first intimation that he was more than a little eccentric came about when our section was at practice on the rifle range. Gerry had sent a man off on some errand, and it seemed to him that the Askari was not moving quickly enough. So he drew his Luger from its holster and started to shoot into the ground just behind the man's heels. We had strong words about this and I had difficulty in persuading the Askari not to report the matter to the OC.

Not long after this Gerry was in trouble again. He knew that flocks of wild guinea fowl were indigenous to Kenya and he set out to get some for the officers' mess. Unfortunately for him, the flock had had their wings clipped, and were the property of a rather blimpish retired colonel whose farm was only a few miles from our camp. By the time the irate colonel arrived on the scene Gerry had already slaughtered a dozen of his birds. One can only imagine the altercation that then took place. Even so, Gerry returned to camp with his birds completely unperturbed and wearing his perpetual grin of contemptuous derision. But that was not the end of the affair.

A few days later, on one of his afternoon peregrinations, Gerry came across a stream full of rainbow trout. Next day he returned with rod, line and appropriate flies and proceeded to denude the streams of fish. While happily engaged in this pursuit an interruption came in the form of none other than the gallant Colonel. The stream was on his land and he had stocked it with trout. This time Gerry returned empty handed, still wearing his contemptuous grin, but hotly pursued by the infuriated Colonel in a rattling old car of 1930 vintage. He was intent on laying his justifiable grievances before our OC.

As a consequence of this complaint the OC decided that he would get Gerry out of the way for a while by sending our section on a task that involved making a stretch of new road from the Northern Kenya border into Abyssinia. Our convoy was made up of two 3-tonners, one 15-cwt truck, a water bowser and a compressor truck, led by the Jeep in which Gerry and I travelled. We carried rations for a month, plus an assortment of hand tools and several cases of gelignite.

We made the first night stop at Archer's Post and with two hours remaining before nightfall Gerry and I set off for a scout round the area in the Jeep; meanwhile, the Askaris, under the supervision of their African NCOs, set up camp. Before long we spotted a female rhinoceros with a calf. I was driving and Gerry asked me to get close to them. I noticed that he was beginning to get excited and was pumping a round into the chamber of his hunting rifle. I told him that he was not allowed to shoot big game unless he had a license, which I knew he did not have. Reluctantly, he applied the safety catch, but pleaded with me to get even closer. I brought the vehicle to within fifty yards, but then the rhino, which is a short-sighted beast, peered in our direction and gave a snort. Then she lowered her head and, without further ado, charged straight at us. I did a wide 'U'-turn, which shortened the gap between us, as the mother rhino was running in a straight line. She was so close that we could hear her heavy breathing; a sound to get our adrenaline flowing. If she had caught up to us she would have had no trouble in smashing our Jeep, and probably us with it. Thankfully our speed caused her to drop back and eventually to abandon the chase, much to our relief, though Gerry had been giggling like a schoolgirl throughout the incident and seemed to be unaware of any danger.

The next afternoon found us in the Marsabit area, which had rocky escarpments and where I knew from previous visits that elephants could usually be seen. Gerry and I were once more having a scout round the area while the troops made camp for the night. Soon we observed a single elephant in the distance. On getting closer we saw that it was a massive bull with very long tusks. I knew from talking with white hunters, the professionals, that lone elephants should be treated with extreme caution. They were often outcasts from the herd, having lost the leadership of it due to the ascendancy of a younger bull elephant. Elephants are gregarious animals and are usually found existing happily in groups of families, so the temper of a lone elephant, and its behaviour, are unpredictable. Nevertheless, I once again acceded to Jerry's request to get closer to the animal, though much against my better judgement. As we slowly got nearer his great ears began to twitch and he eyed us suspiciously. Then, suddenly, his ears came out at right angles to his massive head, up went his trunk to a vertical position and he let out a piercing scream, at the same time breaking into a lumbering run toward us. A quite terrifying sight.

I was expecting his charge and accelerated away from him as hard as possible. The terrain was in his favour as the vegetation in the area was thick, mostly thorn bushes, and we had to swerve to avoid them. The elephant was able to run in a straight line simply by stepping over them. The drumming of his huge feet was frighteningly audible as he pursued us. Then he suddenly just stopped, gave a scream again as though to say 'Let that be a warning to you!' and plodded off in the opposite direction.

Next day we passed Moyale and crossed into Ethiopia and reached the escarpment over which we had to construct a road. It was very steep and its present track was only suitable for camels to pass over. With the aid of the air-compressor truck we were to bore holes in the rock face, fill them with gelignite and transform the track into a road for vehicles. There would be a good deal of work with sledgehammers, picks and shovels, even though the temperature was in the region of 40°C. It was hard work and there was no shade – even the Askaris complained that the sun was burning their skin. To encourage them I frequently used a sledgehammer myself and worked alongside them.

There was nothing in the way of recreation in the evenings. Our small encampment was just a handful of tents out in the middle of nowhere, and with only a few hurricane lamps for illumination. There were no luxuries, only the food and water we had brought with us. Even so, the troop's morale was good and they chattered and sang happily together. Most evenings I would have a mug of tea with them and they would tell me about their war in Burma a couple of years past, and then ask me about my experiences in North Africa and Europe.

Sunday came and the troops were told they could spend the day as they pleased. Jerry and I, with one Askari, Sumoni, went hunting for the pot. We drove for several hours without any sign of game whatsoever. This was disappointing and puzzling too, since we had seen so much game on the journey up from Kenya. Possibly the game had been exterminated by tsetse fly. Visibility was very limited because of the density of the bush and we were forced to make many turns and detours in the hope of finding more open country, but without success. Suddenly we put up a buck and took off in hot pursuit. The buck made a sharp turn to the left, so did we, first on two wheels only, then on no wheels, until the Jeep turned completely over with the three of us underneath it.

Gerry crawled out first, completely unhurt. I soon followed with only a bruised leg, but the unfortunate Sumoni was pinned down by the rear end of the Jeep with only his head and shoulders in view. I managed to find the wheel jack and by raising one end of the Jeep a few inches we were able to drag him free. He was badly shaken but had no apparent injuries. We had been very lucky indeed.

Our efforts to turn the Jeep upright again were made in vain – it was too heavy for us. If we could have found some large rocks to put the jack on we could have done it, or if we could have cut some stout branches to act as levers. But the area was bereft of both these aids. The soil was sandy and there were no trees, only thorn bushes. So I suggested to Gerry that this was a situation where his proficiency in running could be useful. Neither of us was absolutely sure as to which direction the camp lay, but we had left wheel tracks in the sandy soil and Gerry would have these to guide him. It was only two hours before darkness fell so he set off at a run without further ado.

Sumoni and I scouted around to collect dead wood for a fire: as we had no torch we should need the fire for illumination. We had no food with us, but had cigarettes and a can of water, so we would be comfortable enough. By the time night fell we had a good fire going and enough wood to last the night. We sat around chatting and I asked Sumoni about life in his village before he joined the Army. The conversation turned to witchcraft and he told me that if a *machawi* (witch doctor) wanted to kill a man all he had to do was put two crossed sticks on the path to the man's house and the man would surely die. When I asked him how and why, he said that the victim believed so strongly that he was doomed that he very soon after did die.

As we were talking, suddenly a man appeared silently out of the black night and stood looking down at us. He was very thin, tall and black. His fuzzy mop of hair was dyed orange with henna and apart from a thin piece of cloth draped toga fashion from one shoulder, he was completely naked. In his right hand he carried a spear with a long wooden shaft and round his neck was tied a crescent-shaped piece of carved wood with a short leg protruding from it. I learnt later from Sumoni that this latter item served as a headrest when he lay on the ground to sleep. All in all, he was a villainous-looking character. I motioned him to sit and he then made a sign that he wanted a cigarette, which I gave him. I spoke to him in Swahili but he did not understand: he was an Ethiopian and we had no common language. I should have liked to know from whence he came and to where he was going because in the time we had spent in the area we had seen absolutely no sign of any human habitation. So he just sat there staring at us without blinking and without uttering a sound for what seemed a very long time. Sumoni gave his opinion that he was hoping that we should fall asleep and that if we did he would steal our rifles and probably kill us into the bargain. I was inclined to agree with him and kept my hand on my rifle the whole time. After some hours he stood up and left as silently as he had arrived, but I had a strong feeling that he was just outside the range of the firelight and was still watching us. It was a long night and we were both happy to see the dawn break. Two hours later Gerry turned up with a 3-tonner and a dozen Askaris and we soon had the Jeep running again.

The following Saturday was decreed by Gerry to be a 'make and mend' day for the Askaris to give them an opportunity to wash their clothes and to tidy up the campsite. This would be followed on Sunday morning by an inspection parade. Gerry himself took off, saying that he had to consult with the OC at Nanyuki. I was not sure that I believed him – probably the crafty bugger was going hunting. He said he would be back on the Monday morning.

Just before the scheduled parade time on Sunday morning, Sergeant Aloise, an African sergeant, came to my tent and said that the men wanted to speak to me. I went outside to find them drawn up in three ranks but still in their working clothes. Their spokesman stepped forward and complained that the men were unhappy at having to dress up on their day off. It appeared I was facing a mutiny of sorts.

I told them that they were soldiers first and workmen second and that they were committing a serious offence by disobeying orders. I said that if they persisted to be disobedient I should bring up a battalion of KAR to arrest them, then they would all go to prison. This seemed to have the desired effect and they all paraded smartly dressed an hour later, as meek as lambs.

Gerry returned on Monday morning as promised with a large dead antelope on the back seat, which put a smile on the faces of the Askaris. I did not tell him about the mini mutiny as I feared he might start waving his Luger at the miscreants. Three weeks later the job was finished and we were back in the fleshpots of Nanyuki.

A few months later Gerry left for demobilization in the UK. The night before leaving, BNCOs invited him to our mess for a farewell drink as he had been a popular officer. He was smart enough to resist all our efforts to get him drunk and he left the mess in good order. What we did not know was that immediately after leaving, and under cover of darkness, he went to the centre of the squadron's parade square. There he dug a hole in the earthen surface into which he placed a 50lb tin of ammonal blasting powder. He inserted a detonator and guncotton primer into the tin and laid a twin electric cable back to the road edge at the side of the square.

Next morning, an hour before 'reveille' was blown, Gerry was met by an African driver and Jeep at the officers' mess. The rest of the squadron were still slumbering. As they came to the side of the square, Gerry bade the driver to stop and to lift the bonnet of the Jeep. This done, Gerry picked up the end of the cable, which he had previously laid, and touched the two ends of it to the terminals of the Jeep battery. The resulting explosion was spectacular – there was an extremely loud bang followed by a dense cloud of dust rising to a great height.

There was consternation in the camp. Had World War Three started? Had the explosives store gone up? The bemused OC, in his striped pyjamas, stood scratching his head until slowly the truth dawned on him. When questioned, the guard on the gate confirmed that *Bwana*

Ibbottson had left the camp only seconds after the explosion and by now he would be miles away. After a stiff brandy and soda, the OC, who liked a quiet life, decided against bringing Gerry back to face the music. After all, the damage was slight, the Squadron Office ceiling down and some windows broken. But he promised himself that if they ever sent him another officer like Gerry he would leave the Army and become a monk.

Chapter 16

Somaliland

In early 1948 rioting had taken place in Mogadishu, the capital of the former colony of Italian Somaliland, due to the fears of the indigenous Somali population that the Italians would take over the country again when the British occupation forces departed.

There was a British unit, the 1st Battalion, Loyal Regiment (North Lancashire) stationed in the town and 54 Squadron was ordered to join them as quickly as possible. We left Mombasa aboard our old friend HMT *Ascanius*, fortunately only for a short trip of thirty-six hours. For some of our Askaris it was the first time they had seen the sea and their first experience of travel by ship.

When we arrived off Mogadishu we had to disembark onto lighters as the port was too small to take our ship. There was a heavy swell running and one had to pick the right moment to jump onto the lighter, which was rising and falling alarmingly at the gangway. Some of the Askaris got very nervous at this point and had to be encouraged to get off with a helpful push.

We BNCOs were then conveyed to the Loyals' sergeants' mess for lunch. When we arrived there we found a 'Sods Opera' in full swing as the petty officers of a Royal Navy destroyer were being entertained prior to their sailing that evening. The beer was flowing and the atmosphere most convivial, and every guest was obliged to stand up and sing a song. Some of the singing was pretty awful but the numbing effect of the beer helped us endure it.

After lunch we were conveyed to a sandy waste about three miles out of town and told to erect the tents that had been dumped there. Our Askaris set to willingly and by nightfall we were pretty well organized. Just before turning in I was looking at a scarab beetle rolling its ball of dung in front of it when the OC approached and asked me what it was. I explained to him that the beetle laid its eggs in the dung to provide food for its young when they hatched. He was interested and remarked that he had never seen such a thing before. I, knowing he had spent the war mostly in Cairo, cheekily replied, 'No, I don't suppose you would

178

see them in Shepheard's Hotel.' But he did not take umbrage, just smiled.

Next day we were summoned to a lecture entitled *Aid to the Civil Power*. This was given by an extremely tall lieutenant colonel who carried an even taller stick shaped like a shepherd's crook. He prefaced his lecture by admitting that his only experience of this sort of thing was an occasion in Cairo when a riot took place in the street outside the restaurant in which he was eating. He said that he had hidden under the table until it was all over. However, he went on to say that according to regulations the drill was to parade your armed men and then blow a bugle to attract the attention of the rioters, after which a large banner should be displayed with an inscription on it, preferably in their language, saying that the crowd should disperse peacefully, otherwise they would be fired on. This drill would only be carried out at the request of the senior civil authority, confirmed in writing.

'Any questions?' the Colonel barked.

'Yes, Sir,' piped up a pimply subaltern. 'What if we don't have a bugler?'

The Colonel snorted and replied testily, 'Don't be daft man. Any silly bugger can fart down a bugle!'

There were no further questions.

Next day a rehearsal was mounted in order to pass on our newly acquired knowledge to our African soldiers. After explaining to them the object of the exercise they were told to return in half an hour to act the part of a rioting mob. I then assembled a bugler, two men with the banner and a squad of ten Askari with rifles. The mob then arrived on the scene waving sticks, banging drums and shouting threateningly. It was obvious that they were really enjoying this taste of anarchy. The bugle was blown on my command and the banner displayed, but the mob continued to advance towards our line. One Askari was then ordered to shoot the ringleader, which he did, by firing a blank round, and as prearranged the ringleader fell to the ground. At this point the mob should have run away in haste, but such was their enthusiasm that they continued to advance and then swarmed all over us. The banner went flying and my line of armed Askari decided that it was time to retreat to the rear, and did just that. The OC, who had been watching this fiasco, was not pleased. But after two more rehearsals we got it just about right and to his satisfaction.

A few days later the local Somali chieftains were invited to a fire-power demonstration provided by a squadron of locally based RAF Tempest fighter bombers. The target was an old lorry, at which they would fire rockets. In case they should miss it, or in case it did not blow up, I used my SAS expertise by running electric cable to the lorry where I had concealed a can of petrol with a small PE demolition charge attached to it.

The demonstration was a success and the lorry blew up nicely, but the Somali chieftains were demonstrably unimpressed. They were hard men, probably the fiercest fighters in Africa, as the US Army was to discover in the 1990s in Mogadishu when forced to withdraw. Our own Askaris were scared of them, which made them quite jittery when they were on guard duty at night.

On one occasion I was giving my section a lesson on the use of explosives. I had found a length of railway track near our camp, part of the Mogadishu–Villabruzzi (now called Jowhar) line, built by the Italians after the Great War. I wanted to demonstrate how rail could be cut but only had old-fashioned gun-cotton in order to do it. I think I must have overestimated the quantities required because when it exploded a large chunk of the rail penetrated the OC's tent while he was in it. He was quite indignant about it.

This part of Somalia was peopled with all sorts of eccentric characters, and here I refer to the British, not the Somalis or the remaining Italians. Once I went with the OC on a long reconnaissance trip and we crossed over the border into the Ogaden district of Ethiopia, which was notorious for banditry. We came upon a magnificent castle perched on the top of a steep-sided mountain. It had been built for the Duke of Aosta, the pre-Second World War Governor General of Italian East Africa. It was no longer occupied, or so we thought, but when we reached it we were surprised to be greeted by a British major of the paramilitary Somalia Gendarmerie. This body had British officers and Somali troops and was a force to be reckoned with. The Major greeted us in a jovial manner and invited us to join him in a drink of gin – he appeared to have had quite a few already. He then waved airily in the direction of four good-looking Somali girls and remarked proudly that they were his harem. He also hinted that if we fancied any of them that he had no objection.

My OC, who was a rather prim and proper bachelor, was really shocked at this behaviour. It was too near to nightfall to go anywhere else, but he ordered our little party to put up our tents on the outside of the castle and said that we were not to enter it, which was a disappointment to me as I rather liked the jovial major's kind of lifestyle and would have been happy to sample it.

Back in Mogadishu for Christmas we BNCOs decided to brighten up the festivities by mounting a raid just before dawn on the camp of the

180

Loyal Regiment. In front of their warrant officers' and sergeants' mess stood some tall and elegant date palms and these were to be our target. While it was till dark we stealthily approached them and quietly wrapped many turns of Cordtex around the lower trunk of each tree. (Cordtex is an instantaneous detonating fuse and goes off with an impressive bang.) We left a long enough length of slow-burning safety fuse to give us time to get clear of the area in our Jeep. Stopping a quarter of a mile away we watched the trees come down with a bang. Then lights came on in the Loyals' barracks and soon figures were milling round the trees.

Retaliation for this Christmas Day act of vandalism was not long in coming. As we sat down in our mess tent enjoying an early breakfast and having a laugh at the havoc we had caused, we heard the roar of many engines approaching at speed. We dashed outside to see six tracked Bren gun carriers bearing down on our tented camp. Their tactics were simple but devastingly effective – they just drove across the guy ropes of the tents and their metal tracks cut them so that many of the tents collapsed immediately. Their attack only lasted for two or three minutes but it left behind a scene of utter chaos. The Askaris could not understand why they were being attacked by their own side and finally accepted that it was just one more example of the un-predictable and mysterious behaviour of the British *bwanas*.

Our long-suffering OC almost had a nervous breakdown over this incident, but being a decent man, and making allowances for it being Christmas Day, he did not make a fuss about it. He had a bee in his bonnet that when one was away from the permanent camp and on a work detachment out in the bush that one should not make oneself too comfortable and should be able to move off at a minute's notice. I did not see eye to eye with him on this as my philosophy was that any bloody fool could be uncomfortable and that the art of soldiering was to make oneself as comfortable as circumstances would permit.

And so it came about that on one occasion when my section was out in the bush, and miles from any civilization, he paid us a visit. Seeing that we had rigged up a cookhouse and a mess with the use of vehicle tarpaulins and cut-down saplings, he made his usual remark that we might be called on to move at any time and that we appeared to be semi-permanent. He accepted an invitation to lunch, and while he sat waiting in the mess tent I went to the cookhouse and personally supervised the preparation of his meal. This I did by garnishing it with a liberal sprinkling of the local dust. He made no comment when the mess waiter served him with it, but I noticed that he did not eat much of it. He refused an invitation to stay for dinner, saying that he had another section to visit.

There was a good sandy beach near our Mogadishu camp with a small concrete hut, which we BNCOs used as a beach hut and changing room. Then one day we saw that there was a notice attached to it saying that the hut was for the use of officers only. The notice was signed by a captain known to us, and a bit of a snob. We knew that he had recently acquired an Italian girlfriend and wanted to be alone with her on the beach.

The next afternoon I observed the gallant captain on the beach making eyes at his voluptuous paramour. I promptly returned to camp, called together my section Askaris and told them we were all going for a swim. In a few minutes we were at the beach and forty well-endowed Askaris ran naked, whooping and yelling, across the beach and into the sea. The captain looked flabbergasted as his light of love ran off, shrieking wildly, as fast as her shapely legs would take her. He then followed her in hot pursuit.

After this episode the gallant captain must have found another place in which to pursue his amorous dalliances for we never saw him on that beach again. Generally, it was hard to find female company in Somalia, unless, of course, one fraternized with the indigenous Somali women. As the Somalis are mainly devout Muslims, who therefore protect and isolate their womenfolk, the only possibility for a white soldier was to consort with prostitutes – either that or remain celibate. I had heard on the grapevine that there was a very attractive Nubian prostitute on the edge of town who would only sell her favours to white soldiers. One night my curiosity got the better of me and I decided to pay her a visit. Her small house was in an isolated spot and easy to find. I knocked on the door several times without anyone responding. Then the penny dropped: I had been told that the lady was deaf and dumb. So I opened the door, and there she was, sat on her bed.

She motioned me to come inside and to close the door and then gave me a big welcoming smile. She was very black and very beautiful in that her Junoesque body was perfectly proportioned. Furthermore, her skin was like velvet and her flesh firm as India rubber. She was wearing a simple white cotton dress, which was spotlessly clean, just like the rest of her room. To add to the pleasure of the occasion, although she could not speak, she had an infectious giggle and she was fun to be with. She had been making coffee when I arrived and gave me a cupful to drink. While I was sipping it the headlights of an approaching vehicle could be seen through the open window. She immediately motioned me to get under the bed. I did so without hesitation as I suspected that it would be the Military Police and I was right. There were two of them, as from my lowly position I could see two pairs of boots.

As I had come on foot there was no vehicle outside to make them suspicious, and so they never considered looking under the bed. Those spoilsports stayed for over an hour and I almost fell asleep waiting for them to go. They did nothing to improve my dislike of the Military Police. After they had gone I spent a pleasant couple of hours with the girl, but she would not let me stay longer as she conveyed to me by signs that the MPs would visit again later. So I trudged back to camp in a happy mood.

There was a small bar in Mogadishu, popular with British soldiers and run by a vociferous Italian lady, who was quite young. The drinks available were for the most part sweet vermouth or Marsala and the local Gioffi's Gin. Neither were much liked by the troops, who preferred beer, which was not available – but beggars can't be choosers. The sole entertainment was in the form of a wind-up portable gramophone. The majority of the old records had long since been broken and the popular choice of the surviving ones was narrowed down to 'O Sole Mio' and 'Come Back to Sorrento'. These two were played *ad infinitum* until everyone was heartily sick of them.

One night I asked the proprietress if I might walk her home and to my surprise she concurred. The place she took me to was a white mud-walled building about the size of an aircraft hangar, with a crenulated roof like a *Beau Geste* fort. She led me to a corridor within the building and it contained her bed and not one stick of any other furniture. Very strange. We got down to business and what that lady lacked in looks she made up for in energy. The four-mile walk back to camp at dawn felt more like forty miles.

After six months in Somalia our squadron was ordered back to our base at Nanyuki in Kenya. This time we would travel by road. The dirt road was bad in places but the weather was dry and so it was passable everywhere. For a lot of the way it followed the coast. When we reached the small town of Kismayu, on the Somaliland coast, two other sergeants and I were invited by a very charming district officer to drinks at his house, which was on the beach. There we met his equally charming and quite beautiful wife. They lived in an isolated part of the country and they would often not see another white face for long periods, so they were likely to be pleased to have company, particularly as it happened to be New Year's Eve.

The DO's favourite tipple was a dangerous cocktail, which he called a 'half and half', comprising gin and Cointreau in equal proportions. After several of these he suggested that we see the New Year in with a moonlight dip in the sea. We told him that we had no swimming costumes with us, to which he replied 'We never use them.' So off we went, all of us, including his wife, into the warm sea completely starkers. We tried to keep our eyes off the lady in deference to our host, but it was hard to do, and in any case, she did not seem to mind in the least. It was a memorable night and well worth the sore head in the morning.

The next night we camped at Thika waterfalls and the following day were back in Nanyuki again. Somalia had been an interesting experience, but I think that if we had stayed there any longer we should have become as mad as many of the Europeans who live there seemed to be.

One of the last tasks that the squadron was involved in was the destruction of wartime concrete pill boxes that had been built for the protection of Mombasa. This was accomplished by the use of explosives. I was ordered to take an air-compressor truck from Nanyuki to Mombasa and to join the section already working there. I was accompanied by an Askari, and we spent the first night at the transit camp in Nairobi. Next day, in late afternoon we were within twenty miles of Mombasa when we encountered a herd of about thirty elephants, including several young ones. They were on the edge of a large banana plantation and they were having the time of their lives uprooting the plants and tossing them in the air. Those that were not doing that were chewing contentedly, their stomachs rumbling audibly as they did so. It was a vivid demonstration of the problems these huge animals caused when they wandered between human inhabited and cultivated areas.

As we watched, a big bull elephant sighted us and started to amble towards us. The road was narrow at that point as I reversed for about fifty yards but he still kept coming. He didn't appear angry, rather he was just curious. I reversed again, further this time, and he ambled back to the herd. The trouble was that the herd was spread across the road and on both sides of it. I did not want to upset them but by now it was dark and we were due in Mombasa. If we did not arrive they would probably send a vehicle to look for us and I did not want that. So I decided to drive on slowly, at the same time sounding the horn and flashing the headlights, in the hope that this might scare them away from the road. The stratagem worked and an hour later we were at our destination and enjoying cold beer.

In spite of its humid climate I enjoyed Mombasa because its cosmopolitan air compared well with that of the inland towns and villages of Kenya. This was due to the presence of the Arab, African and Indian population of the coastal area, which had been there for hundreds of years and presented a more sophisticated mode of living than was found in the tribal African interior. Also, it possessed some old buildings, a rarity in most of East Africa. In the main these were the homes of Arab traders, but what outshone them all, both in age and appearance, was the huge bulk of Fort Jesus, built in 1593 by the Portuguese. This grim edifice was at that time employed by the British Army as a military prison. One of the BNCOs in the squadron had suffered a month in there for something he was reluctant to talk about. He told us that one of the more useless and frustrating tasks they were made to perform was to go to a large pile of iron cannon balls and carry them one by one to the other side of the fort. There they had to be neatly stacked, and when the last cannon ball was in place, they would start to dismember the pile and carry the heavy balls back to their original place and once again neatly stack them. This sort of thing was pretty well the norm in British military prisons where the object seemed to be not to rehabilitate the inmates but rather to break their spirits.

Further to the promotion of an international ambience in Mombasa was the frequent sight of merchant seamen of many nationalities, who spent their leisure time in the many small bars in the port area. And of course there was a considerable population of the ubiquitous Hindu and Sikh shopkeepers who had settled there.

The demolition task in Mombasa was completed in a few weeks and without injuring anyone, and only causing very minor damage to buildings close to the erstwhile pillboxes, which were destroyed by the use of explosives and pneumatic drills. We then returned once again to Nanyuki.

Rumours had been circulating for some time that a Kikuyu anti-British organization was in the making, though up to now no serious actions had been taken by it. We did not know it at the time, but this organization was the precursor of the Mau Mau uprising, which started in 1952 and ended in 1960.

We were ordered to do occasional night patrols to see if any intelligence could be gained from them. The drill was for a patrol of Askaris under a BNCO to lie in wait first outside the native quarter and to remain there in silence until anyone came by, then to surprise and then question him as to where he had come from and to where he was going. This could be interpreted as interfering with the free movement of citizens, but the facts were somewhat different. Africans did not as a rule like to move about after dark, especially in the bush where there was a danger from predatory animals, and even worse, evil spirits. So if one did encounter Africans after dark they were usually in groups and were probably thieves or up to some other form of skullduggery.

Once during this period I foolishly ventured alone at night into the native quarter. I was worried about the absence of my personal servant, a Jaluo called Augustino, who had been on pass all day and should have reported back to me several hours before. He had a reputation for getting drunk and getting into trouble, unlike my previous personal servant, Tarafa, who had been a paragon of moral rectitude but had now returned on discharge to his home in Ethiopia.

I had decided to go into the native quarter and search for the errant Augustino. The tawdry streets were deserted and I was having second thoughts about being there unarmed. I was about to turn back when I heard voices approaching me. There was sufficient moonlight for me to discern that there were three young Kikuyu men, all carrying stout sticks and swaying drunkenly. I went up to them and asked in Swahili if they had seen any Askaris recently. They answered me in their Kikuyu language, of which I had no knowledge, but the tone of it sounded hostile to me. Then the one nearest me took a swing at me with his stick; as I instinctively stepped back, to my amazement his forward impetus took him ahead with such inertia that he fell flat on his face. His two friends seemed so flabbergasted by this turn of events that they just stood there doing nothing. Perhaps they thought it was white man's magic. I had no illusions on that score, and I got out of there as fast as my legs would carry me, grateful for a miraculous escape. Augustino turned up some two hours later, rather drunk but still able to walk.

I now had only a few more months left to serve in East Africa. I had just been promoted to SQMS and was glad to have a more sedentary job for a while because my health had not been too good prior to this change. During our time in Somaliland I had been struck down with a severe bout of malignant tertiary malaria. The hospital facilities had been quite basic – the hospital itself was just a small house that the British Army had requisitioned. I was put in a room with two other BNCOs who also had malaria. The first night I was there was one of the worst nights of my life. I had a raving fever accompanied by nightmarish fantasies and I perspired so much that my mattress was soaked and there was a pool of sweat on the floor below my bed. The two other lads in the room told me next day that they felt certain I was dying. I was weak for the next couple of days, but after that was soon back on duty.

Since returning to Nanyuki I had had a bout of tonsillitis followed by an outbreak of boils on my legs. They were a mystery to me at the time, but I now think that they were caused by a deficiency of fresh fruit and vegetables when we were in Somaliland. After being back in Kenya for a while my health soon improved. Now I could relax in the QM Stores, lord of all I surveyed. Owing to a shortage of replacements the OC asked me if I would stay on for a few months after my three-year tour finished. He promised me that if I did so then I would have an air passage home rather than going by troopship. I fulfilled my part of the bargain but he was unable to keep his promise and I eventually had to go by ship.

My last few months were happy ones, even though they were routine and uneventful. I would have been quite content to stay even longer, but the War Office had other ideas, so when my replacement arrived from the UK, I had to go. Because I had not held the job of SQMS long enough for it to become a substantive rank I had to revert to my previous rank of sergeant.

So I and another sergeant, who was also tour expired, were told to report to the transit camp at Nyali Beach, just outside Mombasa. The transit camp was a rather ramshackle affair and as we were early arrivals and the troopship would not be arriving for another ten days, we had the camp pretty much to ourselves. No one on the camp staff bothered us and so we spent a great deal of time on the magnificent beach, just bathing and sunbathing. I believe it is now a popular tourist area with hotels and bars and so on, but then it was completely empty, just miles and miles of sandy beach, a real paradise.

Chapter 17

Homeward Bound

Our halcyon days at Nyali passed swiftly and soon we were boarding our troopship in Mombasa port. Her name was HMT *Eastern Prince*, an old-ish cargo-passenger liner, converted to a troopship temporarily and a big improvement on that old rust bucket *Ascanius*.

As a Regular NCO I was detailed by the ship's RSM to take charge of the ship's recreation room and was given three young National Service men to do the work of keeping it clean. It was a great job as at 2300 hrs every night all the troops had to leave the room and I locked the doors behind them. This gave me the huge room to myself, and as it was well furnished with padded benches, I slept very comfortably.

While at Nyali camp my colleague and I had made friends with a WO2 who was also returning to the UK on the *Eastern Prince*. Once on board he asked us if we would like to help him run the ship's tombola sessions. We did not hesitate to accept, because we knew from experience it was an easy way to make money. For the uninitiated, tombola, or Housey-Housey as it was known in the British Army in my days, is a long-established game. It was the only form of gambling officially permitted in the British armed forces. Each player pays for a card on which there is printed fifteen numbers, displayed in three lines of five. The caller, the man in charge, has a bag of counters on each of which is printed a different number. These numbers run from one to ninety. The caller withdraws the counters one at a time and shouts out the number. The players cross out the numbers on their cards when they correspond with those that are being called. Eventually, some lucky person has covered all his numbers on his card and he then shouts out 'House!' His card is checked, and if found correct he receives a cash prize. There are variations on this, such as covering a single line only. These depend on the whim of the caller.

The cash prize, in theory, is the amount of money that is raised by the sale of the cards before the start of each separate game. Officially the soldiers who run the game were allowed to keep 3/6d (17.5p) each for their night's efforts. This paltry sum was treated as a joke, as everyone was aware that those who ran the game kept for themselves a reasonable proportion of the takings. In fact, the ship's RSM, when he authorized us to run the game, made it plain that he and the ship's SQMS expected to receive from us a case of beer each and every night. We did not fail to carry out that commitment.

The British Army had its own terminology for the numbers that were called out. Number one was always 'Kelly's Eye'; seven was 'Lucky for some'; nine was 'Doctor's Chum' (after the infamous No. 9 anti-constipation pill); eleven was 'Legs eleven'; twenty-two was 'Two little ducks'; seventy-six was 'Was she worth it?'; eighty-eight was 'Connaught Rangers' (the old 88th Regiment of Foot); ninety was 'Top of the shop', and so on. An experienced caller could run through all these pseudonyms with hardly naming an actual number at all.

One WO2 friend from Nyali was very experienced and had all his own cards and counters. He even provided my colleague and me with a voluminous canvas bag each, which we tied round our waists and in which we deposited the coins and notes from the sale of the cards. After paying for the beer for the ship's RSM and the SQMS we were each making about £5 a night, which was very good money indeed for those days. We were only challenged once and that was by another WO2 who had counted the tickets sold for one particular game and had worked out what the prize money should have been. He concluded that it was about thirty per cent short. Our WO2, as caller, was suitably indignant and told the accuser that if he wanted he could take over the job himself. This he refused to do, but for the next couple of games we increased the prize money a little in order to keep him quiet. Fortunately the accuser left the ship at Port Said, where we took on board a few hundred more homeward-bound soldiers.

I got to know the ship's RSM quite well and found him to be an interesting character. He had served in the Brigade of Guards before taking on his present job, and during the war had been badly wounded in the legs during the North African campaign. On one occasion some of the young National Service men had complained to me that they had not been able to buy chocolate in the ship's canteen and asked me to take their complaint to the RSM. I went to his cabin, knocked on the door and went in when he called 'Enter'. He was sat on his bunk, wearing shorts, so that I was able to see his extensive wound scars. He was about six feet three inches tall and very lean, and a tough-looking customer by any standards.

To my utter amazement he was engaged in knitting a pair of woollen socks. I had never before seen a man knitting, least of all a Guards RSM.

I hid my surprise as best as I was able and relayed to him the complaint about the chocolate. He snorted with disgust and said, 'My God! What's the Army coming to when hairy-arsed soldiers worry about chocolate!' I felt abashed at his reaction and hastened to assure him that I could not care less about chocolate myself, that I preferred beer. However, he was not noticeably mollified and told me that I should tell the soldiers in question to get stuffed. I passed on these wise words to the young lads, they accepted them without demur and carried on reading the comic magazines to which they were addicted.

At Suez, while our ship waited its turn to pass through the canal, a Dutch troopship passed us, laden with Dutch soldiers going to their East Indies colonies, which have since become Indonesia. There was a war for independence going on there and the Dutch soldiers looked glum as they passed us. They made no response to the jeers of some of our lads, especially when they yelled 'You won't be coming back!' We also passed by an Italian liner full of cheerful Italian immigrants bound for Australia. I doubt if they understood the ribald remarks shouted at them by our lads, they just waved back happily.

The weather stayed fair and the voyage back to England was un-eventful. As the ship sailed up the Solent the decks were crowded with troops all gazing admiringly at the lush green countryside. The vast majority of them were National Service boys at the end of their two years' compulsory service. They had been issued with railway vouchers on board and once they had disembarked they could go straight home. As I was a regular soldier I would first have to report to the RE Depot at Barton Stacey in Hampshire. By now I was within two weeks of the end of my Regular Army engagement, and unless I re-engaged, I would then become a civilian, which I did. And so ends my story – almost.

Envoi

After leaving the British Army I worked for a few years in the Post Office Engineering Department, then passed a Civil Service examination and joined the Waterguard Service of HM Customs and Excise, where I spent the rest of my working life. Some of it was in sea ports and airports in the UK, then twenty-seven years in Cyprus. Four years of that were with the Colonial Customs during the EOKA (Ethnikí Orgánosis Kipriakoú Agónos, Greek for National Organisation of Cypriot Struggle) era, the rest with the UK Sovereign Base Area Customs Service, but that is another story.

The two British SAS regiments were disbanded in October 1945 and some veterans formed the Regimental Association, which, by means of annual reunions and a twice-yearly magazine, helped old comrades keep in touch. The first magazines were not impressive, just a few pages stapled together; nowadays it is a very glossy publication.

Then in 1946 Lieutenant Colonel Brian Franks persuaded the War Office to raise 21 SAS (TA) Regiment, which was formed in early 1947, many of the first volunteers being wartime members of the 1 or 2SAS, SBS or other Special Forces units. Then, in 1951, because of the Malayan Emergency (a guerrilla war between the Commonwealth and the Malayan National Liberation Army [MNLA] from 1948 to 1960), 'Mad Mike' Calvert was asked to form an anti-terrorist unit. It was initially called the Malayan Scouts, then 22SAS Regiment. To my everlasting regret, I knew nothing of this at the time – had I done so I would have gladly volunteered to go back to the SAS for I had always been happy with them. But by the time I did hear of them I was married and had started my new career with HM Customs. The nearest I got to rejoining the Army was shortly after I had joined the Post Office Engineers. I received a letter from the Royal Engineers enclosing a railway warrant and a meal voucher. The letter said that I might shortly receive a telegram telling me to report to an RE Parachute Squadron in London. The Korean War had just broken out and I was on the 'Z' Reserve, which was being recalled. As it turned out, the British did not send airborne units to Korea, so the telegram never came.

When I retired in 1983 at the age of sixty I continued to live in the sunny climes of Cyprus and had lots of leisure time to devote to the SAS Regimental Association. I wrote several articles for the journal, which goes by the name of *Mars and Minerva*, and these resulted in my receiving letters from quite a few old comrades. Chief of these was my old friend Jack Paley, who had been with me in 3 Squadron in France and Italy during the war.

In 1994 I went to the Association's fiftieth anniversary reunion in London, which some 500 members attended, and there met Jack, who had come over from Canada for the occasion. The following year he and I met in Milan and visited the graves of our old comrades buried in the Commonwealth War Graves Commission cemeteries there and at Padua. In Milan cemetery we saw the graves of Lieutenant James Riccomini, Sergeant Sidney Guscott, Corporal Stanley Bolden and Private R. Bruce, the Spaniard. In Padua War Cemetery, not the main city one, which has a British Great War section, we were deeply moved to find, almost side by side (Plot III, left-hand side of the cemetery, opposite the Cross of Sacrifice, Row F, Graves 5 and 7), the graves of Major Ross Robertson Littlejohn and Corporal Joseph Patrick Crowley. Why they were buried with a Corporal Eric Oakley, RASC, died 1941, between them is one of life's minor mysteries, but may they, and 'Freccia' – Major John Prentice Wilkinson, RA and SOE, killed in March 1945 and lying in Plot IV, Row F, Grave 15 – rest in peace.

Then in 1996 we visited France, in particular Alsace and Lorraine, to lay wreaths on the graves of fallen comrades. Here we made lasting friendships with old Maquisards of the French Resistance, who have always held the SAS in high esteem. It is not generally known in Britain the price that these French villages paid for the aid that they gave us during the war. In many of them all the males were taken off to concentration camps in Germany and two thirds of them never returned. Four of us ex-SAS went to Grandrupt in November 2000, and were there presented with the Resistance Medal of the Vosges Maquis.

In the year 2000 a special reunion was held at Wivenhoe Park for wartime members only. About eighty wartime members turned up and we were royally entertained. Some French Resistance men appeared, giving the Association an opportunity to repay some of the generous hospitality we had received from them in past years. Also present were two retired Greek generals who had served with the SAS and SBS in the Mediterranean during the war. To balance that, there were two British generals present, one of them the Chief of the General Staff. The aristocracy was represented by Earl Jellicoe and Lord John Slim. It was a really relaxed occasion, where every member was treated as an equal and privates could share a table with colonels and generals. It was spread over two days and was an occasion to value and remember. Only the SAS could have done it so well.

In late 2002, a friend, Hugh Reid, and I made a two-week trip to visit places where I had served during the war. We made Zurich our base and hired cars in Zurich and Tunis. In France we visited the remains of Natzwiller concentration camp, preserved as a national museum. It is a grim, foreboding place and among the thousands who were murdered there were four SOE girls. We then toured the Great War battlefield at Verdun, another place with a horrendous reputation. So it was with a sense of relief when we moved on in search of the DZ on which I had dropped in 1944. We found the forest itself easily enough, but the location of the DZ was a more difficult task, because the forest appeared to have been abandoned many years before and there was a lot of uncontrolled growth of bushes and saplings. The forestry tracks were also neglected and badly potholed. We came across a clearing that could have been the DZ but I could not be sure as I had only seen it at night, and that was fifty-seven years before.

From the forest we travelled to Sommeville sur Marne in search of my old girlfriend Rejane, and happily found her at nearby Joinville, as narrated earlier. From there we moved on to Sennecy le Grand to see the international memorial with the names of SAS troops of all nations killed in France in 1944. Then it was back to Zurich, from where we headed for Asiago via Bolzano and Trento. We explored the Great War battlefields thoroughly, using Francis Mackay's two excellent guidebooks to the battles in that area, and found them very useful indeed.

I tried to locate some of the partisans I had known in 1945, but only managed to find one. The majority of them were either dead or had moved away from the area. However, I was given a book, written in Italian, describing in detail partisan activity in the Asiago area between 1943 and 1945. It was very well illustrated and I recognized many of the partisans in the photos, and was pleased to find two photographs of my SAS group. Some of the photos are reproduced in this book, with my apologies for the poor quality.

Back to Zurich, thence to Tunis, travelling Business Class, where a delightful air hostess kept us well plied with champagne during the flight, proving that not all Swiss are dull.

Postscript

Regarding the Military Medal that I was awarded in Italy in 1945. I never received the actual medal, probably due to the disbandment of the regiment at the crucial time, and also because I had been posted to East Africa. While I was there, enquiries were made, but no record of the award seemed to exist, and so I was ordered to remove the medal ribbon.

Then in April 2003 the SAS Regiment's archivist, while searching documents in the Public Record Office, Kew, came across a letter from Lieutenant Colonel Franks, dated 4 October 1945, instructing the Chief Clerk of 2SAS to organize, as soon as possible, an investiture for named thirty-one personnel. My name was on that list. Armed with this evidence, the SAS Association made strenuous representations to the MoD on my behalf. However, the MOD replied that it was its firm policy not to make awards retrospectively.

Sad to think that policy takes precedence over righting an injustice. *Ça ne fait rien.*

Cyril 'Charlie' Radford
Cyprus, 2008

Further Reading

2SAS Regiment Operations

France
Roger Ford, *Fire from the Forest* (Cassell, 2003).

Italy
Roy Farran, *Winged Dagger* (Cassell, 2002, reprint of 1948 original).
Robert Hann, *SAS Operation Galia* (Impress, 2009).
Francis Mackay, *Asiago, 15/16 June 1918: The Battle in the Woods and Clouds* (Pen & Sword, 2001).
——, *Touring the Italian Front, 1915–1918* (Pen & Sword, 2002).

Index

198